Katharina Beuter

English as a Lingua Franca among Adolescents

Developments in English as a Lingua Franca

Editors
Jennifer Jenkins
Will Baker

Volume 18

Katharina Beuter

English as a Lingua Franca among Adolescents

Transcultural Pragmatics in a German-Tanzanian School Setting

DE GRUYTER
MOUTON

The project on which this book is based was part of the "Qualitätsoffensive Lehrerbildung", a joint initiative of the German Federal Government and the Länder which aims to improve the quality of teacher training. The programme (support code 01JA1615) was funded by the German Federal Ministry of Education and Research. The author is responsible for the content of this publication.

SPONSORED BY THE

ISBN 978-3-11-221415-2
e-ISBN (PDF) 978-3-11-078657-6
e-ISBN (EPUB) 978-3-11-078661-3
ISSN 2192-8177

Library of Congress Control Number: 2023935961

Bibliographic information published by the Deutsche Nationalbibliothek
The Deutsche Nationalbibliothek lists this publication in the Deutsche Nationalbibliografie; detailed bibliographic data are available on the internet at http://dnb.dnb.de.

This volume is text- and page-identical with the hardback published in 2023.
Typesetting: Integra Software Services Pvt. Ltd. Printing and binding: CPI books GmbH, Leck

www.degruyter.com

Language has no independent existence apart from the people who use it. It is not an end in itself; it is a means to an end of understanding who you are and what society is like.

David Crystal

Contents

Part III: **Discussion**

Appendices

Acknowledgements

Dialogues do not only lie at the very heart of my analyses in this book, which constitutes a revised version of my doctoral dissertation, submitted to the University of Bamberg in September 2019. Plenty of dialogues with most diverse people have also made this research project possible in the first place. I am very grateful to all those who have inspired, contributed to and promoted this work in most various ways.

First and foremost, I would like to thank all participants in my research project, without whom this book would never have come into existence. I express my heartfelt thanks to all students who granted me access to the recordings of their dialogues. I was overwhelmed by their openness and cooperativeness, their sincerity and humour, which kept my spirits high throughout the process of data analysis. I would like to extend my gratitude to all teachers and headteachers involved as well as the students' parents, both in Germany and Tanzania, for their openness towards and genuine interest in my research project and their highly cooperative stance.

Very special thanks go to my supervisor Manfred Krug, whose exceptional academic knowledge and generous support I was able to count on all the way through. He encouraged me to embark on this enterprise, allowed me all freedom necessary to develop my very own research project, while letting me benefit from his astute linguistic comments and pragmatic advice at the same time. My immeasurable gratitude also extends to my second supervisor Barbara Seidlhofer, who spared neither ways nor time to support the advance of my project. I considered myself very privileged to profit from her unprecedented expertise in the research field of English as a Lingua Franca, and her pleasant cheerfulness and academic appreciation very much strengthened me.

While working on this book, I had the advantage of being part of the larger interdisciplinary research project *WegE* ('Pioneering Teacher Education'), generously funded by the German Federal Ministry of Education and Research within the *Qualitätsoffensive Lehrerbildung* ('Quality Campaign for Teacher Education'). I would like to express my sincere gratitude to the local project leadership team Annette Scheunpflug, Barbara Drechsel and Johannes Weber for their trust in my capacities, for all critical appreciation and pragmatic support. I am particularly grateful to the *KulturPLUS* team, which I was very fortunate to be part of as a research assistant within the larger framework of WegE. My heartfelt thanks go to Konstantin Lindner and Sabine Vogt for their inestimable support in providing a stimulating working environment, for encouraging and setting examples of cooperative action, for their academic interest in my work and their many ways of expressing recognition and praise. I would like to extend my gratitude to my col-

https://doi.org/10.1515/9783110786576-203

leagues Adrianna Hlukhovych and Benjamin Reiter, with whom I shared not only an office, but also the experience of working on a large scale research project. Our profound discussions on theoretical, practical and personal matters helped me to stay motivated and focused and to appreciate little steps of progress.

I am very grateful for all further academic advice put into this work. My sincere thanks go to the entire team of the Chair of English Linguistics at the University of Bamberg, the WegE project team as well as local and international audiences in Helsinki, Belfast and London for providing valuable comments and transdisciplinary perspectives on my work throughout all stages. I particularly thank my colleague and friend Anna Rosen for her creative input and our discussions, especially at the very onset of the project. Special thanks also go to Julia Schlüter, Lukas Sönning, Gabriele Knappe, Ole Schützler, Heinrich Ramisch, Fabian Vetter and Valentin Werner as well as Isolde Schmidt, Michaela Hilbert, Laura Murphy, Catherine Irvine and Kenneth Wynne for their valuable questions, their profound advice on linguistic issues, helpful comments on earlier drafts and practical suggestions throughout. Although this work would be different without them, the responsibility for all contents of the final version lies with me as the author alone. I would also like to thank Angela and Peter Webb and their family as well as Victoria Ndossy for their friendship and their help with language questions. I further owe my gratitude to Isabell Walter, Katrin Landwehr and Katharina Scheiner, who pulled the administrative strings behind the scenes in a very professional and most reliable way. Special thanks are due to my persevering student assistants, particularly to Felicia Bayrhof, Veronika Kilian, Alice Limmer and Franziska Schuhmann for their very conscientious support throughout the project.

I gratefully acknowledge the generous financial support not only by the German Federal Ministry of Education and Research, but also through grants issued by funding programmes of the Research Department and the Women's Representatives of the University of Bamberg, which helped me conduct my field research in East Africa and supported the process of publishing this book against all odds of the pandemic. I would also like to express my sincere gratitude to all people at De Gruyter who were involved in the publication process. My special thanks go to Jennifer Jenkins and Will Baker for including the book in their edited series *Developments in English as a Lingua Franca* and to an anonymous reviewer for his or her conscientious examination of the manuscript and appreciative feedback. Their experienced comments and most valuable suggestions have helped sharpen the focus of this book and fill blind spots. I am also highly grateful to Natalie Fecher and Kirstin Börgen, who have led me through the virgin territory of publishing a book in the most supportive and encouraging way I could have wished for.

The present book would never have come into existence without the unconditional support from my family and friends and the significant influence of various companions. I would like to thank Peter Ramroth and Hans Unbehauen for stirring my ambitions in embarking on this dissertation project and believing in my cognitive and creative capacities. My thanks also go to Mathias Gaa and Martin Böhne for raising and fostering my deep interest in and love for the English language and its teaching, in African contexts and beyond. I am very grateful to Neville Alexander for sensitizing me to the social power of language and the wealth of plurilingualism. He encouraged me to strive for significance and taught me to find *my* project. In addition, my heartfelt thanks go to Carole and Ralph Virgo for giving me a second home in English. I am also full of thanks to Tshepho Bodiba for his inspiration and appreciation, his infectious love of life and our unique friendship, which we celebrated in endless ELF conversations. My greatest thanks, finally, go to my family for their unprecedented support and encouragement. From deep within I want to thank my loving parents for holding me and letting me fly, and my siblings for planting in me and nurturing the certainty that I will never walk alone. I am also very grateful to my parents-in-law for their genuine interest in my work and their practical support throughout. Above all, however, I want to thank my husband Stephan for his encouragement and love, his leniency, patience and pragmatic support, and my beloved children for sharing their empathy, for grounding me and revealing to me the best things in life. Ida, Frederik und Jonas: Euch widme ich dieses Buch.

List of figures, maps and tables

Figures

Maps

https://doi.org/10.1515/9783110786576-204

Tables

List of abbreviations

ACE	Asian Corpus of English
ADJ	Adjective
ADV	Adverb
BELF	Business English as a Lingua Franca
BNC	British National Corpus
CA	Conversation Analysis
CEFR	Common European Framework of Reference
COLT	Bergen Corpus of London Teenage English
DCT	Discourse Completion Task
EIL	English as an International Language
ELF	English as a Lingua Franca
EL1	English as a First Language
ELFA	Corpus of English as a Lingua Franca in Academic Settings
EMI	English as a Medium of Instruction
ES	English as a Subject
FOLK	Forschungs- und Lehrkorpus gesprochenes Deutsch
FPP	First Pair Part
FTA	Face-Threatening Act
F-transparency	Formal Transparency
H-transparency	Hearer Transparency
ICA	Intercultural Awareness
ICC	Intercultural Communicative Competence
ICE EA	International Corpus of English East Africa
IFID	Illocutionary Force Indicating Device
IMR	Individual Multilingual Repertoire
L1	First Language
L2	Second Language
LC1	First Linguaculture
LC2	Second Linguaculture
MRP	Multilingual Resource Pool
NS	Native Speaker
NNS	Non-Native Speaker
NP	Noun Phrase
OED	Oxford English Dictionary
OIOR	Other-Initiated Other-Repair
OISR	Other-Initiated Self-Repair
RO	Repeatable (Object)
R1	First Repetition
R2	Second Repetition
RP	Received Pronunciation
R-transparency	Researcher Transparency
SIOR	Self-Initiated Other-Repair

https://doi.org/10.1515/9783110786576-205

SISR	Self-Initiated Self-Repair
SPP	Second Pair Part
S-transparency	Speaker Transparency
TAM	Tense Aspect Mood
TED	Transparency Enhancing Device
TeenELF	Teenagers' Use of English as a Lingua Franca
TIG	Transient International Group
TMC	Transient Multilingual Community
TMG	Transient Multilingual Group
TPA	Transcultural Pragmatic Awareness
TRP	Transition Relevance Place
V	Verb
VOICE	Vienna Oxford International Corpus of English
WE	World Englishes
WrELFA	Corpus of Written English as a Lingua Franca in Academic Settings

Part I: **Theoretical, empirical and methodological foundations**

1 Introduction

From Australia to Zambia, from the Bahamas to Yemen, and from Tanzania to Germany, an increasing number of people all over the globe use English as a shared medium for communication. The number of English speakers is currently estimated at 1.5 billion in total (see Crystal 2012a: 6; Eberhard et al. 2022), with 'non-native' speakers, who account for more than two thirds of all speakers of English, outnumbering 'native' speakers by far (see Eberhard et al. 2022).[1] Global mobility, both long-term migration and short-term sojourns, as well as the rapid spread of the internet continue to bring people from different linguacultural backgrounds together, who – in need of a lingua franca – often resort to English in both real and virtual worlds (see Jenkins 2018: 600). Employed by speakers from most various geographical and social backgrounds in a wide range of domains, English as a Lingua Franca has grown into "a communicative tool of immense political, ideological, and economic power" (Kachru 1996: 910) and has gained a global influence unparalleled (see Seidlhofer 2011: 3).

Following Seidlhofer (2011: 7), I understand English as a Lingua Franca (hence ELF) as "*any use of English among speakers of different first languages for whom English is the communicative medium of choice, and often the only option* [italics in original]". While the use of ELF has become a globe-encompassing linguistic reality, "linguists, teacher educators, and teachers have been told, and have generally accepted, that 'real English' is ENL [i.e. English as a native language]" (Seidlhofer 2011: 23). Over the past two decades, however, a rapidly growing body of ELF research has contributed to making the sociolinguistic reality of ELF visible and accessible to academics and educators alike, exploring ELF from a variety of linguistic perspectives, with a recent emphasis on pragmatics and translanguaging (see e.g. Mauranen 2013; Cogo & House 2018).

Though universally employed, ELF has so far mainly been investigated in a restricted set of regions and domains: while previous studies have centred around business and academic ELF in European and Asian settings (see Seidlhofer 2004: 221–222; Firth 2009: 149; Cogo 2016a: 89; Jenkins 2018: 596; Kaur 2022: 37–38), future research needs to incorporate additional domains and integrate data from further continents (see e.g. Kaur 2016a: 164–166). The present study addresses this desideratum by exploring the interactional behaviour of ELF-speaking ado-

1 As the terms *native speakers* and *non-native speakers* appear particularly challenging in multilingual contexts and against the backdrop of fluid and hybrid conceptualizations of language, they will be used rarely and in inverted commas here (see also Section 2.2.1; Cogo & Dewey 2012: 32; 2017: 102).

https://doi.org/10.1515/9783110786576-001

lescents[2] in an African-European context. Although ELF research is no longer in its infancy, young speakers' use of ELF has received little attention so far (for notable exceptions, see D'Andrea 2012, Vettorel 2013). As Palacios Martínez (2018: 364) notes, however, "[t]eenagers constitute an important sector of society, one which deserves close attention and understanding in its own right". He goes on to observe that "[b]y studying some of the mechanics of their communication, we will be provided with a valuable window onto them as a group." Particularly in view of the ongoing debate about implications of ELF research for English language teaching (ELT), an investigation of the primary target group's use of ELF appears promising.

Research into forms and functions of English in Africa on the other hand is all but new, but has primarily been approached from a variety-centred (see e.g. Mesthrie 2010) or a postcolonial (see e.g. Achebe 1975; Thiong'o 1986) rather than an ELF perspective so far (for notable exceptions, see van der Walt & Evans 2018; Rudwick 2021). Analysing the "new voice coming out of Africa, speaking of an African experience in a world-wide language" (Achebe 1975: 61) in an ELF framework will shift the perspective to African speakers' participation in a global communicative network.

Addressing the urgent need for more "situated, exploratory studies" of a "qualitative, emically oriented" nature (Seidlhofer 2009: 50) while at the same time paying specific attention to the blind spots in ELF research as outlined above, the present study investigates adolescents' ELF pragmatics in the framework of an African-European student exchange. Analyses will largely build on my fieldwork recordings of 26 hours of ELF face-to-face interactions between 30 Tanzanian and German secondary school students aged 15 to 19, compiled into a corpus of about 190,000 transcribed words, but will also draw on fieldnotes, sociolinguistic participant information sheets and retrospective interviews. The overall qualitative approach is complemented by quantitative methods where deemed appropriate for an interpretation of findings. The exploratory study is guided by the following overall research question: How do adolescents taking part in a German-Tanzanian student exchange employ linguistic and paralinguistic resources in English as a Lingua Franca to reach their communicative aims?

As is a common procedure in ethnographically influenced research (see e.g. Starfield 2013: 59; Section 4.4), this broad overall research question will be narrowed down in the process of analysis. As far as communicative aims are concerned, students are found to primarily pursue intersubjective understanding, a management of rapport and the negotiation of identities, which often go hand in

2 On a discussion of terms used to refer to the age group in question, see Section 3.4.

hand. Major linguistic and paralinguistic resources at play will be worked out and further examined in the course of the study. Repetition and repair, the realization of the speech act of complimenting, and the use of laughter receive prominent attention. Particular emphasis is placed on translanguaging as a communicative tool in ELF. These major interactional means and goals will provide the structure for the present study.

The book starts off with an overview of theoretical and empirical foundations of ELF research (Chapter 2, Chapter 3), laying the ground for subsequent methodological considerations and analyses. Conceptualizations of ELF as emerging from previous research pave the way for reflections on the relationship between language and culture in ELF as a transcultural phenomenon. Research on ELF is examined in its interplay with related fields that offer analytical potential, such as interactional linguistics, pragmatics, and intercultural communication research. Theoretical considerations are followed by comprehensive descriptions of methods and data, with the research design being laid out against the background of research interests and objectives (Chapter 4). In a predominantly qualitative approach, conversation analysis (CA) is employed as a major methodological tool for the analysis of the interactional data at the core of the study.

Chapter 5 provides an overview of communicative aims students address in their conversations: the negotiation of meaning, rapport, and identity. The five subsequent chapters (6 to 10) give detailed insights into negotiation processes at work in the present data through a close formal-functional analysis of ELF conversations. Repeating, repairing, complimenting, laughing and translanguaging are investigated with regard to their interactional potential for contributing to the communicative aims as outlined above. The interactional means investigated in detail were chosen on the basis of the following considerations:

- *Salience*: Topics emerging from the researcher's fieldnotes and observations were collated with participants' perspectives retrieved from interviews and contents of previous research. In particular, repetition, repair, and the use of plurilingual resources were brought into prominence as salient communicative means in ELF by all parties.
- *Innovative potential*: Less researched areas in ELF such as laughter and complimenting promise to reveal new insights into general mechanisms at work in lingua franca communication. The innovative potential is also considered high for research on the multifaceted phenomenon of translanguaging in ELF, which has made it to the centre of attention and is now gaining ground in empirical ELF research (see Cogo 2016a: 86).
- *Representativeness*: The linguistic means looked at cover a wide range of domains of language behaviour (see Spencer-Oatey 2008: 21; Section 3.2). While complimenting as a complex speech act, for example, represents the illocution-

ary domain, translanguaging reaches into the domains of discourse and participation, whereas humour and laughter exemplify the stylistic as well as the non-verbal domain. At the same time, the communicative means chosen foreground different functional aspects. While repetition and repair primarily serve the negotiation of mutual understanding, complimenting and laughter play vital roles in the management of rapport, and translanguaging stands in a close relationship to aspects of identification, although no single means is naturally restricted to just one function.

A methodological reflection and a summary of major linguistic findings (Chapter 11) is followed by an exploration of pedagogical implications, both on a theoretical and practical level (Chapter 12). The closing chapter locates the present study and its findings in the larger research context and suggests paths for further investigation (Chapter 13).

2 Language and culture in English as a Lingua Franca

After the phenomenon of English used as a lingua franca had occasionally been referred to in the last two decades of the 20th century (e.g. Hüllen 1982; Knapp 1985; Beneke 1991; Firth 1996; Kachru 1996; House 1999), two seminal publications around the turn of the millennium (Jenkins 2000; Seidlhofer 2001) marked the onset of ground-breaking and ground-gaining research into the nature of ELF. ELF research has since developed into a dynamic field of studies, featuring annual international conferences, the half-yearly published journal *JELF – Journal of English as a Lingua Franca* (edited by Martin Dewey), a comprehensive handbook (Jenkins et al. 2018) and this present De Gruyter Mouton book series *Developments in English as a Lingua Franca* (edited by Jennifer Jenkins & Will Baker). Corpora of ELF in various settings have been compiled and made publicly available (see Table 1).

Table 1: Overview of major ELF corpora.

Corpus		Rough scope	Contents	Director	Reference
VOICE	Vienna Oxford International Corpus of English	1 million words	Spoken ELF mainly in European settings	Barbara Seidlhofer	VOICE 2013
ELFA	The Corpus of English as a Lingua Franca in Academic Settings	1 million words	Spoken ELF in academic settings	Anna Mauranen	ELFA 2008
WrELFA	The Corpus of Written English as a Lingua Franca in Academic Settings	1.5 million words	Written ELF in academic contexts	Anna Mauranen	WrELFA 2015
ACE	Asian Corpus of English	1 million words	Spoken ELF in Asian settings	Andy Kirkpatrick	ACE 2014

ELF research has progressed from an early focus on phonological and grammatical features to an exploration of pragmatic phenomena and larger-scale processes of accommodation and negotiation. Recent research has emphasized the inherently multilingual nature of ELF and focuses on phenomena of translanguaging (see Jenkins 2015: 49). The majority of studies centre upon ELF usage in business contexts (BELF) or academic settings (ELFA),[3] which represent key areas of ELF

3 Overviews can be found amongst others in Jenkins et al. (2011), Seidlhofer (2011), Mauranen (2012) and Jenkins (2015).

https://doi.org/10.1515/9783110786576-002

use. Since the present study is also interested in pedagogical implications of ELF research, it explores the use of ELF among school students in an intercultural setting. The striking geographical confinement of previous ELF research to European and Asian contexts falls short of capturing a representative picture of ELF as a global phenomenon. Although ELF plays a major role in international communication for speakers from Africa, there is a conspicuous lack of relevant data, which the present study seeks to address.

To prepare the ground for further investigations into ELF pragmatics, this chapter will lay the theoretical basis by looking into some more general conceptualizations of ELF, language and culture.

2.1 Conceptualizations of ELF

Proceeding from earlier concepts of ELF which excluded English 'native' speakers from the ELF paradigm (see Beneke 1991: 54; Firth 1996: 240; House 1999: 74; Meierkord 2002: 112), Seidlhofer's widely acknowledged definition – "*any use of English among speakers of different first languages for whom English is the communicative medium of choice, and often the only option* [italics in original]" (Seidlhofer 2011: 7; see Chapter 1) – allows for the possibility of *all* speakers of English to use ELF, regardless of whether they conceive of themselves as 'native' or 'non-native' speakers of English. Any ELF setting will, however, always involve a minimum of two languages, as it is only the presence of different first languages that makes interlocutors employ English as a Lingua Franca with all the implications specified in the following. In her definition of ELF, Cogo (2018b) incorporates a sociolinguistic perspective and broadens the scope of interculturality in ELF settings beyond linguistic diversity, describing ELF as "an intercultural medium of communication used among people from different sociocultural and linguistic backgrounds, and usually among people from different first languages". Accordingly, English is used as a lingua franca in order to mediate between and give expression to different linguacultures (see Section 2.2.2).

With its strong interest in the use of English in various settings all over the world, ELF research is firmly rooted in a Global Englishes framework (see e.g. Pennycook 2007; Crystal 2012a). In the face of terminological fuzziness in the field (see Jenkins 2006: 159–160), the present argumentation follows Baker (2015: 11) in understanding research on Global Englishes as an umbrella term to cover lines of interrelated research such as ELF, EIL (English as an International Language) and WE (World Englishes), all of which share an interest in English(es) used beyond Kachru's Inner Circle countries[4] and no longer accept 'native' standards as the solitary norm-setting manifestations of English. This perspective clearly demarcates ELF from the – deceivingly similar-looking – EFL paradigm (English as a Foreign Language), which has oriented exclusively towards 'native' speaker target norms in English language teaching. As changing paradigms profoundly affect questions of authorization and empowerment, pedagogical implications of the Global Englishes paradigm and ELF-informed approaches to ELT have also occupied researchers and practitioners for meanwhile more than two decades (see e.g. Gnutzmann 1999; Gagliardi & Maley 2010; Bowles & Cogo 2015; Bayyurt & Akcan 2015; Sifakis & Tsantila 2019).

In the "tension between the global and the local" (Cogo 2018b), ELF research explores how discourse in English around the world is shaped by and adapted to various local surroundings. Just like WE research, it is interested in English(es) beyond monolingual and monocultural 'native' speaker settings, and questions the primacy of 'native' speakers and the concept of *'native' speakers* itself (see e.g. Ferguson 1982: xi; Pakir 2009: 233; Widdowson 2012: 10). It also shares with WE research its interest in variation and change as corollaries of language contact (see Schneider 2016; Widdowson 2018), conceptualizing diversity as an expression of development rather than decay (see Kachru 1992: 358). WE research, however, explores individual varieties of English in particular speech communities as influenced by specific linguacultural surroundings in more or less clear-cut geographical regions, mainly in Kachru's Outer Circle contexts (see Baker 2015: 10). ELF, in contrast, cuts across all Kachruvian circles (see Seidlhofer 2011: 81; Cogo 2015: 2) and works on a meta-level in so far as it embraces "contact between these hybrid, contact-based lects – that is, ELF is a higher-order, or second-order language contact" (Mauranen 2018a: 10). This difference in perspective has methodological implications, as WE research correspondingly investigates features of contrasting varieties, while ELF research tries to understand the flexible and adaptive processes of interaction and linguacultural interpermeation at work in lingua franca contact situations. While Schneider's observation of shared "tendencies towards simplicity" (Schneider 2016) in WE and ELF may hold true on phonological and lexico-grammatical levels, ELF pragmatics has been found to operate on highly complex terms (see House 2010; Cogo 2016a: 82).

As to the relationship between EIL and ELF, there is a striking lack of academic consensus. While some studies use ELF, EIL, WE and Global Englishes almost inter-

---

4 On Kachru's highly influential three-circle model, see Kachru (1985). While the model has constituted a central and widely acknowledged force in pushing forward WE research, it has recently come to face increasing criticism in ELF research for placing 'native' speakers central and not capturing the growing blurriness of speaker categories (see e.g. Murray 2012).

changeably (e.g. House 2010: 364), others distinguish between EIL and ELF on the basis of EIL's immanent variety perspective, claiming a close alignment between EIL and WE (e.g. Baker 2015: 10). Seidlhofer (2011: 3–4) differentiates between "localized EIL and globalized EIL", with the former referring to individual varieties of English that emerge in various local contexts of the Outer and Expanding Circle, whereas the latter concept looks at English as a truly international means of communication between people from different linguacultural backgrounds, in other words at English used as a lingua franca. Cutting across all three Kachruvian circles, the ELF lens on Englishes in global contexts encompasses "more transnational, intercultural and multilingual perspectives" (Cogo 2018b) than is the case for contrastive cross-cultural variety research.

Comprising a situationally and contextually dependent means of communication used in emerging *Communities of Practice* (CoP) (Wenger 1998; for its use in ELF-contexts see e.g. House 2003: 572–573; Seidlhofer 2007; Dewey 2009: 74–78) rather than by locally rooted, geographically clear-cut and stable speech communities, ELF transpires as a social practice rather than a closed system (see Baker 2015: 10). In recent years, the concept of CoPs has again come under criticism in ELF research for not being able to capture the ad-hoc and transient nature of many ELF interactions. The concepts of *Transient Multilingual Communities* (TMCs) (Mortensen 2017) and *Transient International Groups* (TIGs) (Pitzl 2018b) have recently been suggested to emphasize this fleeting and dynamic nature in less stable groups of ELF speakers (see Section 2.2.3). They orient towards dynamic processes and micro-diachronic developments in negotiations between ELF interlocutors, so that the social practice approach to ELF is rendered more valid than ever.

Taking into account various scales of social significance, Mauranen (2018a) has suggested a three-pronged categorization for approaches to the analysis of ELF, comprising a macro-, meso- and micro-level (see Figure 1). On a macro-level, ELF is analyzed in the framework of globalization, addressing issues such as language change through ELF or the conceptualization of communities of ELF speakers. On a meso-level, ELF is explored in concrete intercultural interactions. The micro-perspective finally is interested in the intra-individual cognitive side of ELF. It is the meso-perspective (also termed micro-social perspective) that most research concentrates on (Baker 2015: 7) and that is also adopted in the present study. While focusing on small-scale interactions, this approach also allows for an incorporation of global and cognitive issues, thus granting indirect access to phenomena on a macro- and micro-level.

All perspectives on ELF as delineated here have evolved over two decades of growing ELF research and theorizing, which has undergone paradigmatic shifts in the course of its comparatively short history and is still in flux as summarized in Figure 2. Originating in WE variety research (see Jenkins 2015: 53), ELF research

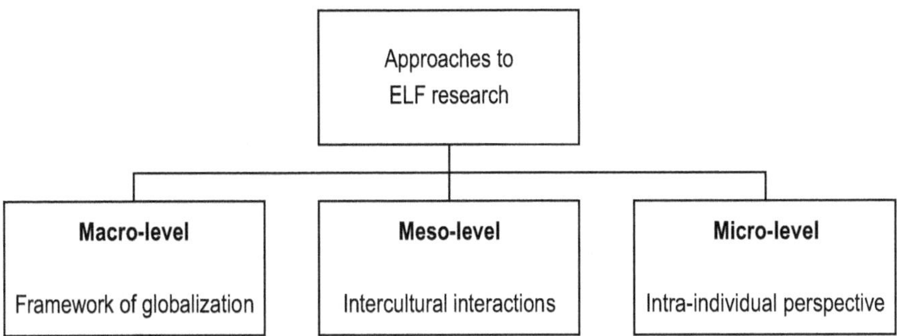

Figure 1: Three levels of ELF research approaches (based on Mauranen 2018a: 8–19).

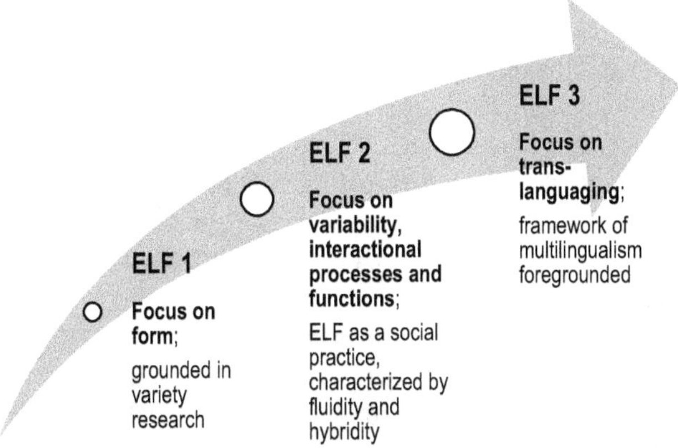

Figure 2: Evolution of ELF conceptualizations (based on Jenkins 2015: 49).

started off with an early focus on forms in an attempt to identify phonological and lexico-grammatical core features (ELF 1) (e.g. Jenkins 2000; Seidlhofer 2001; Kirkpatrick 2007). However, research has shown ELF to be characterized by variability, fluidity and hybridity above all (see e.g. Seidlhofer 2009: 40; Dewey 2013; House 2014: 363–364; Jenkins 2015: 50; Cogo 2016a), so that the conceptual focus shifted as Baker (2015: 7) describes: "ELF is not treated as a variety of English in investigations; rather ELF research is concerned with the variable use of English in intercultural communication". Seidlhofer (2011: 120) emphasizes that "[w]hat is significant about ELF is not the formal properties as such, but how they function to communicative effect". In such a functional and process-oriented approach, which explores the purposeful use of ELF in CoPs, TMCs or TIGs, ELF is reconceptualized as a social practice (ELF 2) (see e.g. Baird, Baker & Kitazawa 2014: 175) or a "kind of language behaviour" (Widdowson 2021: 21). Current research has foregrounded the inherently multilingual nature of ELF (ELF 3), with a retheorizing of ELF as a "multilingua franca" (Jenkins 2015), defined by "its complexity and emerging nature" (Jenkins 2015: 77). In processes of translanguaging (see García & Li 2014) and transculturing (see Welsch 2010: 42–48), linguacultural boundaries are transcended in the "contact zone" (Pratt 1991) that ELF constitutes, with cultural group memberships becoming fluid, and distinct "in-between spaces" disappearing altogether.

The present study traces this conceptual evolution of ELF in so far as it takes formal features as its starting point, but looks at them in their situated occurrence and investigates their context-dependent functions in interactional processes. A particular focus will be laid on the use of multilingual resources in ELF.

As research has found ELF to be characterized above all by fluidity, hybridity and creativity, recent studies have suggested conceptualizing ELF as a complex adaptive system (CAS), locating it in the framework of complexity theory (see e.g. Baker 2015; Frank 2015; Jenkins 2015; Larsen-Freeman 2018). ELF speakers dynamically co-adapt their language situationally in accordance with their own and their interlocutors' language resources in order to co-construct meaning and manage rapport. Common practices of translanguaging (see Section 10.2) further reveal the situatedness of ELF between the global and the local. Current ELF research accordingly places questions of negotiation and accommodation, but also multilingualism, attitudes and identity at the top of the agenda (e.g. Cogo 2018b). These issues set the ground for the present study.

Since its inception, research on Global Englishes in general and on ELF in particular has also addressed applied linguistic issues, for instance by questioning traditional views of language ownership and their consequences for English language teaching (ELT) (see Seidlhofer 2011; Bowles 2015). Especially in oral intercultural communication, ELF speakers often deviate from Inner Circle 'standards', not only because they give priority to content over 'correctness', but also for reasons of identity and rapport. While it is acknowledged that interlocutors' varying linguistic proficiency also influences their use of ELF, ELF research does not conceptualize ELF as an interlanguage, but foregrounds a conceptualization of ELF speakers as pragmatically competent active users and shapers of English rather than 'deficient' learners (see Cogo 2016a: 79; Mauranen 2018a: 10). As *correctness* is a problematic concept in a non-essentialist descriptive paradigm of plurilithic Englishes in flow, appropriateness has been suggested as an alternative leading principle for English teaching contexts (see Seidlhofer 2011: 14; Section 12.1.3).

Constructs of monolithic nation-language-culture units still molding ELT to a large degree fall short of the pluricentric, fluid and hybrid reality embodied by ELF (see Baker 2020: 256–257). It has indeed been claimed that "there is nothing that inexorably links the English language to Anglophone cultures" (Baker 2018a: 29). Kachru (2017: 227) declares that in fact "the English language has now become unique in it[s] cultural multifaces". As the interplay between language and culture appears crucial for any understanding of ELF, it will further be explored in the following.

2.2 Language and culture in ELF research

ELF as "a common medium of intercultural communication used among speakers from different lingua-cultural backgrounds" (Cogo 2016a: 79) seems so tightly intertwined with interculturality by definition that a closer exploration of the relationship between language and culture appears indispensable for a deeper understanding of ELF and related concepts of multi-, inter- and transculturality. This chapter will first reflect on concepts of language and culture and the interplay between the two, before it moves on to explore the location of ELF in research on intercultural communication and the hybridization phenomena of transculturing and translanguaging.

2.2.1 Conceptualizations of language and culture

Definitions of both culture and language have seen a general shift from essentialist-normative towards semiotic-constructionist concepts in the last century (see Risager 2012: 106–107; Frank 2015: 493–494; Beuter 2019c: 16–17, 23–26). Derived from Latin *cultura*, originally denoting the 'cultivation of soil' or 'agriculture' or 'care', the term *culture*, in a clear delineation from *nature*, denotes anything man-made in its broadest sense (see Biebighäuser 2014: 23). The concept of culture has now come to embrace a large range of product- and process-oriented components (see OED, s.v. *culture*, n., 7.a.). In his seminal work on intercultural competence, Byram (1997: 39) conceptualizes culture as "the beliefs and knowledge which members of a social group share by virtue of their membership". Culture accordingly comprises not only a social-collective component, as it creates and strengthens in-group solidarity, but also the potential to differentiate and separate between self and other. Culture is about membership, although people do not possess, but rather construct culture. Current academic discourse is mainly informed by semiotic understandings of culture, building on Geertz' (1973: 89) understanding of culture as "an historically transmitted pattern of meanings embodied in symbols, a system of inherited conceptions expressed in symbolic forms by means of which men communicate, perpetuate, and develop their knowledge about and attitudes towards life". In a social-constructionist broadening of this semiotic approach, human beings are foregrounded as "the social enactors of culture" (Dervin & Liddicoat 2013a: 6), which itself turns "fluid, malleable, subjective" (Dervin & Liddicoat

2013a: 8). Baker (2015: 106) further elaborates on this poststructuralist approach and outlines the role of "fluid culture" in ELF research as follows:

> [C]ulture can be investigated as a process, something we do and this has been especially prevalent in conceptions of culture as discourse, practice and ideology. Culture in ELF communication, and other forms of communication, operates on and across many scales from the local, to the national and the global. However, culture does not neatly fit within each scale; rather conceptions of culture, or cultural systems, involve movement across and between these scales with the boundaries blurred. Indeed, the metaphors of movement and flow have emerged from the discussion as fundamental to understanding culture. Equally crucial has been recognition of the complexity of culture.

In fact, conceptualizations of language, from Latin *lingua*, 'tongue, speech, language', have taken similar turns to those of culture. Structural aspects on the one hand and social-collective characteristics on the other hand are emphasized in the definition of language as a "system of spoken or written communication used by a particular country, people, community, etc., typically consisting of words used within a regular grammatical and syntactic structure" (OED, s.v. *language*, n., 1.a.). Depending on prevailing epistemological streams in linguistics, various aspects of this definition have been foregrounded, with semiotic (e.g. Saussure 1916) and rule-bound generative approaches (e.g. Chomsky 1957) dominating the 20th century. In applied linguistics, the focus shifts to functional properties of language, which is then regarded as "a medium for the creation, communication and interpretation of meanings" (Dervin & Liddicoat 2013a: 11). Recent conceptualizations have emphasized the emergent and constructionist nature of language and have placed it in the framework of complexity theory:

> [T]he phenomenon of language is best viewed as a complex adaptive system that is constantly constructed and reconstructed by its users. Therefore, language should be considered an emergent phenomenon, the result of activity, the collective, cumulative behavior of language agents over time. These emergent phenomena have a strong causal impact on the behavior and learning of each individual language agent. Hence, there is a type of recursiveness to the system in which feedback mechanisms operate as an intrinsic component of it. (Frank 2015: 495)

The emergent and recursive nature of language becomes clearly visible in ELF, which is marked by a high degree of situatedness, accommodation and fluidity. Widdowson (2012: 24) argues that "[t]he study of ELF is [. . .] of particular significance in that it prompts a reappraisal of established, taken for granted ways of thinking about language, especially English." The global spread of English has also increasingly blurred the lines between 'native', 'second-language' and 'foreign language' speakers of English, many of whom live and work in plurilingual contexts (see Sharifian 2017: 102). Cogo & Dewey (2012: 37) claim that the "native/non-native dichotomy is neither appropriate nor useful for an exploration of ELF interactions" (see also Dröschel 2011: 61–62). All of this has led to a "crisis of terminology" (Graddol 2006: 110), which defies any easy solution. Against this background, the present work continues to use the concept of individual named languages, which, however, are conceptualized as hybrid and fluid co-constructions rather than static entities.

2.2.2 The interplay between language and culture

Major overlaps between the conceptualizations of language and culture as dynamic semiotic systems with both individual components and social potential have become evident. The relationship between language and culture, however, proves to be complex. Looking at language as a mere subsystem of culture does not reach far enough. Instead, language serves to abstract, express and communicate culture, can create culture, be drawn upon to decode culture and mediate between cultures in intercultural encounters. According to Busch (2015: 1), "[c]ultural identities and affiliations cannot be maintained but by communication". Language moulds culture and vice versa (see Kecskés & Romero-Trillo 2013: 2). Language and culture "are continuously interacting, influencing each other and consequently restructuring themselves through multiple feedback loops" (Frank 2015: 496).

European thinking, however, had long been dominated by separatist and deterministic ideas of clear-cut language-culture-nation-units as expressed in Herder's influential model of homogeneous spheres (Herder 1774: 56), leaving little space for aspects of hybridity and fluidity. In the early 19th century, Humboldt (1836: 37) further developed ideas of a close relationship between a *volk* ('the people of a nation') and a language, claiming that any language, built around and incorporating a specific worldview, shapes its speakers' thoughts in a particular way. Understandings of language and culture remained essentialist and separatist, which led Wittgenstein (1921: 246) to state almost a century later: "Die Grenzen meiner Sprache sind die Grenzen meiner Welt" [i.e. 'The limits of my language constitute the limits of my world'].

European-American anthropological research around Boas, Sapir and Whorf in the early 20th century elaborated on the idea of languages influencing patterns of thinking in what came to be known as the Sapir-Whorf-hypothesis. "Human beings", Sapir (1929: 209–210) explained, "are very much at the mercy of the particular language which has become the medium of expression for their society. [. . .] We see and hear and otherwise experience very largely as we do because the language habits of our community predispose certain choices of interpretation". In its weak form of linguistic relativity, which proposes a correlation rather than a deterministic relationship between languages, the Sapir-Whorf-hypothesis has remained generally accepted to this day (see e.g. Agar 1994: 71; Danesi & Rocci 2009: 140). Kirkpatrick (2007: 170) claims that "speakers who come to *lingua franca* communication using their own varieties of English will be using varieties of English that see the world in different ways [italics in original]". Sapir further questioned the one-to-one-correspondence between individual languages and cultures, acknowledging the possibility of shifts and multiple references, which any attempt to understand the interplay of language and culture in ELF must necessarily build upon.

While all research outlined so far has focused on the question of how language(s) influence individual and collective thinking and behaviour, from an ELF perspective the opposite and much less frequently investigated approach seems just as promising: How can linguistic phenomena be explored and explained under consideration of cultural conceptualizations and manifestations? Structural and generative approaches dominating linguistic research for much of the 20th century left little space in this regard, with science-oriented linguists exploring context-independent systems and linguistic universals. As ELF, however, is highly context-dependent, research into ELF needs to move beyond formal-structural theoretical linguistics.

From the 1960s, ethnosciences (see e.g. Hymes 1972) and systemic functional linguistics (see Halliday 1979) took up research on context-dependent language use as part and expression of culture from anthropological and linguistic perspectives alike. Building on Saussure's semiology (see Saussure 1916), culture is here understood as a "semiotic metasystem" (Danesi & Rocci 2009: 149), while language is seen as part of this system, but also as "the primary semiotic means of both presenting and creating culture" (Baker 2011:198; see Geertz 1973; Halliday 1979). Linguistic anthropology brings together linguistic and ethnological research traditions and perspectives (see Hymes 1983: 1), also opening the floor for a study of identity through linguistic means. Taking a view on language as a socially relevant activity (Hymes 1964: 5), it adds a functional dimension to the cognitive approach of structural linguistics. Within the framework of linguistic anthropology, communicative competence was first suggested as a central objective for learners of a language (see Hymes 1972).

In further attempts to specify the relationship between language and culture, the concepts of *linguaculture* (Friedrich 1989: 307) and *languaculture* (see Agar 1994: 73; 265) were introduced to acknowledge the realization that "[l]anguage and culture are [. . .] intertwined completely" (Danesi & Rocci 2009: 149) and "constitute a single universe of its own kind" (Friedrich 1989: 306). Drawing on the weak version of the Sapir-Whorf-hypothesis, Agar (1994: 71) argues that "[l]anguage carries with it patterns of seeing, knowing, talking, and acting. Not patterns that imprison you, but patterns that mark the easier trails for thought and perception and action" (Agar 1994: 71). In suggesting to replace the common terminology L1,

L2 etc. by LC1, LC2 and so forth, Agar sensitizes his readership for the intertwinement of language and culture in all settings possible, but is caught in an essentialist viewpoint at the same time, which seems particularly problematic in ELF contexts. Risager (2006: 2; 2012: 105–108) introduces a transnational perspective, separating between individual languages and noncongruent cultures in a differential sense, while at the same time acknowledging the fact that language(s) can never be culturally neutral (see also Seidlhofer 2002: 273; Baker 2018a: 29), as has occasionally been suggested for English as a Lingua Franca (see e.g. House 2014: 364).

The recent transdisciplinary field of cultural linguistics takes up the idea of linguistic relativity from Boasian linguistics and ethnolinguistics and links them with cognitive sciences (Palmer 1996; Sharifian 2017). Cultural linguistics poses

> a framework that is particularly sensitive not only to the role of culture in linguistic choices and perceptions, but also to the role of language in maintaining and transmitting the cultural conceptualizations that these linguistic choices have produced over time under the influence of pre-existing cultural and linguistically entrenched schemas. (Frank 2015: 493)

Cultural cognition emerges from communication and comprises cultural conceptualizations, which differentiate into cultural schemas, cultural categories and cultural metaphors (Sharifian 2015: 477–482). With a schema understood as a "familiar pattern from previous experiences that we use to interpret new experiences" (Yule 2002: 85), *cultural schemas* refer to culturally determined patterns and processes, such as graduation ceremonies, classroom management or greetings, and are constantly negotiated. *Categories* of objects, events and experiences are also culturally constructed and linguistically labelled (Sharifian 2015: 480–481). Categorizations of nouns, for example, are expressed and at the same time influenced by grammatical systems such as gender or noun-classes (see Deutscher 2011; Beuter 2019c). Cultural influences are finally also at play in *metaphors*, which combine two dissimilar domains of experience. When it comes to the constructed seat of emotions, for instance, culture-bound imagery involving bodily organs is frequent, which, however, may range from belly to liver to heart for different cultures (see Sharifian 2015: 482). Cultural linguistics analyzes cultural conceptualizations in their interplay with various fields of language, such as morpho-syntax, semantics, or pragmatics, and will here be drawn upon for an analysis of covert phenomena of translanguaging (see Section 10.4.4).

2.2.3 Cross-, inter- and transcultural perspectives on ELF communication

Considering the close intertwinement between language and culture, and the central role communication plays in connecting the two (see Kuße 2011: 117), transdisciplinary research approaches appear promising. This section will look into the potential that cross-, inter- and transcultural communication research offers for an exploration of ELF interactions and vice versa.

Cross-cultural research takes a comparative stance and contrasts the realization of a particular phenomenon in different cultural contexts (see Jiang et al. 2021: 2; Pitzl 2022: 57) without any obligatory contact or overlap between them. As ELF communication research, however, seeks to explore interactions *between* interlocutors from different linguacultural backgrounds, a cross-cultural approach seems of limited use here.

Intercultural communication research, in contrast, focuses on this very interface between cultures and so promises a high potential for ELF research, all the more as ELF is employed as the communicative medium in a large number of intercultural settings.[5] However, linguistic aspects have long been neglected in intercultural communication research (see Piller 2007: 215; Dervin & Liddicoat 2013b: 8–10), while at the same time linguistically oriented research on ELF, which is defined primarily by its plurilingual and thereby pluricultural nature, has until recently shown limited interest in cultural aspects (see Baker 2018a: 25–33), with some notable exceptions (see in particular Baker 2011, 2015, 2018a and b, 2021, but also Pölzl & Seidlhofer 2006). Culture, identity and intercultural awareness have been outlined as three major strands, with regard to which ELF and intercultural communication research can benefit from each other (see Baker 2018a: 28).

Research on ELF can make an important contribution, for example, when it comes to challenging monolithic notions of national languages and cultures, which are still pervasive in much intercultural communication (and even some ELF) research (discussed e.g. in Piller 2007: 210; Holmes & Dervin 2016: 10–11), still promoted by a powerful public discourse which runs contrary to the post-structural turn in cultural studies as outlined above. It is indeed "the ability of language and culture to come together in novel ways that enables a language such as English to function as a global lingua franca" (Baker 2018a: 29). Research needs to avoid the trap of presuming a priori cultural memberships "by a commitment to studying language, culture and communication *in context* [italics in original]" (Piller 2007: 217). National cultures have in fact been shown to often be of little relevance in intercultural communication through ELF (see Meierkord 2002: 128–129), and constitute just one reference system for interlocutors among many others, such as faith, gender or ethnicity (see Piller 2007: 211). While "suspend[ing] recourse to their own

5 While in a broad sense of culture all interaction could be considered intercultural, Baker (2018a: 27) regards communication as intercultural "when participants and/or researchers regard linguacultural (linguistic and cultural) differences as significant in the interaction", which is the case in the present study (see Section 10.1).

native culture norms" (Kaur 2016b: 150–151), ELF interlocutors are at the same time found to detach their English from its Anglophone cultural background in a process of "'de-anglicizing' their English" (Seidlhofer 2011: xi) and fill it with dynamic cultural contents, which go beyond national references. ELF speakers collaborate, accommodate and negotiate meanings in a "Third Space" (Bhabha 1994: 36–39), co-constructing a "third culture" (see Meierkord 2012: 190), which is characterized by dynamism and fluidity. In this space, interlocutors are *doing* language, identity and culture (see Piller 2007: 211; Holmes & Dervin 2016: 11). In other words, "[c]ulture is a verb" (Scollon et al. 2012: 5), and so are language (see e.g. Jørgensen 2008: 169;[6] Seidlhofer for DYLAN 2011;[7] Ehrhart 2015: 306–307; Hülmbauer 2016: 199–201) and furthermore identity (see Dorleijn et al. 2020: 366 and 369; Section 3.3).

As cultural boundaries are neither clear-cut nor stable in ELF interactions, and cultures themselves become fluid, a transcultural framework keeps gaining ground as a suitable reference system for ELF research purposes (see Baker 2021: 1; Pitzl 2022: 64; Ishikawa 2022: 13). Research on communication as a transcultural phenomenon has emerged within a general post-structuralist *trans-turn* in applied linguistics, which questions existing boundaries in various domains and emphasizes aspects of interwovenness (see Hawkins 2018: 75). Transcultural communication research takes critical intercultural communication research forward, building on the concept of transculturality, which moves away from conceptualizing cultures as separate, homogenous entities as in cross- and intercultural viewpoints, but as internally heterogeneous nexuses characterized by hybridity (see Welsch 2010: 43).[8] Transcultural communication itself has been defined as "communication where interactants move through and across, rather than in-between, cultural and linguistic boundaries, thus, 'named' languages and cultures can no longer be taken for granted and in the process borders become blurred, transgressed and transcended" (Baker & Sangiamchit 2019: 472). Baker & Ishikawa (2021: 184) emphasize that in transcultural communication "cultural and linguistic differences are relevant to participants or researchers but not necessarily linked to any particular group".

---

6 Jørgensen (2008: 169) also uses the verb "to language" and the agent noun "languager".

7 Seidlhofer's authorship of the catchphrase "language is a verb" is attested in Hülmbauer (2016: 198).

8 Addressing a global phenomenon, the idea of transcultural communication has found resonance in various parts of the world. Jiang et al. (2021: 3–4) present the example of the *Tianxa System* (translated as 'All-under-heaven System'), developed by the Chinese scholar Tingyang Zhao (2016) with its aim to "remove the border" and "achieve borderless communication" (Jiang et al. 2021: 3–4), as taking transculturality forward.

A transcultural communication approach stresses the finding that various cultural systems present in ELF interactions are enacted simultaneously (see Baker 2021: 8) rather than side by side or in opposition to each other. Cultural references may include, but are far from restricted to national categories (see Ishikawa 2022: 14; Beuter fthc.). Baker (2021: 9) suggests that for ELF communication "the trans metaphor replaces the inter metaphor to emphasize that in such interactions participants can transgress and transcend linguistic and cultural borders". With regard to the existence of individual cultures he continues to explain that

> in transcending borders we are presupposing their existence but in order to avoid methodological nationalism there should be no a priori assumptions about which categories and boundaries are relevant to interactions. [. . .] [T]hrough the processes of transgressing and transcending boundaries, those very boundaries themselves are transformed, potentially opening up new social spaces and identities (Baker 2021: 9).

These processes of transgressing, transcending and transforming can, amongst others, be laid open through discourse analysis. They also show in various practices of linguistic permeation or *translanguaging* (see e.g. García & Li 2014: 21; Hülmbauer 2016: 195–201; Section 2.2.4 and Chapter 10), in which linguacultural systems permeate each other on all linguistic levels, from semantics and pragmatics to syntax, morphology and lexicology, to phonetics and phonology. As translanguaging phenomena are all abundant in ELF, ELF itself emerges as a linguaculturally not only hybrid, but also fluent phenomenon, which challenges "definite ideas about borders and boundaries between communities, cultures and languages, which had seemed so secure for so long" (Seidlhofer 2018: 97). ELF interlocutors appropriate the English language in a social-constructivist way (see Kohn 2018: 5–6) and turn it into a multilingua franca (see Jenkins 2015; Ishikawa 2022: 3–6), employing their full repertoire to accommodate their communicative needs as arising from situational contexts. This will necessarily involve deviating from English 'native' speaker norms and bring up questions of ownership and authority (see Widdowson 1994: 4–7). In the face of consequent uncertainty with regard to questions of formal correctness, appropriateness has alternatively been foregrounded as a conceptual benchmark in an ELF-aware language teaching (see e.g. Cogo 2016a: 88). Intercultural communicative competence (Byram 1997), intercultural awareness (Baker 2018a) and meta-cultural competence (Frank 2015) have been suggested as learning objectives so as to strengthen skills of adaptation and reflexion (see Chapter 12).

Processes of cultural transgression and transcendence are not restricted to linguistic phenomena alone, but also include other semiotic modes of expression, such as gestures, clothing, music etc. Interlocutors "create meaning and emotional impact through the interaction of modes" (Ishikawa 2022: 11). Hawkins (2018: 56) has proposed the notion of transmodalities "to acknowledge the fluid integration, and mutual informativity, of repertoires of resources in meaning-making processes across local and global encounters and interactions in our globalized world". Translanguaging and transmodal processes illustrate the transcultural nature of ELF interactions.

In the present study, ELF will be conceptualized as a transcultural medium in multilingual interactions (see also Dewey 2021: 609). The influence of national cultures does not cease to exist, but constitutes just one of many factors that may influence interlocutors' conversational choices (see Piller 2007; Spencer-Oatey 2007). In their enactment and construction of identities, ELF interlocutors may also build on their common access to English as well as their shared experiences of 'foreignness' to establish common ground and solidarity (see Beuter fthc.). Recent research correspondingly aims at transcending the "obsession with cultural difference" (Holmes & Dervin 2016: 11), and looks into where culture and identity are made relevant and how they are (co-)constructed and transformed in interaction.

Against this backdrop of non-essentialism and transformation, I also suggest to apply and combine Mortensen's (2017) concept of *Transient Multilingual Communities* (TMCs) and Pitzl's (2018b) concept of *Transient International Groups* (TIGs) as helpful reference systems for various sets of ELF speakers. Mortensen & Hazel (2017: 256) describe TMCs as "social configurations where people from diverse sociocultural and linguistic backgrounds come together (physically or otherwise) for a limited period of time around a shared activity", while Pitzl (2018b: 30) defines TIGs in a similar fashion as "groups of multilingual ELF users who interact for a particular purpose at a particular location for a certain amount of time". Both concepts emphasize the social, fleeting and multi-referential nature of the corresponding configurations, hence appearing suitable for a large part of ELF settings. Pitzl's preference for *groups* rather than *communities* takes into account the fact that interlocutors in many ELF contexts constitute relatively small and short-lived groups rather than more stable communities. Her renewed emphasis on national categories and binary oppositions through the choice of *international* as a premodifier must, however, be viewed critically for ELF contexts as outlined above.[9] I will hence use the blended concept of *Transient Multilingual Groups* (TMG) in the present study.

9 Pitzl herself critically comments on this in a footnote (Pitzl 2018b: 30–31), but continues to use *TIGs* in her subsequent work (see e.g. Pitzl 2022: 64–66).

2.2.4 Translanguaging

With ELF emerging in multilingual contexts, linguacultural concepts of various origins inevitably feed into ELF and are – consciously or unconsciously – used by interlocutors to enhance their communicate effectiveness. In line with a recent trans-turn in applied linguistics (see Hawkins & Mori 2018: 1), searching to account for a linguacultural reality of increasingly blurring boundaries, Pennycook (2007: 47) speaks of "transidiomatic and transcultural practices" at work to refer to "the constant processes of borrowing, bending and blending of cultures, [. . .] the communicative practices of people interacting across different linguistic and communicative codes, borrowing, bending and blending languages into new modes of expression". The Welsh educationalist Cen Williams (2002: 39–41) was the first to use the term *translanguaging* to describe this phenomenon in bilingual pedagogic contexts. While the gerund *languaging* foregrounds "dialogical" and "dynamic aspects" as well as the "fluidity of the communication process" in open linguistic systems (Ehrhart 2015: 306–307), the prefix *trans* adds the aspect of transgression, which here refers to the transgression of alleged boundaries between linguistic codes. The resulting ambiguity between translanguaging (and transculturing) on the one hand, and nameable languages (and cultures) on the other hand, which has previously been pointed to (see Section 2.2.1), cannot be fully dissolved. This ambiguity also becomes apparent in the present study when participants practise translanguaging while openly reinforcing boundaries between clear-cut languages and cultures in discourse (see Chapter 10).

The concept of translanguaging has meanwhile been extended to bi- and multilingual contexts more generally (García 2009: 140) to denote "the fluid and dynamic practices that transcend the boundaries between named languages, language varieties, and language and other semiotic systems" (Li 2018: 9). Languages are no longer seen as separate and closed cognitive systems, but as composing one integrated sociolinguistic repertoire (see Jørgensen 2008: 164–167; Canagarajah 2011: 401; Horner & Weber 2018: 110; Hawkins 2018: 57), one "trans-semiotic system with many meaning-making signs, primarily linguistic ones, that combine to make up a person's semiotic repertoire" (García & Li 2014: 42). It is for interactional linguistic research to find out "how human beings use their linguistic knowledge holistically to function as language users and social actors" (García & Li 2014: 32).

Through their use of multiple linguistic resources, linguaculturally hybrid interlocutors create a translanguaging space, which "is not a space where different identities, values and practices simply coexist, but combine together to generate new identities, values and practices", with boundaries "ever-shifting" (Li 2011: 1223). *Cultural translation* (see Bhabha 1994) takes place in this translanguaging space through a variety of meaning-making processes. Creativity is part of these practices, granting multilingual interlocutors "the ability to choose between following and flouting the rules and norms of behaviour, including the use of language, and to push and break boundaries between the old and the new, the conventional and the original, and the acceptable and the challenging" (Li 2001b in García & Li 2014: 32).

Translanguaging is considered a promising concept for analyzing and theorizing ELF, and theoretical as well as empirical work on translanguaging in ELF is gaining ground (see e.g. Cogo 2012; 2020; Kalocsai 2014; Jenkins 2015; 2018; Ra 2021). This ties in with a recent re-orientation in conversation analysis (CA) to acknowledge and explore heterogeneity and hybridity in talk in interaction after classic CA had been criticized for its monolingual bias by applied linguists (see Kasper & Wagner 2014: 200). The present work will explore processes of translanguaging and meaning-making in translanguaging spaces as they emerge in intercultural interaction (Chapter 10). Linguistic choices will again be analyzed in the framework of larger social processes and functional aspects of ELF – in other words, it is language in use or pragmatics that the focus will be placed on.

3 ELF pragmatics and interactional linguistics

Pragmatics in its widest sense has been defined as “the study of language in use” (Huang 2014: 1). It is here conceptualized as constituting “*a general functional (i.e. cognitive, social and cultural) perspective* on language”, which investigates “*the meaningful functioning of language* in actual use, as a complex form of behaviour that *generates meaning*” (Verschueren 1999: 11 [italics in original]).[10] According to Culpeper & Haugh (2014: 6), pragmatics explores the triadic relationship between linguistic signs, entities these signs refer to, and the users and interpreters of the signs (see Figure 3).[11] As a linguistic approach that centrally “allows humans into the analysis” (Yule 2002: 6), pragmatics seems a particularly promising approach in ELF research, which is interested in context-dependent and dynamic language use by speakers of different linguacultural backgrounds. Interactional functions are explored as they emerge from the interplay between linguistic choices and contextual factors.

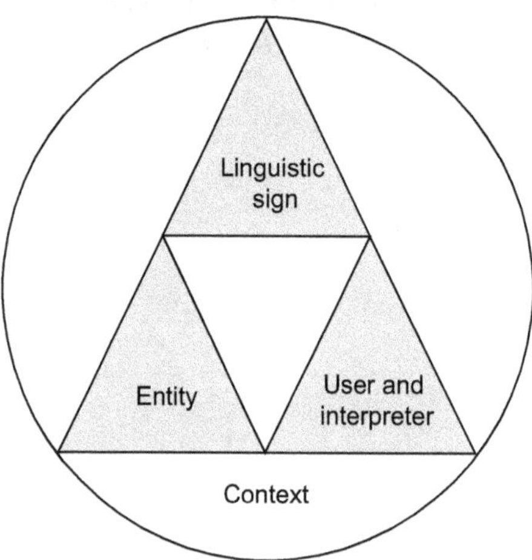

Figure 3: The triadic nature of pragmatics (based on Culpeper & Haugh 2014: 6).

The present chapter starts off with an outline of central concepts in pragmatics relevant to the subsequent data analyses. It investigates how interpersonal prag-

10 For a critical discussion of attempts to define the term *pragmatics* and further elaborations on various perspectives, see particularly Levinson (1983: 5–35).

11 Semantics, in contrast, investigates the dyadic relationship between linguistic signs and corresponding entities, while syntax as a monadic approach looks at forms only (see Culpeper & Haugh 2014: 6; Yule 2002: 4).

https://doi.org/10.1515/9783110786576-003

matics and interactional linguistics may concertedly be drawn upon to explore functions of language use in conversations and how identity comes into play. The final part of this chapter will take up considerations on language and culture and focus on intercultural, transcultural and ELF pragmatics, assembling insights from previous research and theoretical reflections on these more specialized fields.

3.1 Interactional premises

As interactional functions unfold on the basis of formal properties, any understanding of ELF pragmatics requires an investigation of the composition of conversations first. Interactional linguistics (see Couper-Kuhlen & Selting 2018) and conversation analysis (CA) (see Sacks et al. 1974) offer theoretical and methodological frameworks that allow for a fine-grained analysis of interactional procedures (see Section 4.4). Methods not only from intercultural communication research but also from CA and interactional sociolinguistics have hence exerted important influences on ELF communication research (see Pitzl 2022: 60).

With its focus on the analysis of natural interactional data, ethnomethodologically informed conversation analysis promises a high potential for pragmatic research (see Levinson 1983: 294–332), as "[c]onversation and talk in general are the home of language in use" (Gardner 2006: 272). The sociocultural potential of interaction is explored in interactional linguistics from a decisively linguistic perspective, which combines CA methods (e.g. sequential analysis) with linguistic tools (e.g. form-function pairings) (see Barth-Weingarten 2008: 77; Section 4.4). Interested in the interplay between linguistic patterns and interaction, interactional linguistics constitutes "a perspective on language structure and use informed by language's natural habitat in the interaction order" (Couper-Kuhlen & Selting 2001: 1). Building primarily on CA but shifting the focus from ethnology and sociology to linguistics (see Imo 2013: 76), interactional linguistics emerged as a distinct field of study in the 1990s, constituting a "descriptive, functional, linguistically informed approach to language and language use" (Barth-Weingarten 2008: 77). It is grounded in the basic assumption that language and social interaction are mutually dependent (see Schegloff 1996b: 54) and builds on the following suppositions (Barth-Weingarten 2008: 82–86):

- *Linguistic patterns are flexible and adaptable entities, which are collaboratively achieved.* [. . .] Interactional Linguistics conceptualizes language as sets of resources, permitting linguistic practices. [. . .]
- *The relationship between linguistic forms and their sequential interactional context is reflexive.* [. . .]

- *Linguistic forms are tailored to the needs of organizing interaction and interaction is organized by them.* [. . .]
- *The employment of specific linguistic practices in particular sequential environments provides for the interpretation and, thus, the accomplishment of particular actions and activities.* [. . .]
- *Language-specific linguistic forms shape interaction differentially.* [. . .]
- *Linguistic patterns need to be investigated from a holistic perspective.* [. . .] [T]his has come to include a more systematic consideration of non-linguistic means of communication [italics in original].

Both conversation analysis and interactional linguistics conceptualize conversations around turns and sequences (see e.g. Kaur 2016a: 162). Interactional sequences are composed of alternating turns, varying in length between single phonemes and several complex sentences, with one speaker holding the floor until another speaker takes a turn. Turn-taking becomes possible at transition relevance places (TRPs) (see Sacks et al. 1974: 703), which are marked through a combination of prosodic, grammatical and pragmatic indicators (e.g. falling intonation, end of sentence, completion of speech act) (see Gardner 2006: 275–276). While turn-taking normally takes place at TRPs, turns may also overlap to some extent or be separated by periods of silence. The degree to which these deviances are considered normal and acceptable by speakers shows cross-cultural variation (see e.g. Yule 2002: 88).

The internal composition of turns as well as their position within the larger projection of sequences crucially contribute to the collaborative accomplishment of actions through interaction (see Schegloff 1996b, 2007). The formal realization of individual utterances depends on their sequential context, while renewing these contexts at the same time (see Barth-Weingarten 2008: 84). Any analysis therefore needs to take a close look at sequential contexts in order to understand interactional procedures.

Adjacency pairs represent the “minimal interactional sequence” (Clift 2016: 89), consisting of at least two alternating turns produced by two speakers. Interlocutors co-produce adjacency pairs with an expectancy-rising first pair part (FPP) and a responding second pair part (SPP), such as question and answer, or greeting and greeting-in-response. To any FPP there is a preferred SPP, e.g. an acceptance as an SPP to an FPP offer. Dispreferred SPPs are pragmatically marked and precarious with regard to politeness (see Brown & Levinson 1987: 38–43), which is why they are often brought about hesitantly and indirectly, with speakers resorting to mitigators, apologies and appeals for understanding (see Yule 2002: 79–80). The binary structure of adjacency pairs can be expanded in three positions: Pre-expansions pave the way in FPP-position, insert-expansions may occur in between FPPs and SPPs, and post-expansions extend the adjacency pair beyond the end of an SPP (see overview in Clift 2016: 89).

Repair operations represent very common expansions, for instance, covering "practices for dealing with problems or troubles in speaking, hearing, and understanding" (Schegloff 2000: 207; see also Beuter 2019b). Often employed as insert- and post-expansions, they temporarily halt the progression of the interaction. Beyond a correction of errors, repair is also employed for a fine-tuning of particular elements and for making things more explicit (see Kaur 2011: 2706; Kitzinger 2013: 233). Repair may be initiated by either the producer or the receiver of the trouble source (or repairable), and can also be accomplished by either party, which renders a four-fold matrix (see Figure 4). SISR has been found to be the most dominant repair category in general (see Schegloff et al. 1977: 377; Huensch 2017: 358), which may be ascribed to the organization of turns and turn-taking – the first conversational opportunity for repair goes to the speaker – as well as concerns of politeness (see Leech's politeness maxims, Figure 5, Section 3.2). Other-involvement is generally dispreferred (see Schegloff et al. 1977: 362), with OIOR being especially rare (see Clift 2016: 236), due to its potential association with non-alignment or even open criticism (see Kitzinger 2013: 253).

		Accomplisher of repair	
		Self	**Other**
Initiator of repair	**Self**	Self-initiated self-repair (SISR)	Self-initiated other-repair (SIOR)
	Other	Other-initiated self-repair (OISR)	Other-initiated other-repair (OIOR)

Figure 4: Taxonomy of repair (based on Schegloff et al. 1977: 364; Clift 2016: 236).

Exploring the position and composition of turns and sequences constitutes the core of conversation analysis and interactional linguistics, which seek to uncover the substrata of intersubjectivity and processes of jointly accomplished action in interaction.

3.2 Interpersonal pragmatics

While "[t]he very root of the word 'interaction' underscores the centrality of action" (Schegloff 2007: 251), the prefix *inter-* stresses the involvement of two or more people, who do not only negotiate intersubjective understanding but also organize relational matters through interactions. The following section outlines theoretical concepts from *Speech Act Theory* (see Austin 1975; Searle 1969) to the *Cooperative Principle* (see Grice 1975) to *Politeness Theory* (see Leech 1983; Brown & Levinson 1987) and *Rapport Management Theory* (see Spencer-Oatey 2005), all of which serve as a theoretical base for subsequent analyses of interpersonal pragmatics in ELF communication.

Speech acts

The performative aspect of language emphasized by Schegloff is also at the very heart of Speech Act Theory, which is based on the assumption that "to *say* something is to *do* something [italics in original]" (Austin 1975: 12). Austin (1975: 109) proposes that every meaningful utterance or locution is loaded with a functional or illocutionary force, and ultimately provokes a perlocutionary effect. As utterances can have varying illocutionary forces, speakers employ a range of *illocutionary force indicating devices* (IFIDs; see Searle 1969: 62–64; Yule 2002: 49–50), such as performative verbs, stress or intonation, to ensure the hearer interprets the illocutionary force as intended. In addition, certain felicity conditions need to be fulfilled for speech acts to lead to the required ends, which vary depending on the type of speech act. The most general felicity condition, which, however, cannot necessarily be taken for granted in ELF contexts, is for the hearer to understand the language code employed. As in addition the realization of speech acts may considerably differ cross-culturally and cross-linguistically (see Blum-Kulka et al. 1989; Trosborg 2010b), intercultural encounters seem particularly vulnerable to pragmatic misunderstandings.

Based on their distinct illocutionary forces, Searle (1979: 12–20) introduces a taxonomy which comprises five basic classes of speech acts. Following Searle's taxonomy, Yule (2002: 53–55) allocates some general functions to these five basic speech act types:

(1) *Declaration*: The speaker causes a particular situation.
(2) *Representative*: The speaker expresses his or her beliefs.
(3) *Expressive*: The speaker voices his or her feelings.
(4) *Directive*: The speaker wants someone else to accomplish an action.
(5) *Commissive*: The speaker commits him- or herself to some intended future action.

Speech acts unfold their illocutionary force and perlocutionary effects in interaction, which is dyadic by nature. Communicative effectiveness accordingly builds on cooperation between interlocutors, who carefully model their speech acts under consideration of cooperative and politeness principles to reach their goals.

The Cooperative Principle

Communication needs to build on common ground and requires shared principles between the speakers involved in order to succeed. According to Grice's (1975) *Cooperative Principle*, interlocutors normally pay heed to the conversational maxims of quantity, quality, relevance and manner so as to achieve their shared interactional goals by being informative, true, relevant and perspicuous (see Table 2). Beyond what is actually said, implicatures may convey additional meaning (see Grice 1975: 43–44), which hearers can infer on the basis of the Cooperative Principle, drawing on previous knowledge, contextual clues and common ground.

Table 2: Conversational maxims in the Cooperative Principle (based on Grice 1975: 45–47).

	Maxim	Contribution to be...
1	**Quantity**	...as informative as required
2	**Quality**	...true
3	**Relevance**	...relevant
4	**Manner**	...perspicuous

Grice's maxims, however, are often found to be flouted. Speakers may, for instance, withhold important information (flouting the maxim of quantity) or deliberately choose ambiguous expressions (flouting the maxim of manner). These deviations from Grice's Cooperative Principle can often be explained on the basis of the multifunctionality of language (see e.g. Halliday 1976): next to ideational or conceptual functions, interpersonal or relational functions play important roles in communication.

The conversational-maxim view on pragmatic politeness

Interpersonal concerns, in particular issues of (im-)politeness, often account for a flouting of Grice's conversational maxims. Leech (1983) accordingly posits a *Politeness Principle* at work in addition to the *Cooperative Principle*, which decisively influences people's conversational behaviour. He drafts a *General Strategy of Politeness* amounting to the following: "In order to be polite, *S* [self or speaker] expresses or implies meanings that associate a favourable value with what pertains to *O* [addressee or third party associated with addressee] or associates an unfavourable value with what pertains to *S*" (Leech 2014: 90). This overall strategy is further differentiated into ten component maxims (M1 to M10), which pair into five sets with one particular focus each (see Figure 5). Every set again consists of one *O*-oriented and one *S*-oriented maxim each in accordance with the General Strategy of Politeness. All maxims come about with typical speech events, such as commissives for M1 (maxim of generosity) or compliments for M3 (maxim of approbation).

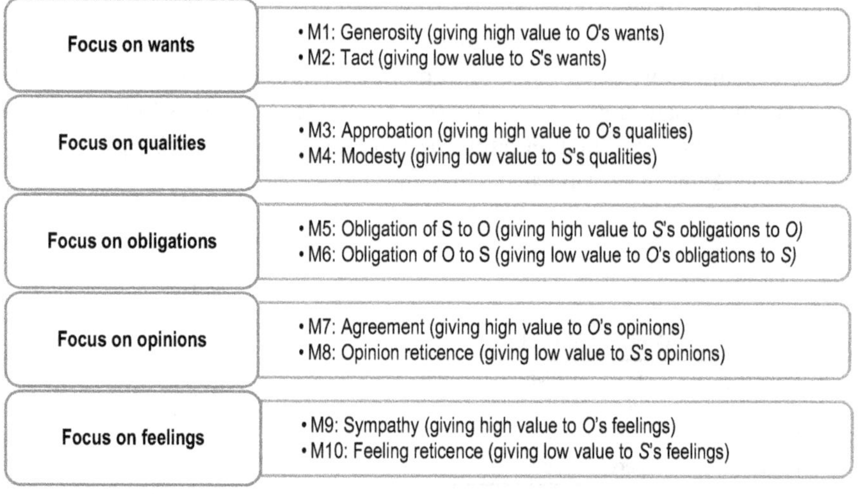

Figure 5: Conversational maxims in the General Strategy of Politeness (based on Leech 2014: 91).

In order to build or sustain rapport, interlocutors will, for example, interact in a consent-oriented way (M7) and largely abstain from self-praise (M4) or other-criticism (M3). The relative importance and pragmalinguistic realization of single maxims may vary with sociopragmatic features of individual speakers, contextual factors and cultural backgrounds, hence posing an interesting field of study in ELF settings.

The face-saving view on pragmatic politeness

Building again on Grice's Cooperative Principle, Brown and Levinson (1987) also place politeness at the centre of interactional choices, but conceptualize politeness as *face work*. They draw on Goffman's definition of face as "the positive social value a person effectively claims for himself [*sic*] by the line others assume he [*sic*] has taken during a particular contact, [. . .] an image of self delineated in terms of approved social attributes" (Goffman 1967: 5). Brown and Levinson (1987: 13) differentiate between positive and negative face, with the former expressing the longing for appreciation and affiliation and the latter referring to the desire for personal freedom and privacy. Both aspects of face may – consciously or unconsciously – be violated in interaction. Criticism of one's person or an affiliated group, for instance, may threaten positive face, while requests, on the other hand, may impose a threat on the interlocutor's negative face. According to Goffman's conversational rules of self-respect and consideration (see Goffman 1967: 6), however, politeness strategies are employed to save one's own and others' face, which are linked in a fragile interdependency. The particular strategies chosen in specific contexts depend on the power structure or vertical distance between the participants, the familiarity and affiliation or horizontal distance between interlocutors, and the degree of imposition (see Brown & Levinson 1987; Spencer-Oatey & Franklin 2009; Leech 2014).

Rapport Management Theory

Brown and Levinson's Politeness Theory has not only been broadly acclaimed and adopted, but has also been criticized for narrowing down politeness to face-concerns, which in addition expose a western cultural bias (see Locher & Sage 2010: 5). Spencer-Oatey (2005; 2008) integrates both Leech's and Brown & Levinson's considerations into the broader conception of her *Rapport Management Theory*: according to her model, rapport does not only build on *face-wants*, but also on *sociality rights and obligations* as well as on *context-dependent interactional goals*. All of these factors mutually influence each other (see Spencer-Oatey 2008: 14).[12]

Interpersonal problems may arise from or worsen through frictions in any one or more of these areas. Not least in their own interest, interlocutors will normally try to avoid this and apply politeness strategies in order to minimize or accommodate disturbances. Appropriate communicative strategies can be drawn from different linguistic domains as depicted in Table 3, with individual options again varying between different linguacultures.

Table 3: Domains of language behaviour influencing rapport (based on Spencer-Oatey 2008: 21).

Domain	Examples
Illocutionary domain	(Composition of) speech acts (e.g. apologies, compliments, requests)
Discourse domain	Topic choice and topic management
Participation domain	Procedural aspects of interaction: overlaps, turn-taking, backchanneling, inclusion or exclusion of participants etc.
Stylistic domain	Forms or address, choice of tone, use of irony
Non-verbal domain	Eye contact, gestures

12 On the usefulness of the rapport management framework for an analysis of relational work in ELF, see also Walkinshaw & Kirkpatrick (2014: 272–274).

3.3 Interaction and identity

Interlocutors are not only concerned with the management of meaning and rapport in their interactions, but also use them as sites for "displaying, constructing, negotiating who they are" (de Fina 2010: 208; Bamberg et al. 2007), in other words, as sites of identification.[13] Whether made explicit or not, identity is considered a salient factor in both language (see e.g. Alexander 2012: 3) and communication (see Jenkins 2007: 202; Svendsen 2015: 14). The negotiation of identities appears particularly fundamental in adolescence, and peer group interactions present "a most important arena for the conversational construction and assessment of social identities of self and other" (Deppermann 2007: 273).

In a poststructuralist and social constructionist perspective, essentialist and static concepts of identity give way to notions of identity as "socioculturally constructed ongoing narratives" (Block 2015: 527; see also Svendsen 2015: 14; Horner & Weber 2018: 118), in a parallel fashion to paradigmatic shifts for the concepts of language and culture as outlined above (see Section 2.2.1; Baker 2015: 106). Identity is regarded as a "social, cultural, and – most fundamentally – interactional phenomenon" (Bucholtz & Hall 2005: 608; Fina 2010: 215; Spencer-Oatey 2007: 642), which suggests a strong alignment between identity studies and interpersonal as well as intercultural pragmatics. Attention in the conceptualization of and research on identity has shifted from monologic approaches to explorations of dialogic co-constructions, with procedural (*identification*) rather than product-oriented (*identity*) views in the centre (see de Fina 2010: 207–208). Integrative approaches further postulate cognitive components at work and conceive of identity as "a crucial social-cognitive mediator that operates between people's social environment and their perceptions and behaviours" (Simon 2004: 42). Next to interactionally negotiating and co-constructing identities, people are believed to "form cognitive representations of who they are that are relatively stable and enduring" (Spencer-Oatey 2007: 642), leading to a dual make-up of identity, which combines emergent social and stable cognitive aspects.

While relational and collective self-aspects provide individuals with a sense of belonging through shared identities, human beings also call upon individual self-aspects at the same time, defining themselves as unique and different from the rest (see Spencer-Oatey 2007: 642; Baker 2015: 112). Joseph (2004: 37) has suggested the terminological pair *identity-as-sameness* and *identity-as-uniqueness* to address these two apparently conflicting sides of identity. This becomes particularly well observable in adolescent peer group interaction, in which interlocutors try to establish a

13 On conceptual overlaps between identity and face, see Spencer-Oatey (2007: 644).

"common we-feeling" (Deppermann 2007: 274), while at the same time striving for individual autonomy. "Adolescents", Deppermann (Deppermann 2007: 273) elaborates, "set themselves apart both intergenerationally from the generation of their parents and from children and intragenerationally from other youngsters who differ in their socio-stylistic orientation. These distinctions are realized by various interactional, emblematic, and actional practices".

People, however, do not only position themselves in interactions, but are also ascribed identities by their interlocutors, which may at times result in contradictory attributions (see Block 2015: 528). Identities are multidimensional in comprising many different categories, such as age, gender, religion, nation, profession or language (see Baker 2018a: 30; for influences of age and language factors in particular, see Rampton 1995). Especially in situations which involve border crossing of some kind (e.g. geographical, cultural, historical) individuals start feeling ambivalent "about exactly who they are and where they belong" (Block 2015: 528), for "asking 'who you are' makes sense to you only once you believe that you can be someone other than you are" (Bauman 2004: 19). Questions of identity are consequently presumed to be highly relevant in intercultural and multilingual, and hence also in ELF settings (see Jenkins 2007: 200).

Necessary as it may be, operating with identity categories may be dangerous as it entails the danger of stereotyping (see Spreckels & Kotthoff 2010: 130), which becomes particularly problematic when identities are reduced to one single category from an outside perspective. Cross-cultural and intercultural research has tended to overemphasize the category of *nation* (see Baker 2015: 109), although nation is not necessarily invoked as a relevant category by participants in intercultural encounters at all (see Spreckels & Kotthoff 2010: 123). Baker (2015: 107) stresses that interlocutors in intercultural encounters draw on local, national and global frames of reference alike. Research needs to investigate which of these and further categories interlocutors actually make relevant in their talk and why they do so (see de Fina 2010: 208).

Language is regarded a key factor in the construction, performance and negotiation of identity (see Creese & Blackledge 2015: 33; Baker 2018a: 30), which it reflects and constitutes at the same time (see Mortensen 2017: 282). Rosen (2014: 23) elaborates on the mutual dependency and interconnectedness between language and identity as follows:

> In principle, identity as a factor in linguistics can work both ways: on the one hand, language crucially contributes to creating a speaker's identity; on the other hand, identity and attitudes (to language) may shape language in determining speakers' choices.

In order to lay open these interconnections, research needs to employ contextually grounded interactional approaches to look into both contents and structures of interaction. Labels, stances, styles, but also entire languages and varieties may prove to be relevant interactional tools in processes of identification (see Bucholtz & Hall 2005: 608).

In ELF communication, one area in which questions of identity become highly relevant is the use of multilingual resources (see Kramsch 2016; Horner & Weber 2018: 104–123), which is also focused in the present study (see Chapter 10). Specifically code-switching has been investigated in previous research as a phenomenon closely linked to questions of identity (see among others Auer 2003; Bhatt 2008; de Fina 2010; for ELF contexts in particular, see Klimpfinger 2009; Pietikäinen 2014; Kramsch 2016). As confirmed in the present study, functions of code-switching include, but are not restricted to, expressing solidarity with a group the speaker feels attached to through linguistic choices (see Jenkins 2007: 200). Especially young people have been shown to exploit multilingual resources to display multiple identities, which are far from limited to ethnic categories, in innovative and often unpredictable ways (see Rampton 1995). Interlocutors in intercultural encounters also draw on multilingual resources to strengthen their shared identity of multilingual individuals, as will be illustrated in the data analyses (see Chapter 10). In exploiting multilingual repertoires, speakers address identity-as-uniqueness and identity-as-sameness at the same time.

3.4 Interactions between adolescents

Questions of identity play a particularly vital role when it comes to interactions among adolescents (see e.g. Nortier 2018: 9; Dorlejin et al. 2020: 366). Djenar et al. (2018: 3) draw a strong connection between sociability and the exploration of identities for young people when they constitute:

> Youth is a time of intense sociability. This sociability is closely linked to young peoples' exploration of their sense of personal identity and their place in larger society. Language provides a vital resource for this sociable engagement and exploration of identity and social position.

Confirming the dichotomy which frames identificatory acts as outlined in the previous section, young people employ their language to explore their own position by demarcating themselves from outsiders, while at the same time expressing their belonging to and solidarity with perceived ingroup members (see Androutsopoulos 1998: 22). Although a considerable body of research on how this finds linguistic expression can meanwhile be recorded (see Chovan 2006: 135), more work is needed to understand ongoing changes in youth language practices, particularly from comparative, pragmatic and conversational perspectives (see Hollington &

Nassenstein 2015: 8). The present study will address this gap and investigate aspects of pragmatics and interactional practices in conversations between adolescents from two different countries.

Considering the variety of terms used to refer to these practices, ranging from *teenage talk* and *teenage speech* to *youth language* and *youth interaction* (see Androutsopoulos 1998: 1; Dorlejin et al. 2020: 368), some terminological explications seem in place. The English language firstly provides various terms to refer to people between childhood and adulthood, such as *adolescents*, *teenagers*, *young people* or *youth*. Although these terms are often used synonymously (see e.g. *teenager* and *adolescent*; *adolescent* and *youth* (OED n.y.); *youth* and *young people* (WHO n.y.)), they come about for many speakers and in different societies and times with slightly distinct denotations and connotations (see Androutsopoulos & Georgakopoulou 2008: 457; UNDESA n.y.). Differences concern age ranges, for example, with the term adolescents roughly covering people aged 10–19, teenagers those aged 13–19, young people 10–24 year-olds and youth 15–24-year-olds (see WHO n.y.). Social criteria have also been discussed as defining factors, such as determining the time between the completion of compulsory education and the taking up of the first permanent job as a criterion for the concepts young people and youth (UNDESA n.y.), which, however, may question some age ranges given above. It is important to keep in mind that, whatever term is used, the group in question constitutes a socioculturally very heterogeneous group with fuzzy age boundaries on both sides. All terms mentioned apply to the participants in the present study and will hence be used in order to include and evoke the various facets mentioned.

As outlined above, young people use language, especially in peer interactions, in particular ways. While the term youth language (see e.g. Nortier 2018: 4–9) seems to foreground linguistic characteristics, youth speech and even more so youth talk move the focus to include an addressee perspective, with youth interaction taking the most decisive dialogic stance and including interactional characteristics beyond the use of language.[14] Rather than comprising homogeneous and static entities, youth language, talk and interaction change depending on their particular users and contexts (see Nortier 2018: 9). Investigations in different subgroups of young people expose the constructive and transient nature of youth language practices (see Djenar et al. 2018: 11).

14 A growing number of these interactions among young people take place in computer-mediated spaces. While research looking into youth language practices in computer-mediated communication (CMC) is thriving (see e.g. Tagliamonte 2016; Androutsopoulos 2018; Siebenhaar 2018; Thode Hougaard & Rathje 2018; Hollington & Nassenstein 2018; Busch 2018; Glaznieks & Frey 2018; Rotne 2018), this area, however, will not be addressed here, as all conversations analyzed took place in face-to-face settings.

Youth languages are commonly viewed as glocal phenomena (see Görke 2018: 119), showing globally shared features and locally influenced heterogeneity alike. The fact that they are primarily used as a demarcation marker (see Chovan 2006: 135) explains the high local variability, transient nature and innovative power of youth languages (see e.g. Androutsopoulos 1998: 19; Hollington & Nassenstein 2015: 3): culturally diverse subgroups coin their own codes and change it again as soon as alleged outsiders start to appropriate parts of it. While youth languages are often stigmatized by outsiders, adults are still found to draw on select features in certain context in attempts to increase their own popularity (see Djenar et al. 2018: 10).

Although youth languages cannot be viewed as monolithic and stable entities but need to be conceptualized as context-dependent and transient social practices, some more general identification markers seem to characterize youth languages through times and places. Table 4 provides an overview of major characteristics without claiming to be exhaustive.

Table 4: Common features of youth languages (based on Androutsopoulos 1998: 7–15; Görke 2018: 103–104; Palacios Martínez 2018: 363 and 382; Djenar et al. 2018: 21; Dorleijn et al. 2020: 370).

Preference for brevity	Shortening of words Syntactic reductions
Creativity	Derivational processes Formation of acronyms Changes in denotation and connotation, particularly for intensifiers, evaluative expressions and discourse markers In English: Use of *be like* as a quotation marker[15]
Use of sound language	Onomatopoeia Use of isolated verb stems denoting sounds as reaction markers
Sociable nature of conversations	Frequent use of address formulae Frequent use of discourse markers Playful and humorous language
Mixing of styles and codes	Stylization Translanguaging

Resorting to and mixing different styles and codes has repeatedly been emphasized as a central characteristic of youth language practices (see e.g. Androutsopoulos 1998: 14; Hollington & Nassenstein 2015: 2; Nortier 2018: 5). The active exploitation

15 Similar processes have been reported for other languages, e.g. quotative *so* in German youth language (see Androutsopoulos 1998: 26).

of multilingual repertoires by adolescents becomes especially well observable in urban contexts (see Jørgensen 2008: 161). It hence comes about with little surprise that translanguaging[16] in various forms emerges as a highly interesting research field within the present study (see Chapter 10), which explores conversational practices between adolescents, who come equipped with plurilingual repertoires and meet in an urban setting (see Section 4.1).

The merging of linguistic codes is a precondition and expression of transcultural practices at the same time. The following chapter will shed more light on transcultural pragmatics and its meaning for the analysis of ELF interactions.

3.5 ELF pragmatics in an inter- and transcultural framework

Interaction in globalized contexts is increasingly often conducted between people of diverse linguacultural backgrounds. In a response to this sociocultural reality, intercultural pragmatics branched off as a distinct subdiscipline within pragmatics in the early 2000s[17] to "investigate[s] how the language system is put to use in social encounters between human beings who have different first languages, communicate in a common language, and, usually, represent different cultures" (Kecskés 2011: 372). Within the recent trans-turn in applied linguistics (see Section 2.2.3), intercultural pragmatics has given birth to transcultural perspectives (see Baker 2018a: 25), which emphasize the permeability of linguacultural systems. While strategies of translanguaging can only be understood and analyzed within a transcultural paradigm, the well-researched field of intercultural pragmatics still provides plenty of tools and findings useful for a sound analysis and interpretation of pragmatic strategies employed in ELF interactions. Processes of linguacultural transgressing, transcending and transforming (see Baker 2021: 9; Section 2.2.3) in ELF communication, however, affect pragmatics just as any other linguistic area. For this reason, I will take a predominantly transcultural stance in analysing ELF pragmatics, while still drawing on and incorporating findings from intercultural pragmatics research.

---

16 Jørgensen (2008: 170) describes these practices as "polylingual languaging" to encapsulate an integration of several codes on the one hand, and the constructive nature of using language on the other. However, the prefix *trans-* in translanguaging is considered to express the dispersion of boundaries between codes by the respective practices more adequately in the present study.

17 The first volume of the journal *Intercultural Pragmatics* was published in 2004. International conferences on intercultural pragmatics have taken place biennially since.

Both inter- and transcultural lines must again be demarcated from cross-cultural approaches to pragmatics, which, rather than looking at jointly achieved interaction, take a contrastive perspective on pragmatics in different linguacultural systems (see e.g. Gumperz & Cook-Gumperz 1981; Blum-Kulka et al. 1989; Geluykens 2007; Trosborg 2010b).[18] While this approach seems of limited use to explore ELF pragmatics overall (see Section 2.2.3), it can still provide interesting insights when it comes to pragmatic transfer or the question of whose pragmatic norms ELF interlocutors follow in particular situations (see e.g. Section 8.4). The focus here, however, will be put on inter- and transcultural perspectives on pragmatics.

Revolving around the same main issues as traditional pragmatics, intercultural pragmatics applies a specific perspective in trying to capture the particularities of intercultural interaction (see e.g. Kecskés & Romero-Trillo 2013: 1). Characteristics arise primarily from the a priori shortage of common ground. As common ground cannot be taken for granted in linguaculturally diverse settings, it must be co-constructed through communication (see Taguchi & Ishihara 2018: 88). Accordingly, interlocutors in intercultural communication "function as core common ground creators rather than just common ground seekers and activators" (Kecskés 2014: 2). As implicatures become unreliable means in contexts of little common ground, interlocutors may become more conscious of the form and content of their utterances (Kecskés 2014: 3). With a prime interest in being understood, interlocutors in lingua franca interactions try to "foresee possible risks to comprehension" (Mustajoki 2017: 62). Conscious recipient design and strategies of heightened explicitness are employed so as to defuse potential uncertainties, which may also arise from varying levels of skills in the chosen lingua franca. Intercultural communication is furthermore characterized to various degrees by multilingual influences.

Intercultural pragmatics has developed a particular perspective on the investigation of intercultural communication. It can be summarized and projected towards a trans-perspective as follows:

– In accordance with the multilingual nature of intercultural communication, intercultural pragmatics itself takes a multilingual stance. Multilingualism is conceptualized as an integrated, non-summative property of speakers (see Canagarajah 2011: 401), which is expected to decisively influence language use in intercultural encounters. This non-summative perspective on multilingualism is shared by and taken further in transcultural perspectives. Multilingual approaches here give way to investigations of translanguaging, where linguis-

18 Cross-cultural perspectives have also triggered a debate about the universality of pragmatic concepts (see Trosborg 2010a: 8). While there is a vigorous East-West debate ongoing, I have not found any indications of a comparable North-South debate.

tic borders are transgressed and transformed. Analyses of translanguaging practices constitute the core of Chapter 10.

- Socio-cognitive perspectives take account of the "double nature" (Kecskés 2014: 6) of human beings as individuals and social beings at the same time, which calls for integrated research approaches paying tribute to both sides. This "double nature" becomes particularly apparent in intercultural encounters such as the one investigated here, where interlocutors on the one hand shape their communicative behaviour against the background of their individual linguacultural origin, and yet communicate in an explicit effort to co-operatively establish common ground and manage new social relations. As linguacultural transformations on both cognitive and social levels are bound to take place, a trans-perspective seems in place again.
- Intercultural pragmatics emphasizes the need for a discourse-segment rather than a turn perspective (see Kecskés 2016: 26), for it is only in moving beyond individual utterances that the socially constructed meaning-making process of intercultural communication can adequately be captured. This seems to be all the more important in a transcultural stance, in which processes of procedural transformation are of primary interest.

As interaction in ELF represents a particular, though not unique, subtype of intercultural communication (see Baker 2018a: 27) with transcultural processes at work at the same time, ELF pragmatics can be understood as a subdomain of inter- and transcultural pragmatics (see Figure 6).[19] Due to the global significance of ELF, research on ELF and ELF pragmatics has developed almost simultaneously with intercultural pragmatics research as an influential strand on its own, carrying the potential of feeding back into its mother domain. Transcultural perspectives have only recently started to gain ground in ELF pragmatics (see Jenkins 2018: 601; Baker 2018b), with ELF itself emerging as a transcultural phenomenon, bridging the inter-cultural gap and deconstructing linguacultural boundaries at the same time.

While early ELF research in its closeness to the World Englishes paradigm focused on systematizing structural features of ELF (see Section 2.1), the recognition of the characteristically flexible and fluid nature of ELF has led to a shift towards an extended investigation of pragmatic processes (see Widdowson 2015: 363). This change in research paradigms has moved ELF closer to inter- and transcultural communication and pragmatics research, though the potential in bringing

---

19 Variational pragmatics (e.g. Schneider & Barron 2008), in contrast, looks at interactions between interlocutors of a particular English variety and compares them with the pragmatics of another, thus falling into the paradigm of cross-cultural research.

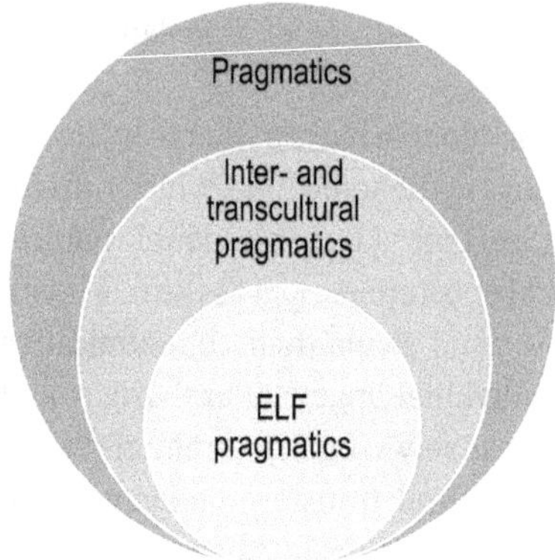

Figure 6: Positioning of ELF pragmatics (own illustration).

these strands together has not been fully exploited yet (see Trosborg 2010a: 30). Both intercultural and ELF pragmatics have also been approached from an interlanguage perspective of L2 pragmatics (see e.g. Kraft & Geluykens 2007; Taguchi & Ishihara 2018: 81). This line, however, has been rejected by the majority of ELF researchers, who emphasize a conceptualization of ELF speakers as competent users in their own right rather than language learners (see e.g. House 2010: 366; Seidlhofer 2011: 24). In the framework of inter- and transcultural pragmatics, strategies found in ELF are correspondingly "not seen as 'compensating' for communicative deficiencies but rather as displays of pragmatic competence by successful multilingual and multicultural intercultural communicators" (Baker 2018a: 33).[20]

Current research on ELF pragmatics focuses on the negotiation of meaning particularly through repetition and self-repair, the employment of interactional elements, idiomatic expressions, and the use of multilingual resources (see Cogo & House 2018: 212; Kaur 2022: 38–40). Three larger strands have been found to be repeatedly addressed in ELF pragmatics research: the use of strategies to raise communicative effectiveness, the use of strategies for accommodation and rapport building, and the use of multilingual resources (see Jenkins et al. 2011; Seidlhofer 2011; Mauranen 2012; Cogo & House 2018; Baker 2018a). Some empirical findings and recent trends in these areas will finally be highlighted and looked at in their relevance to the present study.

---

20 As will be seen, however, linguistic competence such as lexical, structural or semantic knowledge does play a role in the present data when it comes to communicative effectiveness (see e.g. 6.2 and 10.3.4). While the outlined shift of paradigms with its emphasis on communicative competence serves to empower ELF speakers and acknowledge their pragmatic achievements, competence in all communicatively relevant areas must not be taken for granted in ELF conversations, but rather be addressed where the lack of it blocks the way to communicative effectiveness.

Communicative effectiveness

In spite of a lack of common ground, communication in ELF has often been found to be considerably robust and effective, with misunderstandings or miscommunication occurring less frequently than potentially expected (see e.g. Seidlhofer 2004: 218; Kaur 2016b: 136). While in the early days of ELF research the finding that communicative breakdown only occurred rarely was mainly ascribed to the *let-it-pass strategy* (see e.g. Firth 1996: 243–245), which interlocutors employ to keep their conversations smooth and their rapport good, later research found a particular abundance of pre-emptive strategies at work in ELF (see e.g. Cogo 2009: 256; Mauranen 2009: 4; Kaur 2022: 44). Repetitions and self-rephrasing are frequently used as strategies to raise explicitness. Repair as a post-hoc problem-solving strategy (see Chapter 3.1) has primarily been attested as self-repair, with some researchers even reporting a "marked absence of 'other-repair'" (House 2010: 368). ELF interlocutors also resort to metalinguistic comments to expose problems in understanding or to clarify meaning (see Cogo 2016a: 83). As far as the organization of conversation is concerned, turns in ELF interactions have been reported to often be shorter and contain fewer tokens than in English 'native' speaker conversations (see House 2010: 367). Discourse markers such as *I think* or *you know* are often re-interpreted in ELF and become linking and focussing devices (see House 2010: 376–378). The present study corroborates many of these findings, such as the frequent use of repetition and repair, or the brevity of turns, which here shows in complimenting for example. It also contributes new insights into the accomplishment of communicative effectiveness in ELF, such as the use of framing as a pervasive pre-emptive structure (see Section 6.3) or the discovery of the potential of other-repair (see Section 7.4).

Strategies for accommodation and rapport building

Accommodation has been testified repeatedly as a central mechanism in ELF communication to establish both common ground and rapport (see Cogo 2009; Seidlhofer 2009; Baker 2018a; Walkinshaw 2022: 231). Interlocutors engage in collaborative interactional behaviour, which becomes apparent especially in the joint construction of speech acts (see Taguchi & Ishihara 2018: 83). In the present study, the speech act of complimenting will be shown to play a major role in rapport-building (see Chapter 8). In addition, laughter and humour will be explored in their multifunctional potential to contribute to the co-accomplished management of relationships in adolescent ELF (see Chapter 9).

Use of multilingual resources

The involvement of different linguacultural backgrounds is a defining criterion of lingua franca communication. Within the last decade, ELF research has shown an increasing interest in exploring ELF within this multilingual framework (see Chapter 2.1). Recent studies have repeatedly pointed at the versatile exploitation of multilingual resources in various forms of translanguaging, especially though not only in the form of code-switching (see e.g. Klimpfinger 2009; Cogo 2012; 2020; Pietikäinen 2014; Tsuchiya 2020). The present study will investigate the formal and functional range of translanguaging in adolescent ELF and will argue for transparency as the decisive criterion for a classification of translanguaging in ELF and its communicative effectiveness. It is particularly in this area of translanguaging that binary systems of intercultural paradigms hit their limits and ELF exposes its transcultural nature.

4 Methods and data

Proceeding on the assumption that any data analysis and interpretation must necessarily not only build upon a sound theoretical base, but also be preceded by in-depth methodological reflections, the present chapter provides a discussion of methodological choices and a close description of the database. In doing so it addresses a claimed "lack of methodological transparency" (Krug & Schlüter 2013: xxi) generally attested to publications in empirical linguistics and responds to the call for "making methods more explicit" (Krug & Schlüter 2013: xxi). The overall research approach chosen in the present study is of a qualitative, ethnomethodological nature, which allows for a capturing, analysis and interpretation of authentic communicative data in a close-up, context-rich environment (see e.g. Seidlhofer 2009: 56). Against the backdrop of the desiderata and research interests as outlined above, this chapter will first delineate the research design and present the procedure of data collection. It will then provide information on the transcription process and the resulting corpus, before it moves on to present the central methods of data analysis applied in the chapters to follow. Methodological choices will be critically reflected after my linguistic analyses in the final part of this book (Section 11.1).

4.1 Research design

Any decisions on data generation and methods of analysis in the present study directly emerge from the desiderata, questions and objectives as addressed above (see Chapter 1), which are summarized and explored in their respective consequences for the research design in Table 5. The following sections will present details on the implementation of this design.

Overall research approach

Research on intercultural communication may generally build on a collection of authentic interactional data, self-report or survey data and experimental data (see Spencer-Oatey & Franklin 2009: 271–285 for an informative summary of data collection types in intercultural interaction research). While cross-cultural research, mainly for reasons of feasibility when dealing with large amounts of data, has often worked with elicited (semi-)experimental data from discourse completion tasks (DCTs), role plays or multiple choice instruments, the shortcomings of these instruments for research in intercultural pragmatics have repeatedly been spelled out (see e.g. Roever 2013: 242): language use, particularly interactional language use as practised in intercultural communication, is inextricably linked to the very

https://doi.org/10.1515/9783110786576-004

Table 5: Research objectives and design.

Previous findings, desiderata and objectives	Consequences for research design
The overall research objective is English used as a Lingua Franca (ELF).	At least part of the participants need to come equipped with *primary languages other than English*.
ELF research has hardly taken notice of African contexts so far.	The present research deliberately sets a geographical focus and chooses an *African setting*.
Most ELF research has concentrated on adult speakers in business and academic settings.	The present study focuses on *adolescents' use of ELF* in *school contexts*. This is considered all the more relevant as ELF research is mostly conceptualized in an applied linguistics framework with the objective of feeding back into English language teaching and learning.
ELF research is primarily interested in authentic data.	Data are to arise from a context in which ELF is *used naturally* out of communicative necessities.
The lingua franca factor only becomes relevant in dialogic settings.	The approach chosen must be *interactional* rather than cross-culturally contrastive. The study will focus on emerging patterns in conversations, which are dialogic per definition, rather than on language material based on monologues.

sociocultural context it emerges from, a context which (semi-)experimental data are deprived of.[21] Accordingly, authentic interactional data are needed to provide the requested "in-depth, rich insights into specific interactions and their contexts" (Spencer-Oatey & Franklin 2009: 271). As authentic interactional data can be difficult to obtain and time-consuming to handle (see Bondi 2017: 49), however, "[t]here is a relative paucity of research that gathers this type of data", although "there is a pressing need for more studies of this kind" (Spencer-Oatey & Franklin 2009: 271).

When it comes to the pragmatics of ELF, which is embedded in an interactional rather than contrastive cultural paradigm, the investigation of interaction in its natural surroundings becomes almost indispensable. An interactional phenomenon per definition, ELF owes its very existence to its plurilinguacultural context. In line with a large body of ELF research (see e.g. Pietikäinen 2014; Walkinshaw & Kirkpatrick 2014; Pitzl 2018b), the present study therefore draws on a corpus of audio-recorded natural data as its primary data source (the so-called *TeenELF corpus* – 'Corpus of Teenagers' Use of English as a Lingua Franca'), complemented by ethnographic field notes, interviews and questionnaires (see Section 4.2).

21 On the importance of context for any understanding of culture, see also Bamford (2009: 25): "You cannot isolate knowledge from the context that produces it".

For a close, qualitative look at natural interaction as it unfolds through language use in turns and sequences, interactional linguistics has been chosen as an overall methodological approach (see Couper-Kuhlen & Selting 2018). Applying an overall linguistic perspective, it mainly draws on methods from conversation analysis (CA) (see Sacks et al. 1974), which are complemented by an ethnographic perspective (see Hymes 1996). In combining CA and ethnography, interactional linguistics is also closely related to interactional sociolinguistics (see Gumperz 1999), which emphasizes the importance of sociocultural context in interactional research. The combination of a close-up observation of interactional mechanisms through conversation analysis with an ethnographic approach to facilitate the interpretation of linguistic and communicative behaviour on the basis of the situational and sociocultural context has been suggested as a particularly suitable approach for research on ELF (see e.g. Cogo & Dewey 2012: 32), which constitutes a culture- and context-sensitive practice.

In a mixed methods approach (see Ivankova & Greer 2015), methods from quantitative corpus linguistics have further been incorporated where deemed supportive to expose salient sequences or arrive at abstractions of findings. The present interactional linguistics approach thus combines major methods from pragmatics research, namely observational analyses of natural speech stored in corpora, combined with interpretative analyses seeking to find out what particular utterances mean to interlocutors, and formal analyses working against the background of existing theoretical frameworks in linguistics (see also Culpeper & Haugh 2014: 268).

The present study follows an overall approach which Pitzl (2022) has recently termed *micro-diachronic analysis*. While she calls for a "fuller integration of CA, corpus methods and interactional sociolinguistics" (Pitzl 2022: 63) in interculturally oriented studies on ELF pragmatics, her particular concern is on methodological approaches apt to capture transcultural dynamic processes as taking place in transient ELF groups (see Section 2.2.3). Pitzl (2022: 66–67) suggests to primarily base respective analyses on recorded data from authentic interactions, potentially triangulated by elicited data such as questionnaires and interviews as carried out in the present study. The study also meets Pitzl's (2022: 67) request for a combination of content and structure analysis (see e.g. Chapter 10), supported by a qualitative data analysis software (see Section 4.4), and employs conversation analysis, discourse analysis and interactional sociolinguistics alike. Frequency and salience are drawn upon as important aspects to analyze micro-diachronic developments (see e.g. Chapter 9).

The following paragraphs provide information on the setting and the participants of the study, before the chapter moves on to describe the three methodological steps taken to investigate teenage use of ELF – data collection, data transcription, and data analysis – in a way which may provide some further ideas on how micro-diachronic analysis can be put into practice.

Setting

International student exchanges arguably constitute one of the most natural settings for adolescents to use English as a Lingua Franca. Data collection for the present research project was embedded into the framework of a long-standing exchange programme between two secondary schools in Tanzania and Germany.[22] The countries involved were chosen on the basis of the desiderata outlined above and the researcher's previous linguacultural experience, which were expected to help with data analyses especially with regard to multilingual aspects. Groups of students and teachers from both sides prepare annual student exchanges, which regularly take place at one of the two partner schools. While the researcher used the preparation phase for setting up the necessary network, most data were obtained during a one-week exchange between Tanzanian and German students at the respective Tanzanian secondary school in the year 2016.

Primary goals of the exchange programme consist in a dialogic exchange of information, perspectives and experiences so as to provide access to alternative world views, promote intercultural understanding and further a peaceful living together.[23] To reach these aims, participants employ ELF as their transcultural vehicle, and their "only option" indeed (see Seidlhofer 2011: 7; Section 2.1), in order to achieve mutual understanding. Rather than focusing on *learning* English, students here actively *use* English in order to achieve their communicative aims.[24] Set at the learner-user interface, this study reveals the adolescents' learner identity to considerably influence their active use of English, but focuses on language use rather than taking an interlanguage perspective (see also Mauranen 2018b: 106).

Like many African countries (see van der Walt & Evans 2018: 186), Tanzania is linguistically and culturally highly diverse (see Map 1; Schmied 2010: 152; Mohr & Ochieng 2017: 12). Triglossia characterizes its linguistic landscape, with vernacular languages spoken at home, Swahili used as the national lingua franca, and English as an elite international language (see Petzell 2012: 136). Data on the total number of

22 For reasons of confidentiality and research ethics, schools and individual participants involved will not be named but referred to with pseudonyms were necessary.

23 Information obtained from the schools' homepages and personal conversation.

24 In contrast to many language-oriented student exchanges facilitating meetings with 'native' speakers, the present North-South and South-North exchange does not focus on language learning as an explicit objective although the latter one is bound to take place. As successful communication processes, however, pose a prerequisite for the achievement of more explicit goals, such as global learning and a change of perspectives, it comes as a surprise that the language factor is hardly mentioned in some publications dealing with quality standards of North-South student exchange programmes (see e.g. Krogull & Landes-Brenner 2009:16).

languages in Tanzania range between 125[25] (see Eberhard et al. 2019) and 164 (see Languages of Tanzania Project 2009), with numbers varying according to the setting of boundaries in dialect continua (see Wolff 2016: 292).[26] Languages in Tanzania cover representatives of all four African language families (mainly Niger-Congo, but also Nilo-Saharan, Khoisan and Afro-Asiatic languages), plus a few immigrant languages of the Indo-European and Sino-Tibetan language families (see Map 1). With no single language group constituting a clear majority of speakers, Swahili was officially and very successfully promoted as the national language and unifying lingua franca in the young nation-state of the 1960s and 1970s (see Bwenge 2012) and is now spoken by 87 % of the Tanzanian population. At the expense of other African languages the percentage of Swahili L1 speakers is constantly increasing, currently amounting to 28 % of all Tanzanians (based on numbers in Simons & Fennig 2018). While Swahili is mainly used in primary education, politics and the media, higher education[27] and international business are primarily conducted through the former colonial and now second official language English, which, however, is still restricted to an educated elite and hardly spoken as an L1.[28] Code-switching between Swahili and English has become highly common among an urban Tanzanian academic elite, resulting in new linguistic forms summarized as *Campus Swahili* (see Bwenge 2012). Data for the present study were collected in an urban setting. Characterized by an exceptionally high degree of multilingualism, towns and cities represent the overall linguistic situation of Tanzania in a nutshell. Language shift takes place at a fast pace, with Swahili emerging as the primary home language in multilingual families.

Compared to Tanzania, Germany appears linguaculturally more homogeneous on a surface level, as its foundation goes back to the European national movement

---

25 As this number includes languages used for specific purposes, such as religion, there is a slight discrepancy between numbers on the map and in the list.

26 The lack of consistency concerning the exact number of languages in Tanzania also reflects recent theorizing, which increasingly conceptualizes language boundaries as blurry rather than clear-cut.

27 Past decades have seen heated debates about the preferred medium of instruction (MoI) at secondary school level. While in the course of the Swahilization policy of the 1970s the government had announced it an official goal to replace English as a MoI at all levels by the national language Swahili, English has remained the de facto MoI at secondary and tertiary levels throughout. Large parts of the population presently wish to adhere to English, which enjoys high prestige as the language of economic success, but educationalists have recommended a bilingual school policy, and the present government has recently renewed its determination to establish Swahili as MoI (see Mohr & Ochieng 2017).

28 With a total of almost 56 million inhabitants, Crystal (2012a: 64) estimates the total number of English speakers in Tanzania at 4 million, including 52,400 English L1 speakers (Crystal 2010: 371). Due to major changes in demographics, language policies and an increased pace of globalization, the number of speakers is very likely to have risen, though current numbers are not available.

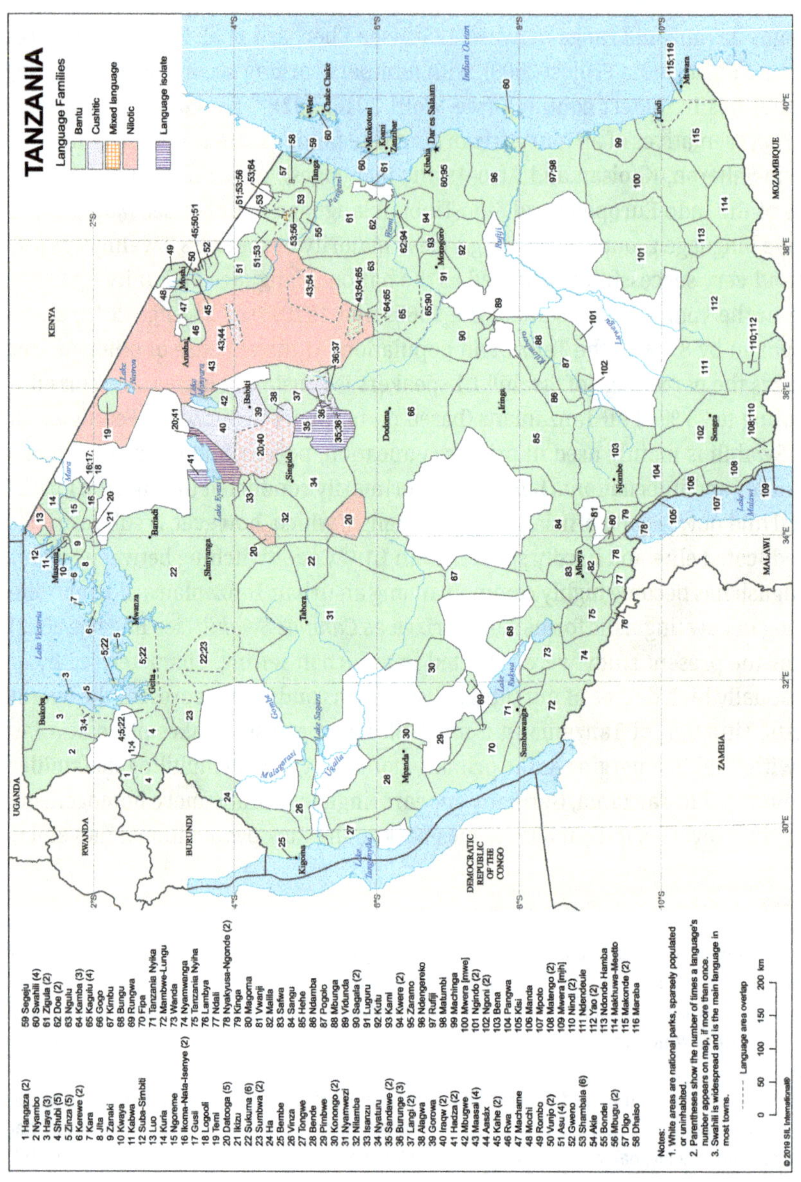

Map 1: Language map of Tanzania © Ethnologue 2019, Eberhard et al. 2019 (used by permission).

of the 19th century.[29] While ideas of linguacultural "purity" and national homogeneity within Germany must be considered to have been illusions from the start, however, migration and globalization have helped further deconstruct the myth of monolithic language-culture-nation-units in the past few decades (see Svendsen 2015: 3). Though 90% of all Germans speak the national language German as their L1, Eberhard et al. (2019) list 25 different languages for Germany, 19 of which are classified as indigenous languages.

In the present study, participants from both countries meet to engage in linguaculturally complex interactions conducted in ELF.

Participants

A total number of 30 students aged 15 to 19 years took part in the exchange, 15 from Tanzania and Germany each. Compiled on the basis of data from participant information sheets (see Section 4.2), Table 6 provides an overview of the group's profile, including the mean age of participants, gender distributions, home languages, as well as the years of formal education in English, both as a subject (ES) and as a medium of instruction (EMI).[30]

Table 6: Overview of participants' profile.

		Tanzanians	**Germans**	**Total**
Age	average in years	17.1	17.5	**17.3**
Gender	female	15	12	**27**
	male	0	3	**3**
Home language(s)	with number of students using it	Swahili (14), English (4), Nyakyusa (1)	German (15), Romanian (1), Russian (1)	
Formal education in ES (English as a subject)	average in years	11	8.7	**9.8**
Formal education in EMI (English as a medium of instruction)	average in years	7.5	1.8	**4.6**

29 European nation states emerged from an internal longing to give political expression to allegedly homogeneous entities of nation, language and culture (see Chapter 2.2.2), whereas the boundaries of what was later to become the nation state of Tanzania were largely drawn by external colonial authorities, who thus created an artificial conglomeration of previously separate linguacultural entities.

30 Individualized information on participants cannot be provided for the sake of anonymity.

The striking imbalance observed with regard to gender can be ascribed to the schools' profiles: While the Tanzanian school is a single-gender institution, its co-ed German counterpart shows a clear majority of female students, probably for curricular reasons.

As far as the linguistic background of participants is concerned, the lingua franca context is made manifest as all students (also) use languages other than English as their respective home languages, predominantly Swahili and German.[31] There is, however, reason to treat the information on home languages with caution: concepts of *home language*, *mother tongue*, *native language* and *first language* are not only highly debated among linguists, but seem to be blurry for multilingual individuals themselves, as excerpt (1) demonstrates. In her information sheet, student LTf[32] states Swahili as her home language and Ndali as her mother's language. In combination with the excerpt below, in which the same student differentiates between her "mother language" Swahili (l. 242) and a "vernacular language" used in her family (l. 246), the difficult conceptualization of *mother tongue* and *home language* in multilingual settings becomes obvious.

(1)
241 **LGf:** [. . .] your mother language is swahili.=
242 **LTf:** =my our mother language is swahili but (.) our FIRST language (0.5) are our vernacular languages. (0.5) yah. tribal languages. but erm (0.5) what connects er all of us (0.5) to speak one language kiswahili.
243 **LGf:** [mh?]
244 **LTf:** [swahili] is what connects (it's) the MAJOR language.
245 **LGf:** and (.) in your family? with you aunt and your [(.) brother and sister?]
246 **LTf:** [↑ah::] (mu:ch) vernacular language is used. (.) we prefer that more. (1)
247 **LGf:** [okay.]
248 **LTf:** [yah.] (.) swahili's (.) sparsely: not that much. (1) yah.
249 **LGf:** and english you learn in school.
250 **LTf:** english i learn in school. (1)

(L1_241-250)

31 The four students who reported to use English at home use it alongside another language.
32 For a decoding of students' pseudonyms, see section 4.2.

While the 14 Tanzanian students filling in the participant information sheet in the present study list a total of 17 different parents' languages (see Table 7), all of them name Swahili as their own home language. 64% use it as their only home language, whereas 36% report on employing an additional language at home (see Table 7), which is mostly English. Ethnically, Tanzanian students identify themselves with one of the more than 120 linguacultural subgroups which build the nation of Tanzania, naming eleven different ethnic groups altogether, which always exhibit close ties to individuals' parents' linguacultural placings.[33] The lack of a one-to-one congruence between nationality, ethnicity and languages used at home for the Tanzanian participants deconstructs notions of closed nation-culture-language units and reveals the speakers' linguaculturally hybrid nature.

The German students in the focus group display a more distinct overlap between notions of nation and home language, with all students employing the national language German as their home language, which is complemented in two cases (13%) by one further language. Parents' languages amount to a total of four. Asked about their ethnic self-identity, however, the German students activate various frames of cultural belonging,[34] drawing on cultural-geographical categories of various sizes (continental, national, regional) to religious affiliations (Protestant, Catholic) to ethnic self-concepts as anthropic beings.

Table 7: Participants' home languages and parents' languages.

	Tanzanian sample	German sample
Percentages		
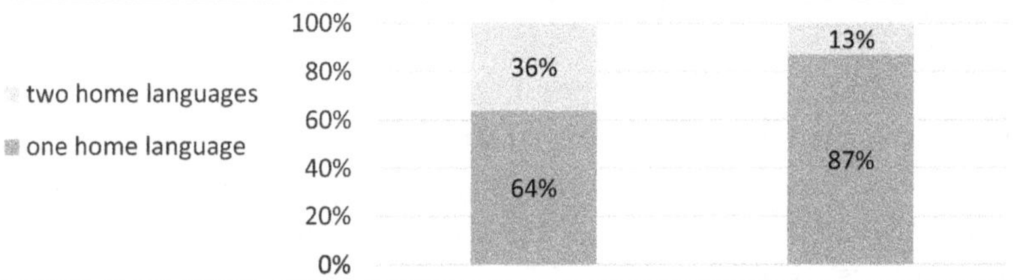 two home languages	36%	13%
one home language	64%	87%

(continued)

33 While *ethnic self-identification* constitutes an open category on the information sheet, the item on *home language* lists Swahili and German as pre-given tick-off categories with one further open slot for other languages (see Appendix B.1), which will have contributed to drawing a picture more homogeneous than the linguacultural reality with regard to home languages.

34 The close affiliations between ethnicity, culture and nation are expressed in standard definitions: The OED online (see OED, s.v. *ethnic*, adj., 1.) defines *ethnic* as "of or relating to national or cultural origin or tradition", and the German *Duden* (see Dudenredaktion, s.v. *Ethnie*, n.; [my translation]) describes an ethnic group as a "group of people (particularly a tribe or nation) that share the same culture".

Table 7 (continued)

	Tanzanian sample		**German sample**	
Absolute numbers of speakers				
	Home languages	**Mother's or father's languages**	**Home languages**	**Mother's or father's languages**
Swahili	14	9		
English	4	1		
Nyakyusa	1	3		
Hehe		3		
Kagulu		2		
Ndali		2		
Manyema		2		
German			15	28
Romanian			1	2
Russian			1	2
Others[35]		10		1

In addition, all students report two or more languages formally studied at school, with Swahili and English playing a major role in the Tanzanian context, and German and English in the German context respectively. As an overall result, the students' "individual multilingual repertoires" (IMRs), defined by Pitzl (2016: 298) as "all the linguistic resources a person has at their disposal" hence vary to a considerable degree. ELF is chosen as a medium of communication in the given situation as it constitutes the only component of the group's shared "multilingual resource pool" (MRP) (Pitzl 2016: 298).[36]

The majority of participants from both countries also report one or more moves of place within their less than two decades of lifespans, which reflects an enhanced mobility and further adds to an individual linguacultural hybridity.

Although the present work does not investigate English as a learner language, proficiency in the language used as a lingua franca undeniably influences communicative processes (see Baker 2015: 112; Piller 2007). A remarkable difference between Tanzanian and German students in the focus group is notable with regard to the years of formal schooling in English. Tanzanian students did not only receive an extra two years of English as a subject on average (11y vs 8.7y; see Table 6),

35 Other languages are Kichagga, Kihaya, Kikurya, Kikwaya, Kinyaturu, Kisimbiti, M'Bena, Mpogoro, Pare, Sambaa, Ukrainian.

36 MRPs in subgroups, however, may show a broader range of linguistic resources. Interlocutors in individual dialogue pairs are seen to switch to French, for example (see C1_163–168), which they have made out as a constituent of their micro MRP.

but also immersed in English as a medium of instruction for much longer than their fellow German students (7.5y vs 1.8y). Although the overall competence in a second or foreign language is subject to much more than quantitative factors alone, German students were particularly impressed by the Tanzanian students' broad vocabulary and reported to profit from the lexical range their interlocutors employed (see Int_GrG; Int_FGf[37]).

With all participants in the exchange "sharing common interests and coming together for certain periods of time to engage in particular activities" (Cogo 2009: 257), they may be considered to constitute a Community of Practice (see Wenger 1998; Seidlhofer 2007). Ethnographic complementary data, which have been considered typical of CoP approaches (see Pitzl 2018b: 28), serve to get further insights into the make-up of this community (see Section 4.2). As the time span of the encounter, however, is very restricted, and further distinctive subgroups – namely the fifteen individual dialogue pairs – can be made out within this larger community, the concept of *Transient Multilingual Groups* (see Section 2.2.3; Mortensen 2017 and Pitzl 2018b) appears more appropriate in the given context.

4.2 Data collection

Conversational ELF data constitute the prime source for the present study. To arrive at a rich and context-sensitive interpretation in an ethnomethodological sense (see Geertz 1973), these data were triangulated by participant information sheets, semi-structured interviews and field notes from participant observation. The research process was designed and conducted in close cooperation with the respective heads of school and accompanying teachers. Following established ethical guidelines, students, and, for participants under-age, parents were previously informed in detail and asked for their written consent on the collection and analysis of data as well as the dissemination of results (see Wray & Bloomer 2006: 173–176). This chapter will portray the process of data collection and introduce the instruments employed.

Dialogue recordings

With a prime interest in natural interaction, the main objective was to produce recordings of authentic dialogues, which constitute "the prototype of language use in social contexts" (Danesi & Rocci 2009: 48). The research project strove at embedding the process of data collection as smoothly as possible into the overall frame of

37 Abbreviations refer to interview data; see Section 4.2.

the pre-existing exchange programme, not only to obtain data as authentic as possible, but also to keep interference for the participants at a minimum. In fact, the research design aimed at contributing to the overall success of the exchange programme with its primary goal of promoting intercultural understanding through an exchange of ideas and worldviews. At the same time, the recordings had to be arranged in a way to make them as accessible and informative for the researcher as possible. In order to meet these demands, the following procedure was adopted.

Students received a short introduction into the project both prior to the exchange and on site, before they were matched into 15 binational dialogue pairs.[38] These pairs remained the same for the rest of the week so as to facilitate a strengthening of relational bonds and allow for both synchronic and micro-diachronic data analyses. Students got together in pairs on four days of the week, picked up a task sheet (see below), then spread all over the school premises and worked on their interactional tasks for about half an hour each day. In an attempt to keep the observer's paradox down to a minimum, the students audio-recorded their own conversations in the researcher's absence (see Labov 1972: 209). In the face of an overall densely packed timetable, this setting allowed for a maximum output of conversational data while reducing the overall time of potentially intrusive recording phases to a minimum.[39]

To ensure dense pair interactions and make the conversations truly meaningful for the students (see Haß 2011: 23 and 189) in times of recording, the teenagers had been involved in putting together topics of their interest prior to the exchange. These clustered around the four major areas *family and friends, nature and society, school and leisure, present and future.* In accordance with a task-based language pedagogy, which seeks to promote intercultural communicative competence through a problem- or product-orientation requiring meaningful communicative action (see Haß 2011: 21–24; 205–207), the students were allocated the task to create and design a so-called *dia|log|book*[40] together, to which each pair had to contribute one page per day. Every pair received an envelope each day containing

38 The matching took place on the basis of two sets of photo cards: Students were asked to choose one card from a set and find their partner.

39 Close observations of free conversations during the remaining time of the exchange, which resulted in a comprehensive collection of field notes, helped the researcher not only to focus on major interactional strategies and patterns, but also to arrive at a rich analysis in an ethnographic sense (see Chapter 4.4).

40 From *dialogue + logbook*; conceptualized by the author for the purpose of this study. In its final version, the dia|log|book documents information that emerged from conversations and which students considered worth noting down, and combines them with a selection of photos. Every student finally received a copy of this book as a keepsake of the exchange.

not only paper and stickers with headings but also a task sheet (see Appendix B.2), which provided all necessary information including some example questions that the students could, but did not have to draw on if they found their conversation in need of new input.

The recordings contain discussions on the respective core topics, interactions pertaining to the written assignments, and casual conversation, which all constituted important parts of the interactions in pairs. Students provided the researcher with a total of 26 hours 16 minutes and 15 seconds of recording from 52 dialogues. Table 8 gives an overview of the recorded material that feeds into the analyses to follow.

Table 8: Overview of recordings (Recording times in hh:mm:ss).

Dialogue pair	**Interlocutors**		**Day 1** *Family and friends*	**Day 2** *Nature and society*[41]	**Day 3** *School and leisure*	**Day 4** *Present and future*	**Total recording time**
Agadem[42]	AGf	ATf	00:34:20	00:33:24	00:38:23	00:32:40	02:18:47
Bilma	BGm	BTf	00:25:54	na	na	na	00:25:54
Charga	CGm	CTf	00:35:05	00:31:22	00:30:04	00:22:10	01:58:41
Douz	DGf	DTf	00:39:24	00:31:59	00:29:44	na	01:41:07
Edimpi	EGf	ETf	00:24:55	00:44:52	00:23:13	00:32:07	02:05:07
Faya	FGf	FTf	00:26:32	00:39:36[43]	00:44:35	00:09:21	02:00:04
Ghadames	GGf	GTf	01:02:16	00:32:26	00:37:11	00:12:25	02:24:18
Hatta	HGf	HTf	00:37:02	na	00:36:00	00:25:26	01:38:28
Ingall	IGf	ITf	00:26:26	00:32:34	00:31:37	00:24:57	01:55:34
Jotwata	JGm	JTf	00:32:39	00:39:28	00:24:06	00:21:38	01:57:51
Kufra	KGf	KTf	00:11:10	na	na	na	00:11:10
Loulan	LGf	LTf	00:37:25	00:36:09	00:06:23	00:18:02	01:37:59

(continued)

41 Anticipating the topic *nature and society* to be the most face-sensitive area of the four, I would have preferred to place it third in the row to facilitate a consolidation of rapport on the basis of less controversial topics first. The order presented here results from a compromise that had to be taken within the larger frame of the exchange programme. Some students indeed reported discussions on Day 2 particularly difficult from an interpersonal perspective, which, however, also provides interesting insights into the interactional management of rapport (see Section 5.2).

42 To ease reference, dialogue pairs were attributed random names of oasis towns following the letters of the alphabet post hoc, which are here listed in alphabetical order. The interlocutors' pseudonyms used throughout consist of an initial letter referring to the name of the dialogue pair the student was part of, another capital letter representing the nationality, and a lower-case letter indicating gender. GTf, for instance, stands for a *female Tanzanian* student part of dialogue pair *Ghadames*.

43 Shaded boxes indicate recordings in groups of three students.

Table 8 (continued)

Dialogue pair	Interlocutors		Day 1 *Family and friends*	Day 2 *Nature and society*	Day 3 *School and leisure*	Day 4 *Present and future*	Total recording time
Merzouga	MGf	MTf	00:41:34	00:36:55	00:30:56	00:23:13	02:12:38
Nizwa	NGf	NTf	00:17:00	00:37:54	00:38:58	00:29:30	02:03:22
Ouargla	OGf	OTf	00:29:58	00:33:45	00:23:18	00:18:14	01:45:15
Total recording time			**08:01:40**	**07:10:24**	**06:34:28**	**04:29:43**	**26:16:15**

Ethnographic complementary data

Conversational data are triangulated in the present study by ethnographic complement data to broaden the interpretative basis and render a "thick description" (see Geertz 1973: 3–30). In the present study, data from participant information sheets, retrospective interviews and ethnographic field-notes gained through participant observation were drawn upon to ethnographically enrich the subsequent qualitative analysis (see Cogo & Dewey 2012; Starfield 2013).

Participant information sheets (see Appendix B) were distributed to the students on the second day of the encounter to elicit sociolinguistic background information on the participants. The design of the information sheet is based on the first page of the Bamberg questionnaire for lexical and morpho-syntactic variation in English (see Krug & Sell 2013: 94), adapted to the target group and research needs (see Appendix B.1). Students were asked to share information regarding their age, gender[44], nationality and ethnic self-identification. The teenagers also answered questions and filled in tables on their own and their parents' education and language profiles. Data on their residence history and previous intercultural encounters, also containing affective questions, were elicited in the third and final part of the participant information sheet. While the sheets on the one hand provide central information on the average age, gender distribution or linguacultural backgrounds of participants, which feed into a detailed description of the sample group as outlined in Section 4.1, data from the sheets are also drawn upon to back up the interpretation of conversational data. The employment of laughter for a management of rapport (see Section 9.2) and translanguaging strategies (see Section 10.3.1), for instance, will partly be read against the backdrop of the speakers' language learning biographies.

44 Binary options in the participant information sheet should be replaced by more open categories in newer versions of the sheet.

In order to strengthen an emic perspective that conversation analysis is interested in (see Section 4.1), semi-structured retrospective interviews (see Mayer 2008; Krug & Sell 2013) were conducted with Tanzanian and German students to elicit explicit statements on the participants' experiences in their intercultural interactions (see Cogo 2009: 259). While an emic perspective is predominantly reconstructed from interlocutors' turns in sequences, (verbal) reactions are sometimes found to be limited or missing in the conversational data. Interviews with "participant-observers" (Cogo & Dewey 2012: 35) can then be useful as "they help identify people's face sensitivities and evaluative reactions, and they can provide insights into the cognitive underpinnings of their reactions" (Spencer-Oatey 2007: 654). Interviews were conducted with two individual Tanzanian students (Int_ETf; Int_HTf) and one German participant (Int_FGf); due to severe restrictions of time, I furthermore organized a group interview with all German students (Int_GrG). Questions progressed from more general aspects concerning the interviewee's experience of the present exchange situation to linguistic and communicative as well as related interpersonal issues, and concluded by a short sequence on metalinguistic awareness and behaviour. Bits of information gained from these interviews are repeatedly drawn upon in the present study (see e.g. Sections 7.3, 9.2, 10.1). In addition, one Tanzanian and three German teachers were interviewed, which provided important background information, but did not feed directly into the analysis of conversational data. Interview guidelines can be found in Appendix B.3.

All data were complemented by ethnographic field notes taken by the researcher as an external participant in the intercultural encounter. Observations focused on the linguistic, communicative and interactional behaviour of student participants. Addressing salient and recurrent features observed, the resulting collection served as a miniature compendium to identify core areas and systematize the subsequent view on the interactional data, while still leaving enough room for new research fields to emerge from the data themselves. Participant observation thus grants a preview to the subsequent fine-grained analysis of the corpus data from audio-recordings.

4.3 Data transcription and corpus compilation

In accordance with the research interest of the present study, all recorded data made available by the students were transcribed sociolinguistically, that is "with a view to capturing detailed subtleties of spoken language" (Block 2015: 535), rather than orthographically. Transcriptions build on Jefferson's transcription system (see Jefferson 2004), with slight modifications and a few additional keys based on the VOICE transcription conventions (see VOICE Project 2007), which pay particular attention to ELF-relevant features (e.g. the transcription of non-English speech). The transcription key as well as a sample extract from a transcribed dialogue are provided in Appendix A. For a facilitation of the process of transcribing, the transcription software *f4* (Audiotranskription n.y.) was used. The resulting *TeenELF corpus* ('Teenagers' Use of English as a Lingua Franca') comprises a total of 190,182 words of transcribed speech.[45] *MAXQDA* (VERBI Software 2022), a software developed for and well-established in qualitative and mixed methods analyses, was implemented for the subsequent process of corpus annotation and data analysis. Categories for annotation emerged from and were adjusted during the conversation analytic process.

4.4 Data analysis within an interactional linguistics framework

As previous data on adolescents' use of ELF are rare, the present study largely constitutes explorative research, seeking to lay bare and investigate major features of teenage ELF interaction. The corpus compiled allows for the required in-depth qualitative analysis of TeenELF pragmatics. With a major interest in linguistic features of interaction, interactional linguistics provides an encompassing methodological framework to explore language use and interactional strategies in the given setting (see Couper-Kuhlen & Selting 2018).

In order to investigate language in interaction along the theoretical premises delineated above (see Section 3.1), interactional linguistics combines methods from ethnomethodology and conversation analysis with general linguistics, interactional sociolinguistics and anthropological linguistics (see Barth-Weingarten 2008: 86). With a distinct focus on linguistic phenomena, the present study primarily draws on conversation analysis as "the most tenable methodology for the analysis of naturally occurring verbal interaction" (Seedhouse 1998: 101), but also resorts to mixed methods approaches to include quantitative analyses where deemed informative. In an ethnographically informed approach, triangulated data are drawn upon for a rich interpretation of findings. Details on the individual methodological strands employed and their application in the present study are provided subsequently.

45 Speaker labels, time markers, passages describing the quality of speaking or providing translations or information on parallel actions are excluded from this count. Contractions such as *I've* or *what's* have been counted as two words.

Ethnomethodology and conversation analysis

Interactional linguistics is grounded in conversation analysis, which in turn has emerged from an ethnomethodological research paradigm (see e.g. Seedhouse 2005: 257; Day & Wagner 2008: 34). Interested in patterns of behaviour in everyday contexts (see Garfinkel 1967: 1), ethnographic research focusses on small-scale settings to conduct in-depth micro-analyses on individual aspects, often drawing on multiple data sources, as realized in the present study. Ethnographic researchers start out from necessarily broad research questions in an explorative, hypothesis-generating approach, as ideas are developed inductively from observations (see Starfield 2013: 51–52).

While ethnography looks into the social, institutional and cultural conditions of human behaviour, conversation analysis narrows the focus down to interactional processes (see Sacks et al. 1974), viewing conversation as "the basic form of speech-exchange system" (Sacks et al. 1974: 730) and thus necessarily social by nature. With ELF research primarily interested in interactional processes and the functional use of language, and ELF itself conceptualized as a social practice (see Section 2.2.1), conversation analysis proves a highly expedient methodological framework, which in fact has been applied in ELF research from its early days (see Kaur 2016a: 161).

Conversation analysis starts from a close observation in the data, from the "empirical bite" (Clift 2016: 31), as it "seeks to discover phenomena in the data, rather than test specific hypotheses about them" (Clift 2016: 31). This data-driven approach or "inductive empiricism" is employed to disclose the interlocutors' own categories and resources (Barth-Weingarten 2008: 87; see also Couper-Kuhlen & Selting 1996: 48) rather than impose pre-existing patterns that may "obscure the very thing that is being investigated" (Sidnell 2009: 169). Instead, conversation analysis investigates "that which the interactants themselves make relevant or talk into being. The constructs studied are therefore those that have reality for the interactants" (Seedhouse 2005: 259).

The fundamental threefold question conversation analysis seeks to answer is "Why this, in this way, right now?" (Seedhouse 2005: 251). Conversation analysis provides the researcher with "the necessary tools to uncover the procedures and methods employed by participants in interaction to produce and interpret talk" (Kaur 2016a: 161–162). Contextuality, sequentiality, and joint construction constitute central concepts in conversation analysis and interactional linguistics alike (see Imo 2013). The analytical focus must consequently be on larger sequences, in which intersubjectivity between the interactants is collaboratively established on the basis of Grice's Cooperative Principle (see Grice 1975; Section 3.2). While sequences comprise one or more turns that cluster to accomplish actions and reactions, turns again consist of various turn constructional units (see Sacks et al.

1974). The sequential organization of turns serves as a scaffolding for interactants and researchers alike. Interlocutors shape their contributions to match the interactional context within a sequence, which in turn affects the subsequent turn, as Watzlawick et al. (1967: 55) summarize as follows: "[E]very item in the sequence is simultaneously stimulus, response and reinforcement". Conversation analysts make use of this interdependency in applying the next-turn proof procedure, in which sequentially following turns are drawn upon as evidence for the action carried out by the previous turn (see Barth-Weingarten 2008: 87). Emerging recurrent cases in turns and sequences can then be compiled to identify more general practices and patterns.[46] Reflexive relationships between form, sequential position and function can be worked out and investigated in their interplay with questions of identity and sociocultural contexts (see Seedhouse 2005: 263).

Linguistic concepts and mixed methods

As outlined above, interactional linguistics can be regarded as a linguistically-oriented differentiation of conversation analysis (see Couper-Kuhlen & Selting 2018), trying to lay bare the mutual relationship between linguistic means and socio-situational needs. Accordingly, linguistic concepts and tools are employed for the description of patterns in interaction (see Barth-Weingarten 2008: 88–89). Form-function pairings and frequency analyses through corpus linguistic methods constitute two central linguistic concepts that are drawn upon repeatedly in the present study.

Investigating language in use, pragmatic research necessarily needs to look at both the realization of particular elements of language and the role these elements play within a particular context. The concept of *form-function pairings*, which is of central importance in usage based approaches of construction grammar (see Goldberg 2013: 27), accordingly runs through the present study like a golden thread (see e.g. Chapters 6, 7, 9). Various examples will also illustrate that the "form-function-context relationship changes corresponding to the shifting attitudes, affect, identities, and relations of speakers" (Taguchi & Ishihara 2018: 82).

In a mixed methods approach so as to make use of "the twin advantages of the use of corpus data in linguistic description" (Mair 2013: 181), the quantitative concept of *frequency* will further be employed in the present study to various ends:

- Frequency analyses will serve to expose short-term diachronic developments and overall tendencies, allowing insights into the relationship between forms and contextual factors (see e.g. Section 10.3.1 on the frequency of code-switching).

---

46 See Watzlawick et al. (1967: 36): "The search for pattern is the basis of all scientific investigation".

- Intra-corpus comparisons of frequency will be used to point to interesting cases, close analyses of which render particularly rewarding insights (see e.g. Sections 9.1 and 9.2 on the frequency and functions of laughter).
- Frequency analyses will also serve to consolidate findings worked out through qualitative analyses as quantification opens the door to cross-corpus comparative studies (e.g. Section 8.2 on formal realizations of complimenting).

In addition to the two general linguistic concepts of form-function pairings and frequency, tools and terminology from various linguistic subdisciplines will be employed as the need arises (e.g. syntax, Section 8.2; morphology, Section 10.4.2; see Imo 2013: 83).

Part II: Communicative aims and interactional strategies

5 Communicative aims in TeenELF

Analyses expose the adolescents participating in the present study to pursue different communicative goals, which can be summarized as the negotiation of meaning, rapport and identity. Next to content and relational aspects, which have been stressed as central in communication research for more than half a century (see Watzlawick et al. 1967: 51; Kaur 2022: 49), students also interact in order to get a clearer picture of who they are, who they want to be and who they appear to be to others. The negotiation of identities appears particularly important in the given age group (see Sections 3.3 and 3.4), gaining force in the face of pluricultural reference systems in the given context.

While this chapter introduces the three macro-aims of intercultural communication separately in order to allow for detailed individual insights, the following chapters will illustrate how students often employ pragmatic strategies in ELF to reach different goals simultaneously so as to maximize their overall communicative effectiveness (see Kaur 2022: 36–37).

5.1 The negotiation of meaning

```
(2)  GTf:  @@@@@ @ (.) don't worry. try try
     GGf:  .hhhhh okay.
     GTf:  (so) [(that i'll)]
     GGf:        [erm:]
     GTf:  understand you.
                                              (G1_147-151)
```

In excerpt (2) from the TeenELF corpus, the students involved make their goal to enhance mutual understanding very explicit. Felicitous interaction indeed centres on mutual understanding. Despite the lack of common ground against the backdrop of diverse linguacultural backgrounds of discourse participants, ELF conversations have repeatedly been found to run rather smoothly and show few misunderstandings or breakdowns (see e.g. Mauranen 2006: 146; Cogo 2009: 255; Firth 2009: 149). While these findings have often been ascribed to the frequent employment of the let-it-pass strategy in ELF (see e.g. House 2010; Murray 2012), more recent studies particularly point to an abundance of collaborative pre-empting, negotiation and problem-solving strategies at work to secure intersubjective understanding (see e.g. Cogo & House 2018). This negotiation of meaning is considered the "key aspect" (Cogo 2016a: 83) of present-day research on ELF pragmatics.

https://doi.org/10.1515/9783110786576-005

In a context in which participants cannot communicate in their respective first languages, the anticipation of difficulties in understanding instigates speakers to put extra effort into the joint negotiation of meanings (see Kaur 2009: 120). Mauranen (2006: 147) observes that "[l]ingua franca speakers [. . .] appear to work hard to achieve mutual understanding, quite possibly on the basis of the natural commonsense assumption that it is not easy to achieve without special effort." In a combination of proactive tactics such as simplification and recipient design (see Mustajoki 2017) and problem-solving strategies in repair sequences, interlocutors monitor and jointly negotiate understanding, thus "establishing common linguacultural ground" (Seidlhofer 2011: 4) as the basis for intersubjective understanding.

In order to raise explicitness and achieve as well as secure mutual understanding, students in the present data make extensive use of repetition and repair, for example (see Chapters 6 and 7). Further interactional strategies which serve similar functions are an abundant use of the progressive aspect in order to increase explicitness as also attested by Cogo (2016: 82), and a transparent employment of plurilingual resources in translanguaging practices (see Chapter 10).

Just as making their wish to understand and to be understood explicit as illustrated in excerpt (2) above, students sometimes also explicitly indicate when mutual understanding has been achieved. In excerpt (3) speaker KGf thanks her interlocutor for her additional effort put into the successful negotiation of meanings.

(3) **KGf:** `[ah okay]`
IGf: `yeah`
KGf: `now i understand [thank you]`

(I3_225-227)

5.2 The negotiation of rapport

Communication, however, is about more than conveying information only. Watzlawick et al. (1967: 54) constitute that "*[e]very communication has a content and a relationship aspect* [italics in original]". Arundale ascribes a very central role to the relational aspect of language, which he considers the central anthropological factor for making us human beings (see Arundale 2010: 159). In the social constitution of interaction, conversational practices can unfold their relational potential. Arundale promotes a social and non-summative conceptualization of relationships as dynamically emerging from people's interacting (Arundale 2020: 248). He considers "[r]elating [. . .] a phenomenon endogenous in the interactional achieving of talk/conduct, rather than an exogenous factor seen to drive or to shape participants' conversational practices"

(Arundale 2010: 155), which exposes the constructionist character of relations as malleable constructs. Interactional linguistics with its detailed descriptions of talk-in-interaction in dyadic units has the potential of crucially contributing to this paradigm (see Spencer-Oatey & Franklin 2009; Couper-Kuhlen & Selting 2018).

International student exchanges, as the one providing the setting for the present study, aim primarily at promoting solidarity and intercultural understanding in order to facilitate an appreciative living-together and secure peace in the long term (see Müller-Hartmann & Grau 2004: 2). Solidarity and understanding can only develop on the basis of felicitous interpersonal relations. These emerge from, change through and find expression in communicative actions.

The participants here detect overlaps in some regards of their cultural identities (e.g. youth cultures, multilingual individuals), and differences in others (e.g. national cultures, linguacultures). These facets of identity constitute face-sensitive factors and as such have to be treated carefully in the communicatively achieved management of rapport: threats to individual or collective components of face may jeopardize relationships.

Due to the participants' similar age and their shared social role as students, group members show no inherent vertical distance from the start. The anticipation of basic equality surfaces in the conversational data in various forms, such as the expectation of a balanced share of turns and numerous instances of negotiating language, content, and organizational matters through interaction. Imbalances can nevertheless be detected in individual sectors, as students for instance show different commands of English or acknowledge cultural sovereignty of interpretation in certain areas.

The horizontal distance between the participants changes during the course of the week: from the first day of their encounter, when students make first contact with peers from a different part of the world, to the end of the week the horizontal distance steadily decreases, although considerable differences between individual groups in the degree and quality of affinity are both observable and reported. The relationships undergo different stages within the short but dense time of the encounter: in between building rapport from scratch to saying goodbye on the last day, students have to negotiate their relationships through challenging situations, but also celebrate happy moments together. The teenagers achieve all this through interaction, applying cooperative principles and politeness strategies (see Section 3.2), consciously or unconsciously, as situationally demanded.

5.3 The negotiation of identity

While students will be shown to often successfully manage both meaning and rapport through their use of ELF, TeenELF interactions also constitute the stage for a further kind of negotiations: in the face of an increased linguacultural plurality, adolescents reflect and enact their malleable identities in ELF interactions (see e.g. Deppermann 2007 for identity in conversations among adolescents; Baker 2015 for identity in ELF). Dorleijn et al explicate the importance of identity work for young people and the role of language therein in the following way:

> There is no professional or lay dispute about the fact that young people, more than older people, are involved in a dynamic process of discovering themselves and the world. They experiment with different identities, and language is an important tool in their identity work. It is, at the same time, the means by which that identity is formed and negotiated in interaction with others. (Dorleijn et al. 2020: 366)

This can be illustrated by a simple, but revealing numerical fact from the TeenELF corpus: *I* and *you* here constitute the two most frequent lexemes in the corpus. In this field of tension between self and other, adolescents co-construct and negotiate their identities. In their contextually changing use of the solidarity-oriented inclusive or demarcating exclusive first person plural pronoun *we*, also ranking among the 10 most frequent words in the TeenELF corpus (rank 7), students fathom varying relations relevant for identification.

It is particularly the first person plural pronoun that demarcates the present ELF interactions from conversations in English as a first language (EL1), as revealed in a cross-corpus perspective (see Appendix C). As Figure 7 shows, frequencies of *I*, *you* and *we* in the TeenELF corpus closely resemble those in VOICE (VOICE 2013), but partly deviate from patterns in EL1 contexts, here represented by the spoken section of the British National Corpus 2014 (BNC2014): while British English L1 speakers in the BNC employ *I* and *you* even more frequently, the first person plural pronoun *we* is used distinctly more often in the two ELF corpora, which may reflect ELF interlocutors' performing and testing of various alignments in complex processes of identification. Content analyses in 20 TeenELF conversations exposed a balanced interest of students in similarities with and differences from their interlocutors (79 vs. 78 tagged instances), which shows the students' orientation to *identity-as-sameness* and *identity-as-uniqueness* categories alike (see Joseph 2004: 37; Section 3.3). Both ELF and EL1 contexts disclose a slight tendency for younger speakers to use *I* more and *we* less often than their adult counterparts.

It is important to note that for all quantitative analyses and cross-corpus comparisons in particular the types of data recorded and context-based influences have to be kept in mind. In the present study, for example, young people formerly not known to each other try to familiarize in the dialogues recorded by asking their interlocutors questions and sharing information about themselves, which leads to frequent uses of first and second person pronouns. The task-based approach is further likely to have contributed to the comparatively frequent use of the first person plural pronoun *we* in the TeenELF corpus.

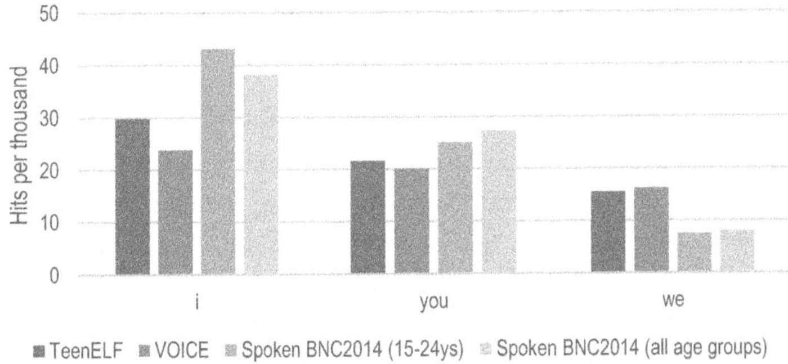

Figure 7: Cross-corpus frequency of select personal pronouns.

In line with the poststructuralist perspective outlined above (see Section 3.3), identity in TeenELF interactions is regarded as a dynamic, multi-faceted and context-dependent concept (see Omoniyi & White 2006). Restricting identity to national categories poses a real-life danger in intercultural communication research (see Baker 2015: 109) and cannot do justice to the complex processes underlying identification work. Interactants are rather found to enact multiple identities in hybrid fashions. While national memberships are repeatedly talked into being as central categories for identification, additional aspects such as learners' identities or adolescents' identities are enacted over large parts of the conversations recorded. Right at the beginning of one of the interviews, a German student foregrounds these latter aspects, which exert a strong integrating force bridging the different national backgrounds:

(4) **FGf:** `Wir sind ja trotzdem alle Schüler - alle Teenager. Und von daher fühlt man sich dann so auf der gleichen Wellenlänge, und das ist einfach das Schöne.`
`'We are all students after all - all teenagers. And so you feel on the same wavelength, and that's just nice.'`

(Int_FGf)

Identity references are established through contents for one thing. Interlocutors for instance express diverging ethnic affiliations when talking about the nature or the society of their home countries and regions, but also converging identities as global citizens, which find manifestation for example in students' talking about movies or pieces of music that both interlocutors are familiar with. The participants expose related learner self-concepts when exchanging information about school, and solidary identities as young people when chatting about friends, love and their relationships with other members of their families, as many examples in Chapters 6 to 10 illustrate.

On the other hand, identification is largely enacted by linguistic means. The idiom *to be on the same wavelength* that the German student uses in excerpt (4) to express identity-based solidarity also translates into the English idiom *to speak the same language* (see OED, s.v. *language*, n., P2.). When communicating in ELF as the predominant global language, students perform their shared identities as global citizens. Mauranen observes that "[s]peakers [. . .] seem to have an awareness of themselves as users of ELF, which for many is a central ingredient of their language identity" (Mauranen 2018a: 12). Extract (5), taken from the TeenELF corpus, illustrates ELF identity at work, which speaker JTf enacts through a negative demarcation from those people who do *not* speak English and consequently lack the "language of communication" to interact with "the foreigner". The use of the third person pronoun *they* (l. 111) creates a demarcating distance.

(5) 109 **JTf:** `the challenge is that in (our) society?`
110 **JGm:** `°hm° (1)`
111 **JTf:** `oh: (.) >(many member of society)< (.) like to talk with the foreigner. (.) but they didn't know HO:W. how the WAY of communicate with them. (1) maybe: they didn't know how to speak (x) english (1) the language of communication with them?`

(J2_109-111)

National, regional and ethnic affiliations, however, remain strong and are enacted consciously or subconsciously through L1 influences (see Jenkins 2007: 202; Mauranen 2018a: 12). Drawing on multilingual resources, ELF speakers in binational dialogue pairs enact their inclusive identities as multilingual speakers capable of communicating in one shared lingua franca, and their strong affiliations to their respective L1 linguacultural background at the same time. Young people have been found to "employ whatever linguistic resources available to achieve their communicative goals, drawing inter alia on their heritage language(s) in interaction" (Svendsen 2015: 23), so that "in opting for a broader understanding of young people's language and identity management there is a need to bridge the gap between traditional language contact studies and studies of multilingualism" (Svendsen 2015: 23). In the present study, TeenELF will be explored within this multilingual framework. While the exploitation of multilingual resources will be shown to centrally contribute to identity work, it is far from being restricted to this function, but rather plays vital roles in the management of meaning and rapport as well (see Section 10.3.4).

6 The use of repetitions in TeenELF

It has been suggested that "the more two speakers have in common, the less language they'll need to use to identify familiar things" (Yule 2002: 7) and that "[t]he amount of talk employed to accomplish a particular social action in conversation is a pragmatic indicator of the relative distance between the participants" (Yule 2002: 82). Against this backdrop, it comes as little surprise that students from different linguacultural backgrounds previously unknown to each other employ "a lot of language" in their talk. In line with previous findings from ELF research (see e.g. Lichtkoppler 2007: 59; Kaur 2009: 120; 2022: 40),[47] repetitions can be found abundantly in the present data.[48] While the recurrent employment of repetitions is well in line with conversational requirements of ELF speakers, further factors encouraging a frequent use of repetitions in the given setting must also be borne in mind: within the task-based set-up of the dialogue pairs, students also employ repetition a lot to negotiate the joint accomplishment of their task, for example (see Section 6.2 on the multi-functionality of repetition).

Extract (6) allows a first glimpse on "language-intensive" talk as employed in TeenELF. Pondering on her preference for company over loneliness, the speaker uses frequent literal repetitions or paraphrases of "(don't) like" and "lonely". The communicative goal of achieving mutual understanding through explicitness here outweighs the competing linguistic endeavour to avoid redundancy.

(6) 149 **NTf:** well (.) i'm afraid of being alone? (.) i don't like to be alone i also (.) i always like to be with other people? (.) i like to be with my family? (.) enjoy them? (.) i don't like loneliness? when you're (.) actually so (.) alone? (0.5) i don't like that.

(N4_149)

This chapter looks into the formal realizations and pragmatic functions of repetition as employed in TeenELF. Special focus will be given to the phenomenon

47 Tendencies to "increase redundancy and transparency" (Schneider 2016: 110) characterize World Englishes alike.

48 As the horizontal distance (see Chapter 3.2) between interlocutors diminishes in the course of the week, fewer repetitions would have to be expected towards the end of the week. While in some pairs this tendency is clearly visible (e.g. L, M, O), other groups seem to behave conversely. Differences may also be ascribed to functional variations of repetitions (see Section 6.2). Detailed quantitative analyses on the basis of larger datasets would be needed to shed more insights into the potential relationship between horizontal distance and the frequency of repetitions.

https://doi.org/10.1515/9783110786576-006

of framing (or distant self-repetition; see Section 6.3), which is very common in TeenELF, but has, to the best of my knowledge, not received much attention in ELF research so far.

Due to considerable overlaps and interplays between repetition and repair, findings on both pragmatic strategies will be integrated and summarized in Section 7.5.

6.1 Formal variation in repetition

According to Kaur (2009: 110), repetition "refers to the practice of re-saying some or all of the elements occurring earlier in an ongoing turn or in a preceding turn". In spite of a "conventional wisdom by which repetition is considered undesirable in conversation" (Tannen 2007: 62), it is pervasive not only in ELF communication, but also in "ordinary conversation" (see Tannen 2007: 101), taking on a variety of forms (see e.g. Lichtkoppler 2007: 46). An overview of parametrical continua, which characterize the formal realization of repetition, is provided in Figure 8.

Frequency	Single repetition		Multiple repetition
Scale of fixity	Literal repetition	Partial reformulating	Rephrasing
Temporal scale	Proximate repetition		Distant repetition

Figure 8: Parametrical continua in the formal realization of repetition (partly based on Tannen 2007: 63).

Repeatable objects (ROs), i.e. objects to be repeated in the course of the conversation, may be taken up once or multiple times, either by the speaker or by the hearer, and can cover the whole range from phonemes to sentences. Along a "scale of fixity" (Tannen 2007: 63), ROs may recur literally ("kind of like complicated", extract (7)), supplemented or reformulated in parts ("everyone takes history everyone takes geography", extract (8)), or rephrased in new words altogether ("the oldest" – "the first born", extract (9)).[49]

49 As the examples show that paraphrasing often goes hand in hand with literal repetition, I do not follow the categorical distinction between the two (see Schegloff 1996a: 179; Kaur 2009: 110), but conceptualize a repetition continuum from word-by-word repetition to paraphrasing (see Cogo & House 2018: 213).

(7) 200 **DTf:** (rain and sunny days) are kind of like complicated? (2) yah: they're kind of like complicated.
(D2_200)

(8) 369 **ATf:** everyone takes history everyone takes geography [. . .]
(A3_391)

(9) 021 **KGf:** do you have a brother or a sister?
022 **KTf:** i have two young brothers.
023 **KGf:** ↑ah so you are the oldest [one.]
024 **KTf:** [£yeah:] the ol[dest£]
025 **KGf:** [@@]
026 **KTf:** @@ the first born.
(K1_021-026)

On a temporal scale, repetition may further be realized proximate to or more distant from the original utterance or repeatable object (RO). While some repetitions are immediately latched on to the RO in either structures of chiasms (A**BB**A) or anadiplosis (A**BB**C), repetitions can also occur more detached from the ROs in anaphorical (**A**B**A**C) or epiphorical (A**B**C**B**) structures (see Table 9). Parenthetical elements can again greatly vary in length, from parts of words to several sentences. The second extract in Table 9 (M2_527) also illustrates the employment of multiple and partly overlapping repetitions in one turn ("for now our our new president (.) our new president").

Table 9: Structural patterns of repetition.

Chiasm	**ABBA**	**NGf:**	[. . .] and **hills we have (.) we have some hills?** [. . .]	(N2_238)
Anadiplosis	A**BB**C	**MTf:**	for now **our our** new president (.) our new president (who've:: starti:: starting:) (.) (the:: erm) (1) presidency (.) last year. (.)	(M2_527)
Anaphora	**A**B**A**C	**CTf:**	[. . .] **i can** walk **i can** talk **i can** see **i can** sing [. . .]	(C4_246)
Epiphora	A**B**C**B**	**ATf:**	the rest of the places i think they **have mountains** (.) the center **have mountains** the north [**have mountains**]	
		AGf:	[okay]	
		ATf:	yeah. the south **have mountains**.	(A2_369-371)

As the examples above also show, repetition may either be self-accomplished (as in excerpt (7)) or other-accomplished (as in excerpt (9); see Cogo & House 2018: 213), and can therefore be referred to as *self-repetition* and *other-repetition*[50] respectively. Figure 9 shows self- and other-repetition plot against the distance between RO and repetition. Communicative functions of repetitions (see Section 6.2) are partly distributed along these lines. Proximate self-repetition, or duplicating, for example, is often employed to enhance explicitness, or for cognitive reasons. While proximate other-repetition (also *echo elements*, *mirror elements*, *shadow elements* or *represents*; see Cogo & House 2018: 213) can be used to address problems or to confirm receipt, distant other-repetition may serve to resume a line of discourse or to signal accommodation. The following section investigates the communicative functions of repetition in more detail. Distant self-repetition or, as I will call it, *framing* is very frequent in the present data and will therefore be dealt with in a separate section (see Section 6.3).

		Distance between repeatable object and repetition	
		Proximate ⟷	**Distant**
Agent	**Self**	Proximate self-repetition *Duplicating*	Distant self-repetition *Framing*
	Other	Proximate other-repetition *Replicating*	Distant other-repetition *Resuming*

Figure 9: Taxonomy of repetition.

6.2 Functions of repetition

A close look at conversational sequences reveals the multifunctionality of repetitions (see Lichtkoppler 2007: 52–59; Cogo 2009: 260; Kaur 2016a: 164). Tannen (2007: 58–62) subsumes the pragmatic functions of repetition under the four categories of comprehension, production, connection, and interaction. These categories find resonance in the functions listed in Table 10, which provides an overview of the functional range of repetitions as elicited from the TeenELF corpus. While the pre-empting of non-understanding through repetitions exemplifies a comprehension-oriented function, for example, gaining planning time and processing new

50 Other-repetition is sometimes also referred to as "allo-repetition" (see Tannen 2007: 63).

information illustrate production-oriented purposes. Expressing affirmation is one example of using repetitions for connective purposes, while repetitions which are employed to signal the end of a sequence serve interactional functions. It needs to be emphasized here that repetitions often serve more than one function, and that "overlapping and interacting functions of repetition are the norm rather than the exception" (Lichtkoppler 2007: 59).

Individual purposes listed in Table 10 will be illustrated in detail in subsequent corpus-based analyses.

Table 10: Functions of repetition in TeenELF.

Raising explicitness and negotiating meaning	Pre-empting non-understandings Addressing problems Solving problems
Cognitive function	Gaining planning time Processing new information Supporting short-term memory
Intensifying	Emphasizing Expressing iterativity or continuity Dramatizing
Interpersonal and expressive function	Expressing affirmation and solidarity Expressing surprise Expressing irritation
Interactional function	Confirming receipt Signalling end of sequence Creating coherence

Raising explicitness and negotiating meaning

Facing "unclear common ground" in an "especially diverse linguacultural encounter" (Cogo & Dewey 2012: 115), ELF speakers often resort to repetition as a useful means to raise explicitness. Interlocutors employ repetition to pre-empt potential non-understandings, but also to address and solve problems in understanding (see Cogo & House 2018: 213; Kaur 2022: 41). Pre-empting strategies are considered particularly important in ELF conversation "as they show how mutual understanding is not taken for granted" (Cogo 2016a: 83). Speaker MTf, for instance, uses this strategy in (10) when she repeats the sentence "they use water transport" (ll. 248; 250) to make sure her partner understands this important part of her narrative. Both MTf and MGf interrupt themselves and continue by repeating and completing their messages (ll. 232; 237; 240), with the effect of offering (part of) their contribution twice, thus enhancing the likelihood of being understood.

(10) 227 **MGf:** [. . .]{reading out} what is the best °movie you have° (.) ever [watched.]
228 **MTf:** [(watched)]
229 **MGf:** °oh.° (.) °that's difficult.°
230 **MTf:** (↑er) (.) anaconda.
231 **MGf:** °anaconda°
232 **MTf:** °yah:° (.) °from ame-° (.) america.
233 **MGf:** °mhm?°=
234 **MTf:** =the biggest snake
235 **MGf:** oh yeah anaconda °yeah.°
236 **MTf:** yah:.
237 **MGf:** °i don't know the (mo-)° (.) °i don't know the movie?°
238 **MTf:** you don't know it?
239 **MGf:** °anaconda? no.° (1) it's from hollywood? or=
240 **MTf:** =you have to s- yeah. you have to search it.
241 **MGf:** okay? [anaconda.]
242 **MTf:** [°(oh yeah.)°] (.) [°(yeah)°]
243 **MGf:** [(it) it's] just anaconda?
244 **MTf:** just anaconda.
245 **MGf:** what is it about?
246 **MTf:** talk about a (.) big snake. (1)
247 **MGf:** oka(@)y?=
248 **MTf:** =snake (.) yeah the people are (.) erm:: (.) in in a: (.) journey. (.) they use er: (1) water transport.
249 **MGf:** mhm=
250 **MTf:** =they use water transport. (.) unfortunately (.) in the (.) ocean there is er (.) erm (.) i don't think it is ocean. (.) like a: river? (.) yah. it is like river. (.) there is a (.) big big big snake.
251 **MGf:** °oa°
252 **MTf:** if you s:ee it (.) by yourself (.) you die before (.) hurt you. (1) you die before it hurt you (.) ↑ew. (1) the big one. (.) [°(yah)°]
253 **MGf:** [yeah] they are (.) like (.) they are really big. (.) yeah

(M3_227-253)

While pre-empting strategies normally come about with zero conversational initiation, problem-solving strategies are often triggered by initiators such as stretches of silence, minimal responses or more explicit prompts such as understanding checks (see Kaur 2009: 111–116).[51] The one-second pause in line 252, for instance, marks a transition relevance place (TRP), which is not taken by MGf. The lack of a verbal response to MTf's depiction of horror ("you die before (.) hurt you (1)", l. 252) seems to make MTf suspect her message might not have been understood. She consequently repeats her statement, enriching her repetition by introducing a subject into a zero-subject construction ("you die before it hurt you", l. 252), thus raising the explicitness of her contribution. At the same time, the repetition serves to intensify the spine-chilling message. When MGf asks about the contents of the movie, MTf draws on paraphrases in addition to literal repetitions ("a big snake" [. . .] "snake", ll. 246; 248), apparently not being sure whether her interlocutor is familiar with anacondas.

While problems in hearing can often be solved by literal repetitions, problems in understanding usually need rephrasing. In (11), the universal open request "huh?" (l. 224; see Clift 2016: 249–250) leaves the kind of problem open to AGf. To secure understanding in any case, she resorts to both word-by-word repetition and rephrasing (l. 225).

(11) 223 **AGf:** `well: (.) my dreams are: that after i finish my a-levels (.) that i can visit the wo:rld?`
224 **ATf:** `huh?`
225 **AGf:** `that i can visit the world so i can go to different countries abroad?`
226 **ATf:** `(oh like) fly and [go somewhere.]`

(A4_223-227)

Other-repetitions can also be used to address problematic items. In extract (14), MGf's repetition of "anaconda" (l. 231) is apparently understood as such by MTf, who offers the paraphrase "the biggest snake" (l. 234) to support mutual understanding. MGf, however, refutes MTf's interpretation of non-understanding by a further repetition of "anaconda" which she frames by the supportive particles "yeah" (l. 235) to confirm her trouble-free receipt of the message.

Cognitive functions

Rather than indicating non-understanding, MGf might have first repeated "anaconda" (l. 231) for cognitive reasons. Repeating the item enables her to process the

51 As the repetition in line 250 is latched on to the backchannel-item "mhm" (l. 249), allowing zero planning time, it is assumed that MTf repeats her sentence without being influenced by MGf. It is for this reason that repetition is here classified as pre-empting rather than problem-solving.

information just gained and search for links to previous knowledge. At the same time, repeating elements may grant the speaker planning time to prepare the following utterance (see Mauranen 2006: 147). Cognitive functions become particularly relevant in ELF contexts, which constitute verbally challenging situations for many participants. Repetitions serving a cognitive purpose often come about with hesitations and pauses signifying the speaker's need for planning time. In (12), ATf indicates that she is not sure about how to continue by stretching sounds and leaving pauses (l. 408). Repeating her previous utterance allows her to hold the floor and continue the interaction even in the face of ongoing planning.

(12) 406 **ATf:** =we go to the church and we have a teacher?
407 **AGf:** yeah=
408 **ATf:** =yeah:: (.) but (2) we (.) we have a teacher? he teaches us the music? we only sing actually.

(A1_406-408)

Interlocutors in TeenELF also use repetitions to support each other's short-term memories. This strategy is often used as a cooperative means when students summarize and write down information for their dia|log|book so as not to forget what they wanted to record. Extract (13) gives an example of repetitions employed as a memory aid. Students talk about the role of families and friends in their lives, collecting and writing down ideas. The new aspect "we celebrate with them: through GOOD times" (l. 442) is repeated in little chunks by both speakers during the process of writing it down[52] (ll. 445; 446; 447; 448).

(13) 442 **LTf:** yeah they help through bad times? (8) also: (.) we celebrate with them: through GOOD times. (1)
443 **LGf:** mh?=
444 **LTf:** =yeah.
445 **LGf:** celebrate?
446 **LTf:** we celbr- celebrate (2.5)
447 **LGf:** together [good times?]
448 **LTf:** [together] good times. (7) mh? (1.5) anything? (1.5)
449 **LGf:** i think °that's it.°

(L1_442-449)

52 The writing process is indicated by prolonged pauses (ll. 446; 448).

Intensifying

Interlocutors also employ repetitions as a stylistic means to intensify the proposition of their message. In the anaconda-extract (10), MTf repeats the attributive adjective "big" twice (l. 250) to emphasize the extraordinary size of the animal in question. The high frequency of this phenomenon appears exceptional in TeenELF, with the number of repeated items often going well beyond the common two (see "many", extract (14), l. 292; "very", extract (15), l. 183).

(14) 290 **LTf:** `[↑well (x) we have many] here like er (.) we have (.) erm hundred and twe- over hundred and twenty tribes.`
291 **LGf:** `wow.`
292 **LTf:** `yeah. (.) many many many many many many`
(L1_290-292)

(15) 183 **HTf:** `=so (1) as:: (.) since back then (.) (she was the) (1) very very v:ery very (.) big help to me?`
(H4_183)

While this strategy may in some instances be ascribed to restricted lexical knowledge, it can also serve as a strategy to make meanings more explicit by making the linguistic form reflect the semantic contents (see "many many many many many many" in extract (14)). In addition, functional-pragmatic transfer appears to be at work: Russell explains, for example, that in Swahili "[t]he use of repetition is a common and very useful way of intensifying or extending the meaning of words" (Russell 2010: ch. 7). When the repeated element is or contains a verb, for example, "repeating [in Swahili] can imply a continuation of the action over a period of time and/or thoroughness and attention to detail in carrying out the action" (Russell 2010: ch. 7). Students transfer this pragmatic phenomenon to ELF, as is illustrated in (16), where NTf complains about the high frequency of exams. She repeats the clause "every month you're doing exams" three times within a short sequence. The first two instances follow each other straight away (l. 034), and the third repetition is further intensified by a three-fold repetition of "exams" (l. 036), which constitutes the semantic core of the objection.

(16) 033 **NGf:** `okay (.) and do you think it's (.) it's (.) very tough that you have so (.) so exams in so many subjects on one day? (0.5)`
034 **NTf:** `↑yes it's little bit tough you know (.) every month you're doing exams every month you're doing exams (.) i kno:w they: they want us to get used to them (.) but you know the we should also: get er leisure time?`

035 **NGf:** [yeah]
036 **NTf:** [s:]tay okay what (.) °wha:t what what what wha:t° (.) we should er (.) also study but not every month we are doing exams exams exams (.) because you ↑know it is a bit tiring

(N3_033-036)

Tautologies, which implement repetition in an idiomatic way, serve a purpose similar to intensification in emphasizing a particularly notable feature of the subject in question. Some turns further on in the anaconda-conversation, the German student enquires about snakes in Africa, whereupon MTf reports of cobras and little snakes (17). She explains Tanzanians' fear of snakes with the tautology "snake is snake" (l. 270). In her subsequent paraphrase "snake is: (.) dangerous" (l. 271), MGf reveals her interpretation of this tautology as an emphasis and generalization of the most significant property of snakes from a human perspective: their dangerous nature.

(17) 265 **MGf:** yeah. okay (1) °(or do)° er but (.) °in tan-° in africa (.) (where) (.) where do the anaconda lives.
266 **MTf:** ↑hm. in africa (.) no:. (.) there is no anacondas. (1) there is (a:) (.) few (.) cobras.
267 **MGf:** cobras.
268 **MTf:** °yeah° cobras (.) (and the snake) (.) the small ones.
269 **MGf:** mhm
270 **MTf:** yeah.° (.) but (er) (.) we('re) afraid of them. (.) becaus:e [snake is snake.]
271 **MGf:** [yeah(@@)h @@@] (.) (snake) is: (.) dangerous.=
272 **MTf:** =°yeah.°

(M3_265-272)

Intensifying through repetition may also have a dramatizing effect, as illustrated in (18). In her narrative about a friend who lost a lollipop to a monkey, NTf repeats her friend's reaction of dismay ("oh my lollipop", l. 371) to make her story more dramatic. High pitch and direct speech further add to this effect in the given example.

(18) 365 **NTf:** a monkey. (.) a monkey took er my friend's lollipop.
366 **NGf:** ↑a[h@]
367 **NTf:** [he] was ea- she was eating it. (.) and she@

368 **NGf:** oh:[@@ h @]
369 **NTf:** [hh she cr@ied s@o much]
370 **NGf:** .h @@ .hh
371 **NTf:** ↑oh my lollipop [my l@ollip@op]
372 **NGf:** [@ .hh]=

(N2_365-372)

Interpersonal and expressive functions

With the repetitional structure in (16), the exam-stricken Tanzanian student also gives vent to her irritation about the situation described. She validates this interpretation explicitly in her final statement "it is a bit tiring" (l. 036). At the same time, other-repetition is often used to express surprise about the previous utterance. The repeated item typically receives high pitch or a rising intonation and is often accompanied by particles articulating surprise such as "oh" or "wow", which all serve to express that the preceding statement is considered extraordinary in some way. In (19), GTf conveys her disbelief concerning the liberal dealing with tattoos at German schools. So dominant is her surprise that she interrupts GGf mid-turn with the high-pitch particle "ha", followed by an understanding check ("it's okay?", l. 827). When this is confirmed, she draws on repetition to voice her ongoing disbelief, with the repeated item "tattoo" constituting the core of GTf's surprise (l. 829). She supports her expression of incredulity by an increase of volume and a sudden rise of pitch ("tatt↑OO"). When GGf's renewed confirmation is once more answered with a high pitch particle of surprise ("↑hu", l. 831), the German student resorts to enhanced explicitness and rephrases her statement to assert her proposition.

(19) 826 **GGf:** [. . .] if we: like to we can: (.) yeah we can wear piercings or tattoo:s (.) it's=
827 **GTf:** =↑ha (.) it's okay?
828 **GGf:** yeah. (.) the [school]
829 **GTf:** [tatt↑OO]
830 **GGf:** it's okay.
831 **GTf:** ↑hu
832 **GGf:** the school can't say er it's: (.) not okay.

(G1_826-832)

On the other hand, other-repetition can also express affirmation and solidarity (see Mauranen 2012: 226; Kaur 2022: 44). In (20), CGm and CTf realize that they like the same kind of movies. They celebrate this similarity in weaving a dense net of co-produced talk, which is tightened by mutual repetitions of various elements ("horror movies", ll. 207–208; "love", ll. 208–209; "funny", ll. 209–210), overlaps and latching, interspersed with laughter. In (21), the repetition of the verb "talk" to express continuation (l. 229) is coupled with repetition for solidarity (l. 230) to the effect that through their interaction the students imitate the content of their talk. LTf thus slips into the role of LGf's friends from home, this way offering right on the first day of their encounter to become LGf's friend as well. Overlap and laughter further contribute to the creation of an atmosphere of familiarity.

(20)	206	**CTf:**	[oh you like] horror movies also?
	207	**CGm:**	also horror movies.
	208	**CTf:**	[i LOVE horror movies]
	209	**CGm:**	[i really love (them)] (.) and also scary movie becau@se i@t's so@ fu@nny
	210	**CTf:**	↑funny@@@@=
	211	**CGm:**	=yeah. [. . .]

(C3_206-211)

(21)	223	**LGf:**	[. . .] at the weekend or in the evening (0.5) we {i.e. LGf and her friends} meet together and (1.5) do some funny things?
	224	**LTf:**	@=
	225	**LGf:**	=@@@
	226	**LTf:**	playing games and everything.
	227	**LGf:**	yeah=
	228	**LTf**	=yah=
	229	**LGf:**	=of course (0.5) and talk talk [talk talk? @@@@]
	230	**LTf:**	[talk talk talk talk talk until] you run out of: words.

(L1_223-224)

Interactional functions

Repetitions may finally help to structure the interaction and create coherence. Going back to the introductory anaconda-extract (10) once more, we see interlocutors making use of other-repetition in a speaker-oriented way to confirm the receipt of a previous utterance and to signal their readiness for the interaction to move on, and of self-repetition to create coherence or indicate the end of a sequence and offer the floor to the other person. In her repetition "just anaconda" (l. 244), MTf, for instance, orients directly to MGf's question (l. 243) and indicates by her exact reiteration uttered with falling intonation that nothing more needs to be added and the conversation can proceed, leaving the floor to MGf once more. MTf's self-repetition "like (a) river" (l. 250) serves a similar function. This time, however, repetition and falling intonation indicate a disposing of her own uncertainties, which she expressed by hesitating through stretching sounds and rising intonation in the first utterance ("like a: river?"). While the first mention, or the repeatable object, and the repetition are only separated by the confirmative particle "yeah" here, this intermediate or parenthetical space, bracketed by two almost identical elements, can be considerably stretched. This phenomenon of framing, as I will call it, as a particular, and in TeenELF very popular, manifestation of repetition will be looked at in detail in the following and final section of repetition.

6.3 Focus on framing

Formal realization of framing

Framing, or distant self-repetition (see Chapter 6.1, Figure 9), is here used to refer to a linguistic practice in which a speaker employs two or more equal or very similar utterances to embrace a parenthetical interior part, which consists of one or more clauses. Repeated elements may range from words to full sentences. Framing can either be realized within one turn (*intra-turn framing*) or stretch over several turns (*trans-turn framing*) as illustrated in Figure 10. While *two-part framing* sees the parenthetical part embraced by a frame-opening repeatable object and a frame-closing repetition, the repeated element can also turn up three or more times in unspecified intervals in *multi-part framing* to the effect of creating a grid or scaffolding rather than a frame. Extract (22) illustrates an example of two-part intra-turn framing ("which year are y[ou]"), while speaker NTf in (23) employs multi-part trans-turn framing ("it is quite/so scary", ll. 264; 266; 272).

(22) 062 **GGf:** so which year are y:- are you third form? or five form? (1) or in year in which year (.) are you? (1)

(G1_062)

(23) 262 **NTf:** [. . .] i've also watched (.) two: egyptian movies. (0.5) hold? (.) the mummy?

263 **NGf:** mh?

264 **NTf:** it is ↑quite scary but it is (.) it is showing the history of egypt

265 **NGf:** ah o[kay]

```
266 NTf:    [and it's] so wonderful? (.) but there's (.) some
            places where it is so scary? (.) er: it is like a b-
            (.) a ba:: what. (.) it is like a ladybug. (0.5) enters
            here in your (.)
267 NGf: o[ah]
268 NTf:  [skin] and then goes [moving and moving]
269 NGf:                       [↑OH no:: oah: @]
270 NTf: and then come outs like here
271 NGf: ↑uuh::=
272 NTf: =£it's so scary£
```

(N2_262-272)

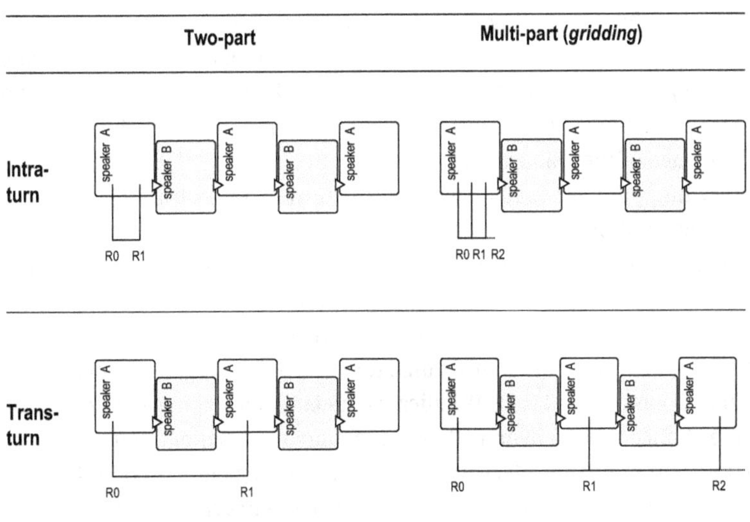

(RO = repeatable object; R1 = first repetition, R2 = second repetition)

Figure 10: Forms of framing.

Functions of framing

Interlocutors employ framing in TeenELF to various ends. Repeated items run through interactional sequences like a golden thread, making the interaction coherent, explicit and transparent. This strategy can provide a helpful scaffold in many ELF settings and other intercultural contexts, where interlocutors cannot necessarily build on common ground (see Cogo & Dewey 2012: 115; Kecskés 2014: 2), and also beyond. Individual communicative functions are achieved in an interplay between the framing elements and the parenthetical part, which may vary in their semantic relations.

If the parenthetical content, whether self- or other-accomplished, digresses from the frame-opening statement, the repetition serves to return to the first mentioned topic, indicating that the speaker considers the issue central but not discursively completed yet. Accordingly, the frame-closing element does not necessarily have to mark the end of a sequence, but may also take up an interrupted thread, which may then be spun further. Speaker NTf in (23) introduces the movie as "quite scary" (l. 264), but quickly moves into a different direction, revelling in the "wonderful" depiction of Egypt's history (ll. 264; 266). A particular movie scene in her mind, which she relates subsequently, makes her return to her previous assessment ("it is so scary?", l. 266), with a rising intonation indicating her intention to hold the floor and share further details.

In most cases, speakers fill the interior part of a framing construction with explications of their frame-opening statement, paraphrasing, extending or explaining their message, as NTf does in the second part of the extract, describing one particularly scary scene from the movie (ll. 266–270). The frame-closing repetition (l. 272) then serves to underline and emphasize the opening statement, highlighting the central message of the elaborate contribution. In (24), CTf's statement "for me, school is everything" (l. 088) opens another trans-turn two-part framing sequence of this kind. Triggered by CGm's disbelieving reaction "really" (l. 089), the Tanzanian student offers arguments for her opinion (ll. 092; 094). She marks the end of her explications by a short pause before she resorts to the conjunct "so" to finally lead back to and emphasize her original utterance (l. 094).

Extract (24) also exposes an interactional function of framing. The repetition of "for me, school is everything" (l. 094) indicates the end of a sequence, offering the addressee the chance to take over. Falling intonation and a salient pause serve to mark the transition-relevance place after the frame-closing element (l. 094), upon which CGm takes the floor (l. 095), repeating parts of the previous utterance again to express addressee orientation and create coherence.

```
(24) 088 CTf:  for me:: (.) school is: everything.
     089 CGm:  really
     090 CTf:  yeah:=
     091 CGm:  @@@
     092 CTf:  =because (1) it's hard to find (.) something to do if you
               don't have education. (.) especially here (1) because we
               don't have (.) music or fine arts so you [can't]
     093 CGm:                                           [okay?]
```

094 **CTf:** say: if i (.) go academically (0.5) no (.) so for me school is everything. (1)
095 **CGm:** for me school is an important part n- but not (0.5) the only part of my life

(C3_088-095)

Framing may finally also be used as a universal means to continue the talk in the face of difficulties in production. Returning to a previous, pre-formulated theme grants the speaker a low-cost and interactionally efficient tool to re-focus a troublesome conversation. What is to become the parenthetical part of a framing construction in (25) starts off as an attempt to explain and elaborate on the frame-opening element "different to YOUR summer" (l. 302). When faced with difficulties in conveying her thoughts as she cannot recall the English term for either *muggy* ("schwül", l. 304) or *humidity* ("Luftfeucht[igkeit]", l. 306), and neither gets support from her German classmate in this group of three, IGf returns to her original statement (l. 308) to close the unfinished sequence, thus allowing the conversation to move on.

(25) 302 **IGf:** but er i think it's very di- er different to YOUR summer because=
303 **KGf:** =yeah
304 **IGf:** here is a (.) erm (.) we say it in germany. <L1de> schwül {muggy} </L1de> with
305 **KGf:** [it's very]
306 **IGf:** [mhh it make-] it makes you tired because you have so (.) much (.) s- erm o too in your (2) <L1de> was [is er Luftfeucht-] {what [is er humidi-]} <L1de>
307 **KGf:** [yeah]=
308 **IGf:** =mmh we don't know the- the word but our summer is (.) er. (.) different to your summer=
309 **KGf:** =yeah=
310 **ITf:** =[mmh]

(I2_302-310)

7 Repair strategies in TeenELF

In the negotiation of meaning, the phenomena of repetition and repair, both highly frequent in the TeenELF corpus, often go hand in hand. As illustrated in the previous chapter, repetition can serve the initiation and accomplishment of repair. Just as the functional use of repetition amounts to much more than repair, however, so must any discussion of repair go beyond repetition alone. In this chapter, repair will be introduced as a formally diverse and functionally versatile cooperative achievement of central importance in TeenELF. As will be demonstrated, the negotiation of intersubjective understanding through repair is also closely connected to interpersonal factors. This chapter starts off with a formal analysis of repair and moves on to investigate linguistic objects of repair, before it analyzes functions of (non-)repair in its communicative contexts. The subsequent section is dedicated to an exploration of other-involvement in repair, which stands out in the TeenELF data recorded in the given school setting. A summary of major findings for repetition and repair is provided at the end of the chapter.

7.1 Formal realization of repair

Employed as a communicative practice to deal with problems in the production or reception of speech (see Schegloff 2000: 207), repair is a common phenomenon in intercultural communication and ELF in particular (see Baker 2011: 201), and also omnipresent in the TeenELF data. Repair can be initiated and accomplished by either self or other (see Figure 4, Section 3.1). In line with general interactional research that has pointed to the preference of *self-repair* over *other-repair* (see Brown & Levinson 1987: 38–43; Kitzinger 2013: 232), *self-initiated self-repair* (SISR) constitutes the most frequent type of repair in TeenELF by far:[53] students amend and fine-tune their own utterances to maximize the potential of being understood to their satisfaction. Student HTf in (26), for example, changes her pronominal subject from "he" to "she" (l. 277) as she refers to a female Tanzanian singer.[54]

53 As, however, SISR is not only pervasive but at the same time multifarious in nature (see also Kaur 2011: 2704), it defies quantification in a corpus of the given size. Small-scale counts suggest that the share of SISR covers considerably more than half of all repair operations in TeenELF.

54 Pronominal gender mix-ups, though not confined to Tanzanian speakers in TeenELF (see e.g. AGf in A1_277), appear to expose an influence of the Swahili noun class system, which does not distinguish between masculine and feminine gender.

https://doi.org/10.1515/9783110786576-007

(26) 255 **HTf:** [. . .] have you ever heard about lady jaydee? (1)
256 **HGf:** no.
257 **HTf:** oh yes. he: (.) she has been in germany about five years (past)?
(H3_255-257)

Other-initiated self-repair (OISR) ranks second in frequency, occurring more than four times as often as the two remaining types in the TeenELF corpus (OISR: 218 instances; OIOR: 49 instances; SIOR: 47 instances).[55] In order to secure intersubjective understanding, hearers intervene and ask speakers to provide repair of their original utterance, no matter whether or not there has been an "objective linguistic mistake".[56] In (27), AGf initiates repair through an alleged repetition ("liking", l. 073) of the trouble source ("lacking", l. 072). Assuming the problem accordingly to be one of hearing rather than understanding, ATf tries to accomplish repair by literally repeating the repairable in response to AGf's question (l. 074). Flagging her response by a code-switched particle of recognition ("ach", l. 075) and repeating the word in question correctly now, AGf signals a proper hearing. Her renewed repetition, now with rising intonation, however, suggests a problem in understanding in addition and thus serves as another repair initiator. Accordingly, this time, ATf does not only accomplish repair through another repetition but through offering a paraphrase for the problematic item. In her response, AGf once more repeats the word in question (l. 077); rising intonation and hesitation markers such as sound stretches, pauses, laughter and fillers ("er::", "well::", l. 077), finally followed by a meaningful answer to the original question, indicate that this last repetition serves cognitive functions (see Section 6.2) and repair has finally been accomplished.

(27) 072 **ATf:** so:: {reading from task sheet} is there anything lacking in your life?
073 **AGf:** liking?
074 **ATf:** lacking.
075 **AGf:** <L1de> ach {oh okay}</L1de> lacking. lacking?
076 **ATf:** yeah lacking like (.) you don't have it in your life?
077 **AGf:** lacking? er:: (2) well:: @@ it's difficult to say because (.) i'm the only (.) child of my parents [. . .]
(A4_072-077)

55 Due to the multifaceted nature of repair realization and resulting challenges with regard to coding and tagging, absolute numbers need to be treated with caution, but can only indicate tendencies. On the difficulties of pragmatic corpus annotation, see also Weisser (2015: 84) and Chapter 11.1.
56 While the term *correction* refers to the replacement of errors or mistakes, *repair* includes correction but is not limited to it (see Schegloff et al. 1977: 363).

In accordance with previous findings from conversational research (see e.g. Schegloff et al. 1977; Clift 2016: 236), other-accomplished repair is far less frequent in TeenELF than self-accomplished repair. There is nevertheless a surprisingly high frequency of *self-initiated other-repair* (SIOR) and the otherwise extremely rare type of *other-initiated other-repair* (OIOR) in the present data, with more than 40 instances identified for each type. In SIOR (see (28)), hearer involvement in repair is encouraged by a speaker experiencing difficulties, which he or she may express explicitly or indicate through the use of hesitation phenomena (see Mauranen 2013: 238). Student EGf draws on metalinguistic devices ("i don't know how to say", l. 206) to retrieve lexical support from her fellow student, which is promptly provided (l. 207) and accepted (l. 208).

(28) 206 **EGf:** `if (.) in germany somebody does the: (.) i don't know how to say.`
207 **ETf:** `horn?`
208 **EGf:** `horn (.) it's a:: a sign for be careful and it's very dangerous so (.) we never use it [. . .]`

(E2_206-208)

OIOR, in contrast, comes about "uninvited", wherein lies its particular face-threatening potential. In (29), FGf interrupts her fellow student mid-turn to initiate and operate a semantic repair, suggesting *war* (l. 683) as a contextually more appropriate term for *crisis* (l. 682), which is then taken up by the first speaker (l. 684). In an attempt to explain the unexpectedly frequent occurrence of OIOR in TeenELF, Section 7.4 will explore this phenomenon in more detail.[57]

(29) 680 **HGf:** `yeah you know (.) at the moment in our country a lot of (.) people from abroad come to our country. (.) because for example in syria?`
681 **FTf:** `°mhm?°=`
682 **HGf:** `=there's a crisis. so (.) many [(.) pe-]`
683 **FGf:** `[a wa:r]`
684 **HGf:** `yeah. a war @ yeah. there's war.`

(F2_680–684)

57 OISR and OIOR are sometimes found to be combined, with the speaker first repairing an item in question and the hearer adding another paraphrase to either fine-tune the meaning or indicate his or her understanding.

7.2 Targets of linguistic repair

The previous extracts also illustrate that objects triggering repair cover a wide range of trouble areas from phonological over grammatical and lexical problems to pragmatic and conceptual discrepancies. While repair is often used for conceptual fine-tuning and paraphrasing, many grammatical errors, in fact, remain unrepaired, as demonstrated in (30), where neither the double marking of the past ("**did** you **had**") nor the contextually 'non-standard' use of the indefinite article *a* rather than *an* before the vowel-initial noun *exam* are commented on by either side. Mistakes going unrepaired may not be detected by interlocutors none of whom speaks English as a first language. They may, however, just as well not be considered relevant for mutual understanding so that students rather let them pass than interrupt the flow of speech. While the decisive factor for other-initiated repair to set in seems to be an ensuring of understanding, speakers often use SISR to align their speech with an underlying norm. Although there is hardly any danger of being misunderstood, speaker AGf in (31) repairs the verb *look-[ing]* to *watching*, probably recalling the once-learned idiomatic collocation 'to watch TV'. Presenting oneself as a competent speaker of English thus also seems to play a role in repair.

(30) 012 **AGf:** `did you had a exam la- yesterday?`

(A2_012)

(31) 229 **AGf:** `so: well i think everybody in germany likes football and the national team (.) erm:: yah i think everyone is look- er: watching it when it's in the t v? especially the national team [. . .]`

(A2_229)

In retrospective interviews, Tanzanian as well as German students often name pronunciation differences as a major obstacle to mutual understanding (see e.g. Int_FGf; Int_ETf). Variation in the TRAP vowel (RP /æ/), which is neither part of the Swahili nor the German phonetic inventory, for example, often leads to misunderstandings as further explored in Section 10.4.1. In (32), this gives rise to an elaborate OISR sequence, as *tax* is mistaken for *text*. Students employ understanding checks (l. 543), repetitions (l. 544) and paraphrases (ll. 545; 546; 548) to expose the misunderstanding, which can only be solved when both students expand and contextually embed their ideas (*text – messenger*; *tax – to pay taxes*). In her closing turn (l. 549), LTf corroborates the successful negotiation of understanding through repair by the high-pitch and prolonged discourse marker "↑oh:", a confirmative paraphrase ("so you want to become a: (0.5) in charge of taxes", l. 549) and her reference to the *Tanzanian Revenue Authority* (l. 549).

(32)
542 **LGf:** i want to (.) go to the <pvc> tex {tax} </pvc> office.
543 **LTf:** text office?
544 **LGf:** <pvc> tex {tax} </pvc> office.
545 **LTf:** you want to become a (messenger)? (1)
546 **LGf:** er:m: ts (.) i work at a <pvc> tex {tax} </pvc> office so (.) i: (.) look (.) that (.) all the people?
547 **LTf:** mh?
548 **LGf:** pay their <pvc> texes {taxes} </pvc> [in the right way.]
549 **LTf:** [↑oh:]y- (.) so you want to become a: (0.5) in charge of taxes. (0.5) ↑i like it. (.) that's also great (.) so here we have that (.) authority names na- we name it t r a.(.) tanzan-tanzanian revenue authority.

(L2_542-549)

Repair does not only address mis- or non-understandings arising from phonological variation, but also frequently attends to lexical problems. If speakers cannot recall or feel uncertain about particular lexemes, they often initiate repair, thus indicating that intersubjective understanding is at stake. In (28), EGf finds herself in lack of the lexeme *horn*, which first becomes observable through hesitation phenomena such as a prolongation and a pause (l. 206) and is finally explicitly expressed in the metalinguistic comment "i don't know how to say" (l. 206). This concession serves as a repair initiator, which is promptly answered by other-accomplished repair with ETf providing the item in question ("horn", l. 207). Employing rising intonation, ETf imparts a suggestive character to her repair, which renders the repair cooperative rather than corrective.

At other times, lexemes may be readily available but speakers realize in the course of their utterance that a different expression might be conceptually or idiomatically more suitable. In (30), for instance, AGf interrupts herself in the middle of a word ("la-"), choosing the adverb "yesterday" instead. It stands to reason whether AGf initiated and accomplished repair after realizing the non-idiomacity of "last day", or the semantic error of "last week/month". Conceptual modification is also at work in (29), where "crisis" (l. 682) undergoes repair and is converted into "war", which is accepted as more suitable by both speakers (ll. 683; 684).

7.3 Communicative functions and effects of repair

While repair is primarily directed at the modification and negotiation of meanings, it often has significant impacts on rapport at the same time. Interpersonal impacts of repair may greatly vary depending on the formal realization of repair and its situational context. The negotiation of understanding through repair and its interpersonal effects are investigated in the present section (see also Beuter 2019b). After illustrating how understanding is achieved through repair in TeenELF, it moves on to explore interpersonal effects of repair, such as the building or jeopardizing of rapport. The final part of the section looks at examples of failed or misinterpreted repair and their potential effects on rapport.

Achieving understanding through repair

Students primarily initiate repair to negotiate and fine-tune meanings and secure intersubjective understanding as illustrated in extract (33), where interlocutors employ a range of repair mechanisms for the negotiation of understanding. From the very beginning (l. 290), we see the German speaker making extensive use of SISR. He frequently cuts himself off, hesitates, uses fillers such as “er”, “erm”, “oh” or “i think”, also draws on L1 resources (see “irgendwie” {somehow}), then repeats himself, starts anew and inserts passages. He does not realize, however, that one of the central lexical items he uses to carry his message, namely *muezzin*, poses a challenge for his addressee, probably for phonological, but potentially also for lexical reasons. The addressee, on the other hand, follows a let-it-pass strategy for quite some time. As the Tanzanian speaker, however, seems to realize that the item in question will neither become clearer in the course of the interaction nor turn out to be irrelevant, she decides to initiate repair (l. 291). Her question interrupts the German speaker in mid-turn, a conversationally highly dispreferred position (see Clift 2016: 247–248), underlining the urgency of her question. As she uses the category-specific question word *who* to elicit the subject, she manages to turn the German speaker's attention directly to the repairable, despite its distance. The German student first repeats the repairable, then paraphrases and provides additional context for the word *muezzin* (l. 292).

This paraphrase, however, produces a new repairable, as the German speaker cannot recall the lexeme *mosque*. He hesitates and initiates repair by help of a paraphrase and the metalinguistic concession of not knowing the lexical item. Upon this, the Tanzanian speaker steps in and operates self-initiated other-repair, supplying the word searched for (l. 293). In the following turn (ll. 294; 296), the German speaker, now aware of the possibility of further problems, pre-empts the critical item *minaret* by paraphrasing it and finally closes the first frame by returning to the previous repairable *muezzin*, explaining it in further detail, while also drawing on creative means such as using sounds (l. 296). The Tanzanian speaker finally signals understanding, although it appears that she has still not activated the English lexical item for the word looked for (l. 297). With her final statement, she indicates that the conversation can now move on.

(33) 290 **CGm:** what i really though- when i first came here (.) at the hotel (.) er the (.) <pvc> muezzin <ipa> ʻmuɛtsi:n </ipa> </pvc> (.) called and (.) i (.) thought er oh. (0.5) it (.) was (.) in germany we only know the bells if they're ringing (.) (at) the church towers? (.) and here it's the <pvc> muezzin </pvc> and i think it's (1.5) it's <L1de> irgendwie {somehow} </L1de> (1) i think it's (.) great how he sings and so i think it's
291 **CTf:** who is that?
292 **CGm:** erm the <pvc> MUEZZIN </pvc>. erm the one who is in the (1) the (0.5) the church where muslims go to how it's [called]
293 **CTf:** [oh] the MOSQUE.
294 **CGm:** yeah. (.) and [on the]=
295 **CTf:** [ah]
296 **CGm:** =mosque there is >er in germany we call it< <L1de> minarett <ipa> ʻmɪnaʁɛt </ipa> </L1de> s- it's the tower? (.) and on that (.) the (.) muezzin (.) calls and so <sing> ah:: </sing> and so (.) calls er. (.) to pray.
297 **CTf:** aouh. (0.5) the er yeah:. (.) it's different.

(C1_290-297)

Building rapport through repair

O'Neal (2019: 213) has pointed to the finding that "repair sequences are much more than just the resolution of an interactional problem".[58] Enhancing clarity

58 O'Neal's (2019) study, set in a Japanese-Filipino business ELF context, focusses on the effect of repair sequences on subsequent linguistic feature selection. Although this micradiachronic focus has not been taken here, it would be very interesting to further investigate whether repair sequences also have an effect on subsequent feature selection in the TeenELF corpus and how this ties in with relational issues as studied in the present chapter.

through repair can go hand in hand with a promotion of rapport if repair is successfully brought about, as demonstrated in excerpt (34), in which students ATf and AGf share their worries. The repairable, which contains a phonetic rather than a lexical deviation from 'native' speaker norms – *two* pronounced as [tju:] – is demarcated by the speaker herself upon the first mention through hesitation and rising intonation (l. 430). In a self-initiation repair process, AGf draws on a metalinguistic question, which includes a repetition of the repairable ("you know it the c o <pvc> two <ipa> tju: </ipa> </pvc>", l. 430) to make sure her interlocutor understands her message. Due to a lack of verbal reaction, indicated by a one-second pause, the producer of the trouble source herself comes up with an explanation, which, however, still fails to help the addressee understand. Whether consciously or not, the Tanzanian speaker now retrieves the decisive problem solving strategy by asking her German dialogue partner to "write" it down (l. 431). In what follows, both speakers see this strategy work, and the German speaker explicitly accepts the repair offered by her dialogue partner by the confirmative particle "yeah" (l. 436) and the metalinguistic comment "that's what i mean" (l. 438). She attaches an apologetic explanation (l. 440) as a face-saving strategy to counter the potential face-threat that other-correction brings about. As can be seen in the final sequence, however, the relationship between the dialogue partners does not seem to have suffered at all. Both speakers express their shared joy in the face of this collaboratively achieved success in the negotiation of meaning through extensively laughing together (ll. 440–442) and thus assure each other of their sound relationship.

(34) 429 **ATf:** =in germany?
430 **AGf:** erm:: (.) well the global warming (.) of course erm (1) well (.) i think in germany (.) in the moment we have many fears about the c o (.) <pvc> tue {two} <ipa> tju: </ipa> </pvc> you know it the c o <pvc> tue </pvc>(1) well erm: when you drive a car what they (.) come out of the car and (.) think many people in germany: fear the erm: results they will (think) [-cause of this.]
431 **ATf:** [oh you can write] this. (1)
432 **AGf:** erm::
433 **ATf:** in germany? (8)
434 **AGf:** {writing} results (3) of (1) c o you write it like this=
435 **ATf:** =oh carbon dioxide.
436 **AGf:** yeah [@@ @]
437 **ATf:** [@@@]

```
438 AGf:  that's what i mean @@@
439 ATf:  @@@
440 AGf:  i don't have chemistry so: @ i don't (.) just know (.)
          this [@@]
441 ATf:       [@@@]
442 AGf:  @ okay.
```

(A2_429-442)

Jeopardizing rapport through repair

Relational concerns, however, can also lead to the failing of repair. The Tanzanian student JTf in (35) talks about natural resources that can be found in her home country. Singling out Tanzanite as "the unique one" (l. 083), she triggers a repair sequence, which, however, remains incomplete. In the course of the conversation, the German speaker mainly uses the discourse marker "mhm" as a default back-channel item (e.g. l. 082). Deviating from his standard pattern by using a higher pitch "ah" (l. 084), he signals surprise, which the Tanzanian student, however, does not receive as a repair initiation and therefore simply answers with a confirmative "yes" (l. 085). Consequently, the German speaker turns to a stronger repair initiator[59] and repeats the assumed repairable ("unicorn", l. 086), exposing to the analyst the source of trouble. The Tanzanian student now recognizes the need for repair and offers a paraphrase for *unique* ("it's found in tanzania only", l. 087). This, however, does not solve the problem for the German speaker, who resorts to a last weak repair initiator ("ah okay?", l. 088), probably hoping to receive further clues. When these are not offered, he decides to employ the let-it-pass strategy and initiates an abrupt topic change (l. 090).

In retrospective interviews students disclosed that, when faced with understanding difficulties, they would generally ask for clarification no more than twice, feeling further requests to be impolite and embarrassing (see Int_GrG). In essence, then, positive rapport here outranks the management of understanding and causes students to leave repair incomplete.

59 For a categorization of repair initiation types along a scale from weaker to stronger, see Clift (2016: 251).

(35) 081 **JTf:** `also (.) there is minerals (.) like (.) diamond copper (.) gold gypsum magnetite`
082 **JGm:** `[mhm]`
083 **JTf:** `[there]'s some iron (.) and the unique one which is tanzanite`
084 **JGm:** `↑ah`
085 **JTf:** `[yes]`
086 **JGm:** `[the] unicorn?`
087 **JTf:** `(.) it's found in tanzania only`
088 **JGm:** `ah okay?`
089 **JTf:** `yeah.`
090 **JGm:** `a::nd (.) what can you say about your society?`

(J2_081-090)

Promoting solidarity through failed repair

Face concerns, however, do not constitute the only factor leading to a potential failure of repair. Repair may also remain incomplete because interlocutors are simply unable to find a satisfying solution to their problem. Rapport may then even benefit from a shared lack of knowledge, as demonstrated in (36). While in this sequence, in which students exchange details about their respective school lives and find themselves in the process of writing major aspects down for their dia|log|book, repair attempts fail again, the relational outcome differs notably from the previous example. Due to deviant conceptualizations of day times – in Swahili, 1 pm corresponds to *saa saba* ('7 o'clock') (see Section 10.3.4), while in Germany people use *13 Uhr* ('13 o'clock') rather than 1 o'clock in timetable contexts – both students have problems with the English time concept and manage to increase confusion rather than truly correct each other. What is particularly interesting here is the final sequence: the teenagers admit that they do not have a solution ("we are not sure", l. 459), but they do not see this as a problem ("it's fine"; "she'll[60] understand", ll. 460–461) and comment that "it doesn't matter" (l. 456). Their indifference does not pose a communicative problem insofar as intersubjective understanding is secured despite the lack of a concrete solution to their dilemma.

60 The pronoun "she" refers to the researcher, who lateron compiled the separate pages into one dia|log|book.

From their shared lack of knowledge, the students appear to draw solidarity and further construct their co-identity as 'non-native' speakers of English.[61] This is expressed by the change of pronouns from first person singular *I* to an inclusive and shared first person plural *we* (ll. 456–459), which is further strengthened by a demarcation from a third person *she* (l. 463). The speakers confirm the positive effect of this unsolved repair sequence on their relationship by extensively laughing together (ll. 462–463) before finally turning to something else.

(36) 431 **ATf:** {writing} school in germany? (9) school in tanzania it's erm:: let's say:: er::
432 **AGf:** maybe starts at?=
433 **ATf:** =starts at (.) yeah. {writing} starts at (2) seven thirty? is it p m? or [a m?(.)@@]
434 **AGf:** [a m (.)] a m @@
435 **ATf:** {writing} seven thirty a m an:d ends at (3) ends at (2) erm: two thirty? (2) thirty? (2) a m? we have (even) a- afternoon classes?=
436 **AGf:** =yah. (2)
437 **ATf:** we call them remedial classes? (2) {writing} classes (2) classes (4) a::t (1) erm:: (.) we start afternoon classes at s- at one?
438 **AGf:** okay. (1)
439 **ATf:** it's two hours? one (.) one hour each subject? [so we]
440 **AGf:** [mhm?]
441 **ATf:** study two subjects (.) in the afternoon.
442 **AGf:** okay.
443 **ATf:** erm::? {writing} one p m to:: (4)
444 **AGf:** i think it's p m (1)
445 **ATf:** er?
446 **AGf:** yah it's p m because (.) it's (.) after: (.) lunchtime.
447 **ATf:** an:d before lunchtime?
448 **AGf:** it's a m (.) er:: it's p m (.) wa- wa- wait.
449 **ATf:** @@ let's (.) [use this.]
450 **AGf:** [no well] well.
451 **ATf:** erm:=

61 Hülmbauer (2009: 335) further illustrates how ELF speakers benefit from what she calls their "shared non-nativeness".

452	**AGf:**	=no (.) it is b- (2) before twelve o'clock it's p m? an::d
453	**ATf:**	@
454	**AGf:**	after twelve o'clock [it's]
455	**ATf:**	[okay.] (2)
456	**AGf:**	isn't it? ah:: (1) i'm not su::re? (1) but i think (.) well it doesn't matter.
457	**ATf:**	@ @@
458	**AGf:**	we just (.) yeah. just yeah.
459	**ATf:**	we are [not sure.]
460	**AGf:**	[it's fine.]
461	**ATf:**	she'll understand.
462	**AGf:**	@ [@@@@@@]
463	**ATf:**	[@ @]

(A3_431-463)

Tellingly, this repair sequence starts off (l. 444) with an otherwise conversationally very rare instance of OIOR (see Clift 2016: 247), which is normally strongly avoided for fear of face-loss. It seems unproblematic here particularly because of the positive relationship that has been established in the course of previous interactions within this dialogue pair, which enables the speakers to openly negotiate meanings in an emerging *third space* (see Section 2.2.3). Speakers make these negotiations possible through openly marking the subjectivity and tentativeness of their contributions by help of hedging devices (e.g. "maybe" and rising intonation, l. 432; "i think", l. 444), not insisting on their own version to be the only correct one, and encouraging each other to further contribute, for instance by frequent confirmative backchanneling ("yeah"; "okay", e.g. ll. 436; 438).

Misunderstandings arising from pragmatically misinterpreted repair

While repair is mostly operated for an enhancement of understanding, a pragmatic misinterpretation of intended repair may also have the opposite effect of leading to rather than solving misunderstandings. Extract (37) illustrates a communicative situation repeatedly occurring along similar lines in TeenELF, in which a positive reaction to a negative question causes confusion. FTf's positive response "yes" (l. 018) to FGf's negative utterance "and next week there're also no [exams]" (l. 017) is open to different interpretations. As inferred from her reaction ("yes there (are) okay", l. 019), FGf interprets her partner's positive response as a repair of her own utterance, concluding that there will be more exams to come the following week.

FTf, however, may not intend to repair FGf's assumption, but rather verify the declarative question by a positive answer. This interpretation is contextually suggested by FTf's previous and subsequent elaborations "no more" (l. 014), emphasized by the paraphrase "we already finished" (l. 016), and "december"[62] (l. 020) when read against the backdrop of discourse on the same topic as conducted by her fellow Tanzanian students in other dialogue pairs (e.g. G2_057; G3_26–27; L1_640). Whether or not intended and received meanings finally match, must remain open as no further conversational clues are given and the interlocutors enter into a prolonged stage of silence (l. 021), walking around in search for a place to sit.

(37) 006 **FGf:** ho::w many exams (.) do you have to do? (1) [(x)]
007 **FTf:** [today] is only one.
008 **FGf:** only one.
010 **FTf:** yes
011 **FGf:** a:nd is there (.) is there tomorrow?
012 **FTf:** no::
013 **FGf:** and this (.) er this week no (.) [no more (.) (tests)]
014 **FTf:** [no: no more]
015 **FGf:** [bu::t]
016 **FTf:** [we already] finished
017 **FGf:** ↑ah:: we- (.) oh okay. (.) that's great. (1) a:nd next week there're also no
018 **FTf:** [yes]
019 **FGf:** [exams.] yes there are okay.
020 **FTf:** december (1)
021 **FGf:** okay. (20)

(F3_006-021)

7.4 Other-involvement in repair

In accordance with conversation organization and principles of politeness, repair is both self-initiated and self-accomplished (SISR) in the present data in the vast majority of cases. OISR ranks second, with the hearer indicating a trouble source the speaker might not have noticed and giving the speaker the opportunity to amend the problem. In addition to these two common types of repair, however, TeenELF

62 The dialogue was recorded in late October.

also shows a considerable degree of other-accomplishment in repair. Even OIOR, otherwise very rarely used for fear of face-loss, is not uncommon here, with more than four dozen documented cases in 26 hours of communication. This discovery is in line with the finding that teenage talk tends to be more direct than adult interaction (see Palacios Martinéz 2018: 365). In an attempt to find further reasons for the high incidence of other-involvement in repair in TeenELF, the present section explores objects and functions of OIOR in the present data, and inspects how situational factors, face concerns and questions of identity come into play.

Objects and functional range of OIOR

Just as repair in general, OIOR can be used to correct more obvious errors and mistakes, for example spelling mistakes or a mispronunciation of proper names, but is often employed to negotiate understanding, fine-tune utterances or express subjective disagreement. Objects triggering OIOR cover a wide linguistic range from pronunciation deviations over malapropisms to a perceived inappropriateness of discursive explicitness. While the total number of coded OIOR sequences (n_t=49) defies a sound quantitative analysis, spelling mistakes (n_{sp}=10 instances) and lexico-semantic inaccuracies (n_{ls}=9) stand out as the two most frequent initiators of OIOR in TeenELF. The prominence of spelling as an object of repair in OIOR (e.g. *Tansania* vs. *Tanzania*, E2_161–171) suggests a lower tolerance towards deviation from 'standard' norms in written language than in spoken language. Lexico-semantic problems (e.g. *a.m.* vs. *p.m.*, A3_443-463) are addressed to secure mutual understanding. Variation in pronunciation and spoken grammar, in contrast, is only commented on if intersubjective understanding is in danger.

Conversational sequences show OIOR to cover a wide functional range from a correction of norm deviations over a negotiation of meanings to an expression of stance and, if applied ironically, also a potential promotion of rapport (see Table 11).

Table 11: Functions of OIOR in TeenELF.

Addressing norm deviations	Correcting errors and mistakes Seeking affirmation in the face of unclear norms
Negotiating meaning	Addressing misunderstandings Fine-tuning Raising explicitness
Expressing stance	Evaluating Negotiating appropriateness
Promoting rapport	Boosting solidarity

Addressing norm deviations through OIOR

A spelling disparity ("Tansania" vs. "Tanzania") constitutes the object of repair in (42), illustrating the most common type of OIOR in TeenELF with regard to the type of repairable. A close look at the sequence in combination with the respective entry in the dia|log|book (Figure 11) facilitates detailed insights into conversational mechanisms at work and motivations behind OIOR, which is here employed to correct a supposed spelling mistake. While ETf first follows a let-it-pass strategy as can be deduced from an uncorrected first entry of "Tansania" in the dia|log|book (see Figure 11), she decides to point to the spelling mistake when the item in question turns up a second time. While repair is otherwise often used for a negotiation of meanings, intersubjective understanding does not appear to be at stake here. It is more likely that the speaker here employs repair because she is worried about handing in a deficient contribution to be distributed in class. The situational context with its task-based assignment seems to play an important role for the frequency of OIOR.

This particular instance of repair seems all the more significant as the item in question is of such central situational importance, as it not only directly touches ETf's national identity as an important facet of her self-concept, but also refers to the country where the students meet. This may also explain why EGf's reaction in (38) turns out unexpectedly elaborate in the face of a mere spelling mistake. Repeated apologies (ll. 167; 171), laughter and discourse particles to express worries ("oh oh oh", l. 169) reveal a sensitivity to face issues inherent in OIOR: correcting here introduces a vertical distance (see Section 3.2) into a formerly balanced relationship, and the sudden realization of having got a central aspect wrong in some way causes EGf to apologize. When this is granted by ETf at the end of the sequence ("it's okay", l. 172), balance seems to be restored (see balance principle in Brown & Levinson 1987: 236).

(38) 161 **EGf:** {writing "Tansania"}
162 **ETf:** it's not <pvc> tans:ania </pvc>. tanzania. ah: @@
163 **EGf:** with z?
164 **ETf:** tanzania. not <pvc> tansania </pvc>.
165 **EGf:** so i [write (.) with z.]
166 **ETf:** [tanzania (.) with z.]
167 **EGf:** oh: sorry.
168 **ETf:** @@@
169 **EGf:** oh oh oh @@
170 **ETf:** @@

171 **EGf:** i'm sorry.
172 **ETf:** it's okay. (18)

(E2_161-171)

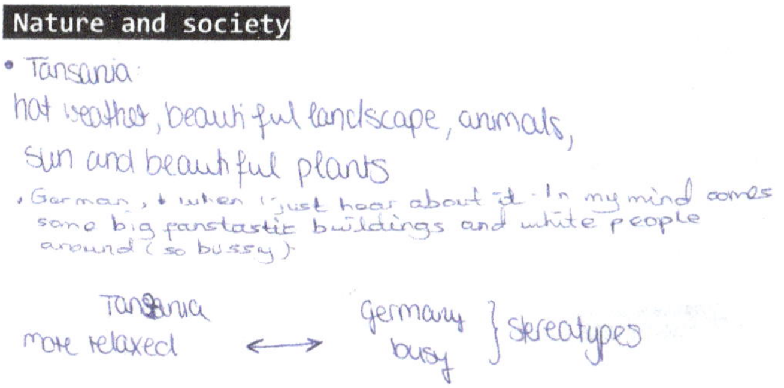

Nature and society

• Tansania:
hot weather, beautiful landscape, animals,
sun and beautiful plants
• German, + when I just hear about it. In my mind comes
some big fanstastic buildings and white people
around (so bussy).

Tansania more relaxed ⟷ Germany busy } stereotypes

Figure 11: Dia|log|book entry *Tans/zania*.

The spelling mistake displayed here shows influences of underlying languages at work, with *Tansania* representing the German way of spelling. When students openly expose linguistic transfer as a reason for deviances from 'standards', this may have the effect that face in a repair situation is restored through a foregrounding of the speakers' shared identity as multilingual language users, rather than through apologizing for any shortcomings as language learners.

Speaker CGm employs this strategy in (39) with far-reaching consequences. While CGm enters notes into the dia|log|book, CTf points to the fact that *Africa* should be spelled with a *c* rather than a *k* (l. 255). When CGm explains his way of spelling by linguistic transfer at work (l. 256), CTf may want to reject this explanation by opening an adversative statement ("but", l. 257), but then joins in the discourse on plurilingualism, commenting that in Swahili, just like in German *Afrika* is also spelled with a *k* (l. 257). In the light of this similarity, the students agree on leaving OIOR unaccomplished here, signalled through CTf's finalizing comment "it's okay" (l. 257) and the unchanged entry in the notebook (see Figure 12). ELF speakers here consciously flout 'standard' English norms in favour of new rules that give expression to their shared multilingual identity.[63] The interlocutors here

63 See also Crystal (2012b): "Spellings are made by people. Dictionaries – eventually – reflect popular choices".

illustrate Canagarajah's (2007: 927) observation that "[m]ultilingual speakers are not moving towards someone else's target; they are constructing their own norms".

(39) 353 **CTf:** so lots of raw mat[erials] in africa=
254 **CGm:** [mh?]
255 **CTf:** =↑africa is with a c. (1)
256 **CGm:** oh: in germany it's with a k @@
257 **CTf:** but if it's (.) if it's in: kiswahili it's with a k. (1.5) it's okay

(C2_353-357)

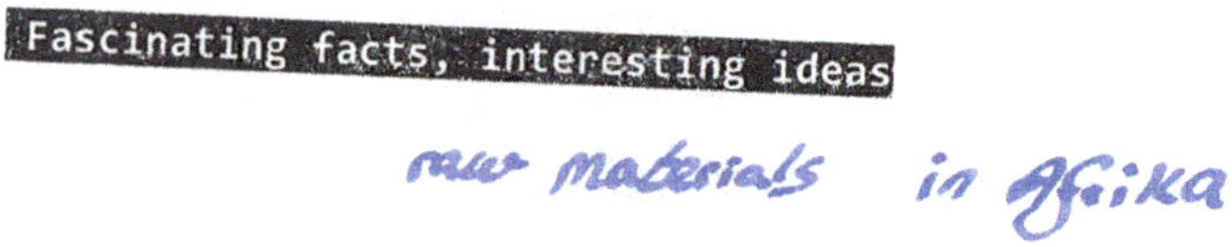

Fascinating facts, interesting ideas

raw materials in Afrika

Figure 12: Dia | log | book entry *Afrika*.

While underlying norms are a recurring issue in OIOR, they are not always negotiated dialogically. In (40), KGf operates a repair of the noun phrase "no much time" (l. 178), which is considered ungrammatical against 'standard' English norms. KGf's repair, however, is delayed and brought about with a markedly soft voice (l. 181), suggesting that the utterance is not to be understood as an open correction, but rather directed at herself rather than at her interlocutor. The 'error' detected does not impede mutual understanding, but clashes with the language norms KGf has studied, which she reaffirms in her repair operation. An explicit acceptance does not seem to be expected and is not provided either, as KTf carries on without taking overt notice of the repair (l. 182).

(40) 178 **KTf:** and (0.5) i spend very little time with my family actually maybe (until on) (.) holidays i can: spend my time with my: youngest brothers (.) a:nd other friends but (.) i have (.) no much time with my family.=
179 **KGf:** =yeah:
180 **KTf:** yah:
181 **KGf:** °not much.°
182 **KTf:** cause i like singin? (.) [. . .]

(K1_178-181)

Negotiating meaning through OIOR

OIOR, however, goes beyond a negotiation of norms and often addresses problems in understanding, which sometimes become apparent through spelling as illustrated in (41). Phonetic levelling of the final fricative has here led to a mixing-up of "laugh" and "love", which only shows in spelling when GGf enters "laugh" into the dia|log|book (see Figure 13). When GTf realizes the misunderstanding, she initiates repair (l. 024) and provides the intended lexeme. GGf implements the repair in the dia|log|book, replacing "laugh" by "love".

(41) 018 **GTf:** for me when (.) when (person loving me) it's make me happy. (2)
019 **GGf:** <family> (.) [i think we]=
020 **GTf:** [l- love]
021 **GGf:** =can write it (1) and (.) and [laugh]
022 **GTf:** [(x)]
023 **GGf:** too? (1)
024 **GTf:** ↑ah (↑no) (.) ↑this. (2)
025 **GGf:** (oh that) (lo-) [(that love)]
026 **GTf:** [yea:h.]=
027 **GGf:** =okay yeah. (2)

(G4_018-027)

Figure 13: Dia|log|book entry *laugh/love*.

Negotiating meaning and securing mutual understanding also figure prominently when objects of OIOR go beyond spelling. Extract (42) shows two students employing other-repair repeatedly as a means to gradually increase lexico-semantic appropriateness. HTf starts off presenting her ideas on what school is about, namely a "place where [...] (you can change) ideas and you can see different kind of people" (l. 547), which HGf summarizes and amends to "school as a place of exchange a:nd [...] (social-)" (ll. 550; 552). HTf suggests the term "commuting" (l. 553) to abbreviate and state the message more precisely. As in doing so she resorts to a malapropism, however, HGf steps in to provide OR once more, offering the lexeme "communication" instead (l. 554), which finally, in its verbal form, finds entry into the dia|log|book.

(42) 547 **HTf:** (we're) at school (1) (in the) place where you can: (1) °(you can change)° (.) ideas and you can see different kind of people (because)=
548 **HGf:** =°okay?°
549 **HTf:** actually=
550 **HGf:** =school as a place of exchange an:d
551 **HTf:** yeah=
552 **HGf:** =(social-)=
553 **HTf:** =commuting.
554 **HGf:** °commu-° (.) °communi-cation?°
555 **HTf:** °(yeah)°

(H3_547-555)

Speaker CGm in (43) employs OIOR as a means to raise explicitness though neither norms nor understanding are in danger. Rather than truly correcting his interlocutor's choice of words ("u k"; l. 067), CGm draws on the long version "united kingdom" (l. 068), which is less prone to mishearings or misunderstandings than its abbreviation, to make sure he understands correctly.

(43) 067 **CTf:** [. . .] i've always wanted to live in the s- in the u k.
068 **CGm:** the united kingdom (1) the united kingdom is a nice country. it rains a lot and then it's cold. (.) so may@ be@ you ha@ve to mi@nd i@@t.=

(C4_067-068)

Expressing stance through OIOR

OIOR accomplished negotiations may not only evolve around norms and meanings or raise explicitness, but may also address values and appropriateness in a given context, as illustrated in (44). In her repair reaction "it's (.) not really a problem" (l. 059), GGf neither addresses a norm deviation nor a misunderstanding, but qualifies GTf's statement ("a problem (to you) (1) [is] [. . .] your health", ll. 056; 058) with regard to its content.

(44) 056 **GTf:** a problem (to you) (1) [is]=
057 **GGf:** [er:]
058 **GTf:** =your health.
059 **GGf:** it's (.) n:ot really a problem.

(G4_056-059)

Face concerns in OIOR

While OIOR serves important functions in the negotiation and fine-tuning of norms, meanings and stance, it remains delicate from a rapport point of view: uninvited correction, criticism or disagreement intrinsically threaten the addressee's positive face. For this reason, interlocutors frequently employ the let-it-pass strategy rather than repairing, or delay their intervention as far as possible to grant the speaker the option for self-correction. If they do consider an intervention necessary, speakers will normally try to minimize the face-threat by resorting to face-saving strategies adjusted in directness: the higher speakers esteem the face-threat, the more indirect will be their strategy chosen (see Brown & Levinson 1987: 59–60).[64] On a continuum from highly direct, bald on-record to indirect, off-record tactics, Figure 14 gives an overview of strategies. Examples illustrate how these strategies are employed in the present data.

Extract (45) illustrates how the speaker adjusts her level of directness in repair as the need arises. The object of repair is an alleged spelling mistake in the plural of *mango*.[65] In her first attempt to initiate repair, LTf pays heed to communicative politeness by resorting to a rather indirect strategy, using hesitations ("er:"), hedges ("i think") and the modal auxiliary "should" in her request (l. 381). Positive politeness becomes visible in the repeated hearer-oriented affirmative particle "yeah" (l. 383). When repair, however, is not accomplished by LGf, LTf abruptly interrupts her row of assenting "yeah"s by a blunt "no" (l. 383). This very direct strategy is employed as a measure of emergency to prevent further harm, as LGf has apparently begun to "dis-correct" the item in question. In a post-hoc effort to mitigate this face-threatening on-record interjection, LTf delivers a general statement to justify her repair initiation ("they are written", l. 383) and then starts to explain the repair expected step-by-step in an elaborate trans-turn instruction, paying close attention to LGf's actions ("and then you (add here) e s. em. (.) there is m a n g o between", ll. 383; 385; 387), until the repair is finally jointly achieved, as the entry in the dia|log|book reveals (see Figure 15).

LGf closes the repair sequence not only by showing that she has finally come to realize the mistake in question, but also by an expression of gratitude ("thank you", l. 388). Thanking her interlocutor for providing new insights, LGf alleviates the face-threat inherent in criticizing and being criticized, changing LTf's role from that of a criticizer to that of a supporter. In a complex interactional process, the students thus manage to accomplish OIOR while mitigating the face-threatening act.

64 Brown & Levinson (1987: 60) point to the finding that an inappropriately direct strategy may make a face-threatening act appear more threatening than it actually is.

65 The OED online (see OED, s.v. *mango*, n.1.) lists two plural forms of *mango*, namely *mangos* and *mangoes*.

			TeenELF Examples		
Direct	Bald on-record	Blunt no	**ATf:**	**=no**:: career is written like c a r r e r [sic]	(A4_408)
		Isolated repaired item	**CGm:**	erm (0.5) about sixty percent are christians? […] and thirty percents are (.) nothing? (0.5)	
			CTf:	**pagans**.	(C1_326-327)
	On-record + redressive action (positive politeness)	Yeah + repaired item	**GGf:**	you wanna be a pharma?	
			GTf:	**yeah a pharmacist?**	(G4_051-052)
	On-record + redressive action (negative politeness)	General statement	**ITf:**	=[no **the**]=	
			IGf:	[yeah.]	
			ITf:	=**question is (.) says** that (.) what's comes to your mind first when you think of my country. (1)	(I2_137-139)
		Hedging and hesitation	**ATf:**	erm::? {writing} 1 p.m:: to:: (4)	
			AGf:	**i think** it's a m. (1)	(A3_443-444)
		Elaborating	**CGm:**	my brother is (.) sixteen.	
			CTf:	@	
			CGm:	i'm eighteen=	
			CTf:	=one year difference.	
			CGm:	**it's (.) sixTEEN so** it's TWO years.	(C1_031-035)
	Off-record	Repetition of repairable	**ATf:**	so you guys use these pens to write in your?	
			AGf:	erm: (.) no normally we use <pencil>?	
			ATf:	**<pencil>**	
			AGf:	but (.) sometimes we have to write something erm: (.) coloured so (.) then we use them.	
			ATf:	we only use black (.) or [blue]?	
			AGf:	[okay] @@	
			ATf:	you'll: use a pencil to draw?	
			AGf:	yeah.	
			ATf:	(only that's what i s-) so it's (.) either black or blue [pen.]	
Indirect			**AGf:**	[okay.]	(A3_509-518)

Figure 14: Directness in TeenELF OIOR (general categories based on Brown & Levinson 1978: 68–70).

(45) 381 **LTf:** er (.) also coconuts mangoes? (1) we grow mangoes here? (1) oranges? {LGf writes “coconuts, mangos”; see dia|log|book} (3) er: (1) i think you should add (.) e here. (.) yeah (.) yeah yeah here. (.) mang[oes.]
382 **LGf:** [an] e?
383 **LTf:** yeah- no- mangoes they are written em mango? (.) and then [you]
384 **LGf:** <L1de> [ach] {oh} </L1de>
385 **LTf:** (add here) e s.
386 **LGf:** so (.) there [is an e?]
387 **LTf:** [em] (.) there is m a n g o (.) between of (.) [yeah.]
388 **LGf:** [ah] okay. (.) so. [(.) thank you?]
(L2_381-388)

Figure 15: Dia|log|book entry *mango(e)s*.

Even OIOR strategies towards the more direct end of the scale are not necessarily perceived as face-threatening but may be interpreted as cooperative behaviour instead. This is especially the case if repair items are used for semantic fine-tuning rather than phonetic or grammatical correction. In (46), the repair operation that turns *knives* (l. 317) into *irons* (l. 318) can be read as a paraphrasing expression to indicate shared understanding rather than vertical correction. Speaker NGf does not seem to perceive a face-threat in this direct repair, as she continues the conversation hardly paying any attention to the repair at all (l. 318). As we have seen in extract (33) where *crisis* is changed to *war*, the hearer may repeat, accept and actively apply the newly suggested item in the ongoing conversation, signalling agreement with the adequacy of the repair item.

OIOR may even be used to promote solidarity between interlocutors, as can be demonstrated in (47). OIOR – “the wonderful picture” undergoes repair and is changed to “the most beautiful picture” (ll. 257–258) – is here used to boost an inclusive *WE*-compliment (see Section 8.1) on the students and their friendship.[66] Irony and laughter, common means for managing rapport in TeenELF (see Chapter 9), are used in this sequence to further strengthen solidarity.

66 The picture in question is a photo showing the two interlocutors.

(46) 317 **NGf:** : yeah (.) i (.) and i like hugh jackman? he's one of the (.) the actor of the erm (.) ones with the this (0.5) the fingers (.) and he has like (.) knives [in them?]
318 **NTf:** [er like] irons.
319 **NGf:** yeah (.) a:nd (.) erm (.) yah. i really like this movie (1.5)
(N3_317-319)

(47) 257 **OGf:** =(an:d) there is enough (.) space for the wonderful picture.
258 **OTf:** °yeah. the most° (.) °beautiful picture°?
259 **OGf:** @@
(O4_257-259)

OIOR and identity

The relatively high overall frequency of OIOR in the present data seems to some degree attributable to the fact that students also work on a written task, as spelling mistakes account for a high percentage of OIOR. Misunderstandings and errors to be addressed by OIOR show more clearly when they appear on paper. Explicit negotiations are then found to be necessary if an interlocutor wants to find his or her stance correctly and clearly presented in a jointly worked out product. A combination of oral and written tasks thus provides a comprehensive arena for elaborate negotiations of meaning, which also carries important pedagogical potential (see Chapter 12).

The findings presented above, however, also suggests that, in addition to explanations on the basis of writing, young ELF users may be particularly prone to other-involvement in repair due to a conducive interplay of various components of identity (see Figure 16):

- As *multilingual individuals*, teenage ELF speakers do not take intersubjective understanding for granted and are familiar with the constant need of negotiating meaning. Seeing repair as a necessity to achieve mutual understanding, they don't hesitate to initiate or accomplish it when the need arises.
- As *learners*, teenaged ELF speakers are conscious of their own fallibility and ready to accept correction as a necessary measure to achieve progress. They appear particularly willing to admit help in the present setting as it is offered

by peers.[67] Their learner identity will also help students to accept that some problems do not have easy solutions.

- As *students*, teenaged ELF speakers have learned to fulfil tasks conscientiously. They consequently use repair to perfect their assignments.
- As *critical adolescents*, teenaged ELF speakers emphasize their right to hold and share their personal opinions. They use repair to express their individual viewpoints that might differ from previous statements.
- As *competent communicators*, teenaged ELF speakers attempt to make communication as effective as possible, using other-repair for example to raise explicitness or reduce redundancy.

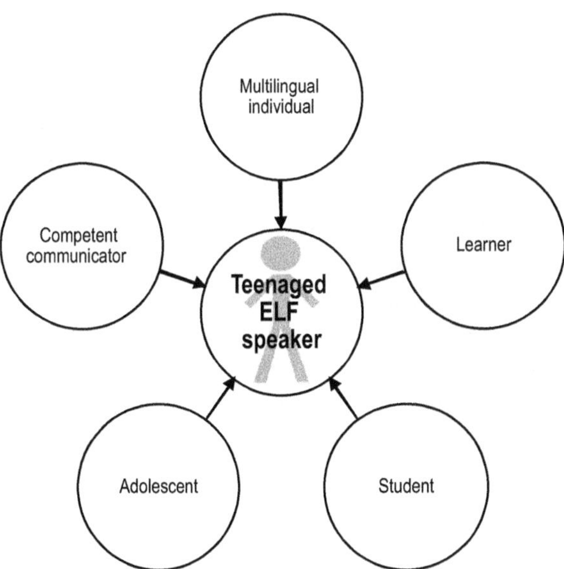

Figure 16: Components of identity contributing to the frequency of OIOR in TeenELF.

7.5 Summary of findings on repetition and repair

Chapters 6 and 7 have explored the polymorphism and multifunctional use of repetition and repair as omnipresent and partly overlapping phenomena in TeenELF. Mainly employed for an enhancement of explicitness and the negotiation of mean-

67 On the positive influence of peers on learning processes, see e.g. Topping et al. (2017); Deutsch & Rohr (2018).

ings, both strategies have also been examined in their interpersonal potential and their interplay with aspects of identity. Framing, or distant repetition, has been revealed as a central interactional device to raise explicitness and impart cohesion at the same time. TeenELF interaction has also been shown to be conspicuously open to other-involvement in repair, which has been explained by an interplay of various factors of identity.

Analyses of repair in TeenELF have further exposed the conceptual blurriness of *errors* in the light of fluid norms and the need for a reconsideration of concepts of proficiency (see e.g. Cogo & Dewey 2012: 168; Jenkins 2017: 560). While students' use of repetition and repair display an inherent norm orientation, it is not always clear which norms are in operation. The question of norms, the treatment of errors and the understanding of proficiency becomes particularly relevant in educational contexts (see Chapter 12).

Repetition and repair reflect an essentially cooperative behaviour, which in the present data also figures for instance in frequent utterance completions, the use of metalinguistic devices or recipient-designed interaction. Lingua franca speakers have been found to exhibit "a strong motivation for mutual understanding" (Mustajoki 2017: 70). The fact that the students taking part in the present exchange had invested a lot of time and money to make this exchange happen[68] suggests that they had a genuine interest in their interlocutors' lives and ideas. This is bound to have increased their willingness to engage in extended collaborative repair, in order to make meanings as clear as possible and guarantee intersubjective understanding. The task orientation – here the assignment to jointly create a book – is almost certain to have further increased the students' efforts to attain high levels of clarity and assumed correctness. The present study has also laid open the pedagogical potential of a combination of oral and written tasks, as misunderstandings may become more transparent when written down and can then be thoroughly negotiated in talk-in-interaction.

Adolescent students in a learning environment like the given one appear particularly likely to accept help offered by peer interlocutors. TeenELF participants repeatedly emphasize their exchange partner's openness, easy rapport building and an overall sound relationship they experience in interacting with their dialogue partners (see Int_ETf; Int_FGf; Int_HTf). While repeated halts in progressivity may obstruct the building of rapport, it seems to be primarily the positive peer-to-peer-relationship which makes the extensive other-involvement in repair possible in its various manifestations. As has been shown, the joint accomplishment

68 Students had prepared for their encounter for more than a year, collecting information, preparing presentations, working to collect money etc.

of repair can further boost solidarity and facilitate even stronger bonds between interlocutors in a positive circle.

The following chapter focuses on an interactional phenomenon which stands out in its significance for the management of rapport in TeenELF: the speech act of complimenting.

8 The speech act of complimenting in TeenELF

> `i don't know what (.) what makes me happy. (.) i think (.) sometimes (s) also little (.) things can make you happy like if you: (.) i don't know if somebody compliments you or something like that`
>
> (DGf in M4_256)

Apparently well aware of the positive effect of complimenting as expressed by one of the participants in the introductory quotation, students do not spare compliments in their TeenELF interactions.[69] Holmes defines a compliment as "a speech act which explicitly or implicitly attributes credit to someone other than the speaker, usually the person addressed, for some good (possession, characteristic, skill, etc.) which is positively valued by the speaker and the hearer" (Holmes 1988: 446). As speakers employ them to express their (positive) feelings about something, compliments belong to the class of expressive speech acts (see Section 3.2). Complimenting displays a twofold structure (see Golato 2005; Duan 2011: 356): any utterance of a compliment is followed by a meaningful compliment response (including zero response), so that complimenting presents itself as a truly dialogic speech act. In the interactional realization of compliments and compliment responses, principles of politeness play a major role (see Section 3.2).

The following analyses will look not only into the nature of objects receiving compliments, but also into the formal realization and the functional range of complimenting. Furthermore, the nature of compliment responding and relevant sociocultural aspects in TeenELF will be investigated.

8.1 The semantics of complimenting

Compliments have been found in previous studies to primarily address appearance, possessions, abilities, accomplishments and character traits (see Wolfson 1983: 90–91 for American English; Holmes 1986: 496 for New Zealand English; Golato 2005: 27 for German). All of these categories can also be detected as objects of complimenting in the TeenELF corpus (see Table 12).

Although the full range of assessables (i.e. objects receiving compliments; see Golato 2005: 27) is covered in the present corpus, there is a striking scarcity of appearances[70] and concrete objects as targets in TeenELF compliments, with

69 In total, 321 instances of complimenting have been tagged in 26 hours of speaking time.
70 Appeareances have been attested as highly relevant, for example, in American English (see Manes 1983: 98).

https://doi.org/10.1515/9783110786576-008

Table 12: Objects of complimenting in TeenELF.

Object category	Example		
Appearance	**HGf:**	i i saw your pictures i was like yeah she's modelling. [@@@@]	(H3_290)
Possession	**CTf:**	it's a really nice pen	(C2II_160)
Ability	**OGf:**	you can so (.) er you sing so good it (.) it sounds (.) so cool and so nice and wonderful (and) (.) i like it.	(O2_046)
Accomplishment	**DGf:**	@ i just say so many things and you wrote it down in: one sent- sentence it's SO(@) good @@	(D3_250)
Trait	**NGf:**	[. . .] you have a lot of (.) joy: and you're (.) you're often really happy and you (.) you show it to other people that you're happy and you're (.) really (.) erm (.) open too: (.)	(N2_046)
Behaviour	**NGf:**	when we came yesterday you just sat with us and (.) you asked so many questions and we just (.) could speak with you although (.) we didn't actually know you but it was: (.) it was so nice	(N2_046)

the school and its premises where the students meet forming a notable exception. Apart from this, the adolescents rather address particular ways of living, ideas or achievements; they focus on abstract possessions, such as talents and traits, as well as particular behaviour and successfully accomplished tasks rather than concrete objects. Students repeatedly compliment each other with respect to their perceived openness, for example, but also to friendly and peaceful ways of living together in their home country, beautiful singing as well as ideas for and entries into the dia|log|book. If the choice of objects considered apt for complimenting reflects sociocultural values, as has previously been proposed (see Manes 1983; Holmes 1988; Yuan 2002), these findings may suggest a rather non-materialistic and process-minded value orientation of the adolescents involved.

What strikes as ELF-particular is the high frequency of language-related compliments in TeenELF conversations. Students compliment on each other's home languages (see (48)), but also on competences in English (see (49)), which are frequently addressed in the interview data as well, exposing the students' metalinguistic awareness.

(48) 256 **ITf:** and also (.) i like your language (the way) you are talking [but]
257 **IGf:** [ohh]=
258 **ITf:** = i don't understand [it?]
259 **KGf:** [@@]
260 **IGf:** [oh.]=
261 **ITf:** =but i can (.) (heard) it.

(I2_256-261)

(49) 091 **HTf:** [. . .] i: have my uncle over there? {i.e. Canada} (.) a:nd yeah. (.) he (was having a (.) xx) s:even [years?]
092 **HGf:** [that's why]
your english is so great i guess.
093 **HTf:** @@@ actually: er erm (.) he's not s:o- (.) he's not coming into tanzania: frequently? but (1) yes we do communicate? [. . .]

(H4_091-093)

Complimenting in TeenELF is not necessarily restricted to assessables of a single addressee. Explicitly or implicitly, many compliments are directed at possessions, traits etc. of a larger group that the compliment receiver is part of or relates to. For a differentiation along these lines, the following taxonomy based on personal pronouns is suggested, with lower-case letters referring to single referents and capitals indicating group references (see Table 13), making it possible to distinguish between personal pronouns in the 2nd person group, which is found to be most salient in complimenting.

Table 13: Taxonomy of complimenting based on addressee of compliment.

	Singular	**Plural**
1st person	*I*-complimenting	*WE*-complimenting – Inclusive – Exclusive
2nd person	*you*-complimenting	*YOU*-complimenting
3rd person	*(s)he*-complimenting – Self-related – Other-related	*THEY*-complimenting – Self-related – Other-related

In addition to prevalent *you*-complimenting, the TeenELF corpus also shows an abundance of *YOU*- and inclusive *WE*-complimenting, i.e. compliments that are addressed at both speaker and hearer. *YOU*-compliments are mostly based on either national (or continental) categories, which are especially drawn upon when contrastive ways of living are assessed, or to the school community the addressee is part of. Inclusive *WE*-compliments are often used towards the end of dialogues for a positive assessment of a jointly achieved product (here especially entries into the dia|log|book), as illustrated in (50).

(50) 598 **OGf:** `i like our sheet.=`
599 **OTf:** `ah::.=`
600 **OGf:** `=it's [cool.]`
601 **OTf:** `        [@]@@@=`
602 **OGf:** `=@@=`
603 **OTf:** `=@ @ (haha:)`
604 **OGf:** `do you like it?`
605 **OTf:** `yeah. (.) i like it.`
606 **OGf:** `some(x it's great)`

(O1_598-607)

While OGf expresses her appreciation of their common achievement no less than three times (ll. 598; 600; 606), OTf shows herself somewhat hesitant to join in and only does so after an explicit elicitation (ll. 604–605). In her hesitant behaviour, OTf pays tribute to the modesty maxim of politeness (see 2.3.2). While inclusive *WE*-compliments generally make up for a flouting of this modesty maxim to some degree through a positive enforcement of solidarity,[71] exclusive *WE*-complimenting and *I*-complimenting lack this force and are hence very rare, though not altogether absent.[72] Speaker ETf in (51), for example, praises her own cooking abilities, which EGf first answers with a shy laughter (l. 265), and later on with a polite expression of recognition (l. 267).

(51) 264 **ETf:** `i know how to cook.`
265 **EGf:** `@@ [yes?]`
266 **ETf:** `    [but the] tradition(al) ones. i know how to cook.`

---

71 Students also employ inclusive *WE*-complimenting in a humorous way, playing with a flouting of the modesty maxim but marking it as ironic through exaggeration and accompanying laughter. For an example, see excerpt (47), Section 7.4.

72 In the strong sense of Holmes' (1988: 446) definition (see Introduction to Chapter 8), first person singular-addressed praise may not even be considered part of the paradigm of complimenting.

267 **EGf:** oh wow.
268 **ETf:** mhm.

(E1_264-268)

In order to comply with the modesty maxim, students also use strategies to accomplish self-related praise more indirectly, such as interrogative "fishing for compliment"-structures eliciting compliments from the hearer (see (52)), or passive voice constructions (see (53)). In (52), CGm first receives an affirmative answer as the preferred second pair part to his question (ll. 119-120), which finally leads to an open other-compliment on his pen (l. 122). In example (53), speaker DTf comments on the beauty of her country, which might have easily been interpreted as arrogance by her interlocutor, had she not chosen a passive voice construction ("we are blessed with", l. 060), which modestly presents the Tanzanian people as the receivers of an external blessing rather than the possessors of a praised good.

(52) 119 **CGm:** do you like the pen?
120 **CTf:** yeah (1.5)
121 **CGm:** erm: my mother erm. (0.5) it was a present from my mother in the fifth grade it's now (.) i think eight years ago? @ @@=
122 **CTf:** =it's nice

(C2_119-122)

(53) 060 **DTf:** i think tha:t we are blessed (.) with [many landscapes]
061 **DGf:** [@@@]
062 **DTf:** in tanzania.

(D2_060-062)

(S)HE- and *THEY*-complimenting remains rare in the TeenELF data, though individual instances of adolescents' positively commenting on an absent person's traits can be found: students for example praise their teacher's personality and counselling competences or their president's policy as in (54), which indirectly paint a background of positive living conditions. The overall scarcity of 3rd person complimenting, however, may be attributed to its lack of direct relevance for a promotion of the adolescents' prevalent communicative aims: the negotiating of meaning, rapport, and identity.

(54) 122 **DTf:** [. . .] since our new president came in he's doing be- (.) much better things. [. . .]

(D2_122)

8.2 Formal realization of complimenting

Previous studies have emphasized the formulaic nature of complimenting (see Manes & Wolfson 1981; Holmes 1988; Golato 2005; Trosborg 2010a; Duan 2011), with regard to both syntactic patterns and lexical choices. This formulaic character makes the speech act easily recognizable for the interlocutor, minimizing the danger of misunderstandings (see Manes & Wolfson 1981: 124).

The formulaic quality of complimenting can also be observed in the TeenELF data. Students clearly favour the syntactic structure *NP {copular V} (ADV) ADJ* to express praise, approval or congratulations, as for example in "all of you students were so motivated" (H3_142) or "it's really delicious" (C1II_044). This particular syntactic pattern accounts for almost half of all instances of complimenting. Figure 17 charts this and further syntactic structures as used in the 321 examples of complimenting tagged in the TeenELF corpus (see Introduction to Chapter 8) against the backdrop of findings from a study on complimenting in American English everyday conversations (Manes & Wolfson 1981).[73] Categories were adapted from Manes & Wolfson (1981: 121). The striking dominance of type 1[74] *NP {copular V} (ADV) ADJ* in the TeenELF data is in line with Manes & Wolfson's findings (1981: 120). It is followed in TeenELF by the pattern *(ADV) ADJ (NP)* (e.g. "very nice", K1_209; "good job", I2_689), which students employ in almost a quarter of all cases. This observation stands in stark contrast to Manes & Wolfson's findings, who only assign rank 7 to this type (1.6%, see Manes & Wolfson 1981: 121). The popularity of this pattern in TeenELF, which has also been attested for other ELF contexts (see Thompson 2022: 153), may be explained by the attractiveness of short and grammatically straightforward, yet pragmatically versatile constructions for ELF users (see also Dröschel 2011). It is also in line with the finding that short syntactic structures appear popular in youth languages (see Androutsopoulos 1998: 7). While the further overall ranking of syntactic patterns in TeenELF complimenting resembles Manes & Wolfson's findings, some patterns hardly feature in the TeenELF corpus at all. The scarcity of type 5 in TeenELF may be explained by its marginalization particularly through type 2, which can be read as an abbreviation of type 5. Patterns 7 and 8 are deemed unusual among young speakers and are hardly or never employed by TeenELF students.

73 The comparison of data from different studies and sources bears the general problem that comparability is distorted by diverging research designs, different times of data collection etc. Diachronic developments in particular will have to be borne in mind for the present comparisons.
74 As Manes & Wolfson neither label nor number their types, counting of types here follows frequencies as they occur in TeenELF.

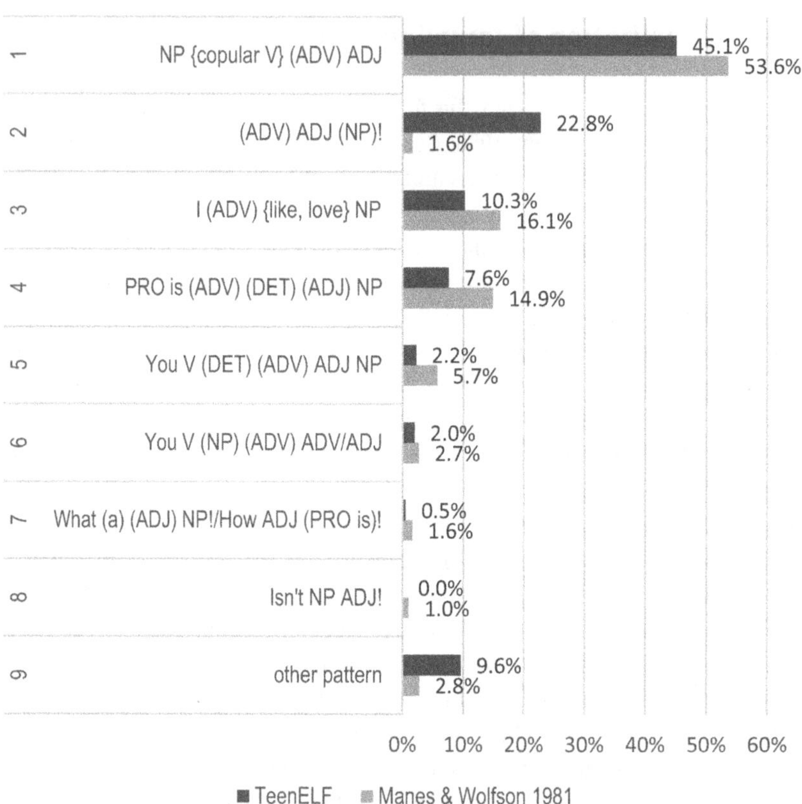

Figure 17: Syntactic patterns of complimenting in a comparative view.

Relatively high figures for category 9, which comprises any other kinds of syntactic patterns, suggest that TeenELF speakers employ an overall greater variety of syntactic patterns in complimenting than the reference group. Students use complex patterns, for instance, to express compliments in a more indirect way (see also Holmes 1986: 486), such as in (55), where IGf wraps her praise in a hypotactic *THEY*-compliment.

(55) 199 **IGf:** `(or) when people think about tanzani:a (1) <erm: i think> (.) they:: (.) <think abou:t friendly happy people> (1) yeah.`

(I2_199)

Several types can also co-occur in one speech act of complimenting as extract (56) demonstrates. Type 1 ("it was so cool (.) [when] [. . .] you are singing la- [yesterday]", l. 042) here combines with type 6 ("you sing so good", l. 047), and type 3 ("i like it", l. 047).

```
(56) 042 OGf: [. . .] it was so cool (.) [when]
     044 OTf:                            [yeah.]
     045 OGf: you are singing la- [yesterday]
     046 OTf:                     [@@]
     047 OGf: you can so (.) er you sing so good it (.) it sounds (.)
              so cool and so nice and wonderful (and) (.) i like it.
                                                        (O2_042-047)
```

The positive value of a compliment finds expression in the choice of words. In the vast majority of cases, this positive force is carried by an adjective (see Figure 17), which is often further emphasized by intensifying adverbs such as *really, very, so, perfectly*. Extract (60) has exposed some examples such as *so cool* (l. 042), *so nice* and *wonderful* (l. 047). While TeenELF students use 33 different adjective types (e.g. *sweet, peaceful, charming*) in a total number of 339,[75] four adjectives only (i.e. *good, great, nice, cool*) make up for almost three quarters of all cases (74.4%). This again corroborates the formulaic character of complimenting that has been attested cross-culturally (e.g. Manes & Wolfson 1981 for American English; Holmes 1988 for New Zealand English; Golato 2005 for German). The choice of favourite lexemes, however, partly differs from previous findings, as illustrated in Figure 18, where adjectives used in complimenting are ordered by their frequency in the TeenELF corpus. TeenELF data are here charted against data available for American English (see Manes & Wolfson 1981) and for German[76] (see Golato 2005). The top three adjectives in TeenELF – *good, great* and *nice* – also figure among the top six[77] in Holmes' data on New Zealand English (see Holmes 1986: 490).[78]

The four adjectives used most frequently for complimenting in TeenELF are *good, great, nice* and *cool*. While *nice* (and German *schön*) as well as *good* (and German *gut*) rank high in both studies of comparison, too, and *great* also features among the five most frequent adjectives in Manes and Wolfson's study, *cool* clearly stands out from the TeenELF data. Denoting especially something stylish or admirable in its colloquial use (see OED, s.v. *cool*, adj., 8.a.), *cool* is used particularly by young people. It has found entry with this same meaning into the German lexicon

75 The type-token-ratio (TTR) for adjectives which are used as elements that carry the positive value in compliments amounts to 9.73% in TeenELF compared to 13.19% in Manes & Wolfson (1981), so complimenting is lexically less varied in the TeenELF corpus.

76 Golato (2005: 82) compares her findings on *gut* and *schön* with the corresponding English adjectives *good* and *nice*, although a perfect semantic and pragmatic congruence cannot be expected.

77 The remaining three adjectives adding up to the top six are *lovely, beautiful* and *neat*.

78 As percentages cannot be calculated from Holmes' (1986) publication, her data have not been charted in Figure 18.

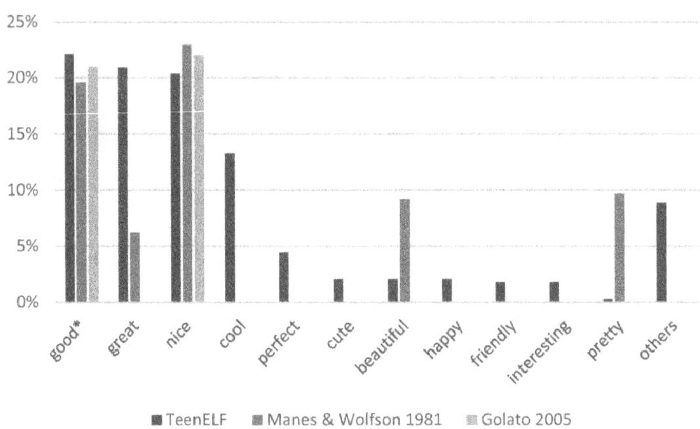

*Quantitative data are available only for the five most frequent adjectives in Manes & Wolfson (1981), and for the two most frequent adjectives in Golato (2005). Absent bars accordingly do not necessarily imply zero frequencies.

Figure 18: Adjectives carrying the positive force in complimenting.

as an English loan (see Dudenredaktion, s.v. *cool*, adj. 4.) where it is also predominantly used by the younger generation.

Additional cross-corpus comparisons can shed further light on questions concerning potential influences of age, first languages and/or the lingua franca context on prominent linguistic phenomena such as the frequent use of *cool* in TeenELF. Table C.1 in Appendix C provides a comprehensive overview of the corpora drawn upon here for comparison (namely VOICE, the spoken sections of BNC1994 and BNC2014, COLT, ICE EA and FOLK). Due to major differences in the compilation of these corpora with regard to size, time of recording, speech event types etc. as shown in Table C.1, however, results from cross-corpus comparisons (Figure 19) have to be treated with extreme caution and can only indicate tendencies.[79] As far as the item in question is concerned, the cross-corpus comparison suggests that *cool* is particularly popular among young people (see Figure 19; COLT > Spoken BNC1994; Spoken BNC2014 (15-24ys) > Spoken BNC2014) and has experienced a diachronic rise in popularity (Spoken BNC2014 > Spoken BNC1994; Spoken BNC2014 (15-24ys) > COLT). While *cool* is rarely used in spoken ICE East African English,[80] Figure 19 attests a high frequency of *cool* in spoken German contexts (FOLK), which almost measures up to the correspond-

79 On the problematic nature of cross-corpus comparisons, see e.g. Hundt (2015: 383–386) and Vetter (2022: 76).

80 Low numbers may also be accounted for by the high degree of monologues and scripted speech events in ICE EA.

ing frequency in the spoken section of the BNC2014, and surpasses frequencies in COLT and Spoken BNC1994 by far. Young age and German LC1 combine for half of all TeenELF speakers, leading to an abundance of *cool* in the TeenELF corpus in their interplay, so that *cool* can also be considered an important identity marker.

Figure 19 shows similar mechanisms at work for the appreciatory particle *wow*, which is frequently used to either express or enhance a compliment in TeenELF in addition to adjectives and verbs that convey positive assessments. Higher frequencies in VOICE and lower frequencies in FOLK for *wow* as compared to *cool* suggest a lingua franca factor rather than LC1 influences affecting frequencies of this versatile particle in TeenELF, which seems to be further corroborated by high frequencies of *wow* attested in ACE as another ELF corpus (see Thompson 2022: 153). Young age emerges as a decisive factor once more, with frequencies in COLT and Spoken BNC2014 (15-24ys) surpassing frequencies in the respective reference corpora (Spoken BNC1994 and Spoken BNC2014).

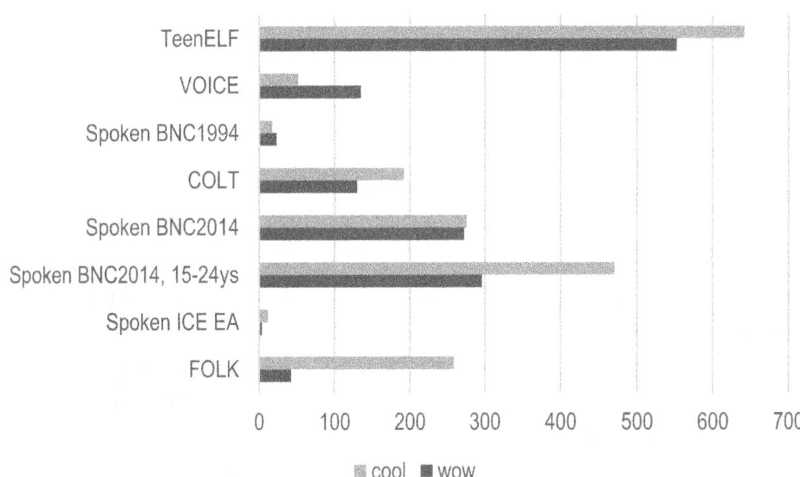

Figure 19: Frequency of *cool* and *wow* in select corpora (hits per million).

The relative scarcity of *beautiful* and *pretty* in TeenELF (see Figure 18) can be explained in the light of preferred topics of compliments as outlined above: both adjectives are predominantly used to assess appearances and objects, which, however, form a minority of compliment targets in TeenELF (see Section 8.1).[81] *Good*, *great*, *nice*, and *cool* in contrast constitute semantically more open adjectives, which find universal use in TeenELF.[82]

While comparative and superlative forms of adjectives are generally rare in compliment structures (see Golato 2005: 82), the intercultural ELF context triggers an occasional use of these forms. Complimenting is then embedded in a contrastive context, as illustrated in (57) and (58). In the first example, speaker MGf's compliment on her interlocutor's language, which includes the comparative form "nicer", works against the backdrop of her previous devaluation of her own language. Complimenting is often found to be coupled with self-criticism, which serves to further enhance the compliment and shows the reflection of self-concepts at the same time. Rapport building and identity work are simultaneously in operation here.

(57) 067 **MGf:** `oh. (.) i don't like german. (.) i i think (1) °hm° (.) °i can think (kusw- i ki-) kiswahili is (a) nicer language.`

(M2_067)

(58) 067 **CGm:** `but you REALLY got a nice school yard. er so (.) i really like it at (.) at our school it's not as nice as it's here`

(C1_389)

The positive force of the compliment can also be carried by a verb. Studies have exposed the two verbs *love* and *like* to be clearly favoured in corresponding contexts (see Manes & Wolfson 1981: 118; Holmes 1986: 491). TeenELF students align with this finding, but show a clear preference for the verb *like* (see Table 14). TeenELF compliments often come along with a good amount of laughter, which strengthens the major interactional function of complimenting in the present data, namely the expression and promotion of solidarity (see Section 8.3).

---

81 Language change does not seem to play a role with regard to the relative scarcity of *beautiful* and *pretty* in TeenELF when compared to Manes & Wolfson's (1981) data. Normalized frequencies of both items are significantly higher in Spoken BNC 2014 than in Spoken BNC 1994.

82 High frequencies for *nice* and *cool* have also been attested for ACE (see Thompson 2022: 155).

Table 14: Verbs carrying the positive force in TeenELF complimenting.

Verb	TeenELF example			Number of occurrences
like	**CGm:**	i also like your culture	(C1II_204)	32
love	**EGf:**	i love the school garden	(E3_013)	4
appreciate	**HGf:**	christians and muslims liv:e together just in peace and.= [. . .]° i guess that isn't (.) usual always. because there are a lot of wars. (.) because of rel- religion [. . .] yeah. (.) but i i really appreciate °that.°	(H1_715-719)	2
Others	**MTf:** **MGf:** **MTf:**	i (.) i prefer talking like that. like german? yeah	(M2_064-066)	6
Total				44

8.3 The functional range of complimenting

While the "reinforcement and/or creation of solidarity appears to be a basic function of compliments in our society" (Manes & Wolfson 1981: 124), complimenting can serve a range of further functions, such as keeping a conversation smooth, eliciting information on how to obtain the compliment target, or mitigating face-threatening speech acts which are to follow (see Trosborg 2010a: 5; Duan 2011: 356). Especially the category *(ADV) ADJ (NP)* so popular in TeenELF turns out to be functionally highly versatile.

Functions of complimenting in TeenELF can be allocated to five major categories: interpersonal functions, content-oriented functions, interactional functions, speech-act-supportive functions, and identificatory functions (see Table 15). Boundaries are hardly clear-cut, with particular functions being foregrounded rather than executed exclusively.

Interpersonal functions

In line with previous findings, TeenELF students primarily use complimenting for interpersonal functions, such as the building and maintaining of solidarity. In (59), students are deeply engaged in relational work and employ compliments to express appreciation and pay respect. Speaker NTf prepares her compliment by elaborately describing the situation and behaviour her compliment will refer to (ll. 123; 125). NGf confirms that she shares this perception by backchanneling an

Table 15: Functional categories of complimenting in TeenELF.

Interpersonal functions	Building and maintaining solidarity
	Expressing respect
Content-oriented functions	Interest in compliment target
Interactional functions	Opening a conversation
	Keeping a conversation smooth
	Closing a sequence
Speech-act-supportive functions	Strengthening thanks
	Strengthening comforts
	Mitigating criticism
Identificatory functions	Performing identities
	Ascribing identities

approving "yes.:", which gains force through lengthening of the coda consonant (l. 124). On the basis of these shared recollections, NTf then presents her compliment, separated from this "preface" by a short pause and further exposed by help of the opening particle "well" (l. 125). She reinforces it by not only employing the intensifying adverb *really*, but also by repeating the compliment in a different form ("i really appreciate the way that you (.) reacted when you see my home?", I *ADV V NP*; "you reacted quite good?", You *V ADV ADJ/ADV*). The procedural nature of the compliment target, which is not unusual in TeenELF (see Section 8.1), finds expression in the complex noun phrase that serves as a direct object in the first sentence ("the way that you (.) reacted when you see my home", l. 125), and in the predicate of the second sentence ("reacted quite good", l. 125). The combination of first and second person agents in this twofold compliment exposes the matter to be an interpersonal one. NTf further underlines this by adding the effect of NGf's behaviour on her feelings (l. 127). This openness is taken up by NGf in her final response (l. 128), which mirrors the previous sequence: NGf compliments on her interlocutor's behaviour by stressing the positive effect this has on herself ("i'm (.) so glad that you say this", l. 128). Both students expose their vulnerability in this sequence, but manage to interactionally use it for a strengthening of their relationship by paying each other respect through complimenting on each other's sensitive behaviour.

(59) 123 **NTf:** well erm (.) i'm also happy that you are here i could see you you went (in for) my home (.) and you're welcomed (.) and you felt as it if it was your home?

124 **NGf:** yes.:

125 **NTf:** =you didn't feel like awkward or something like that? (.) well i really appreciate the way that you (.) reacted when you see my home? you reacted quite good?
126 **NGf:** [@]
127 **NTf:** [and] actually i felt good about that.
128 **NGf:** oh i'm (.) so glad that you say this.
129 **NTf:** er (.) is there <pvc> anythink </pvc> (.) anything lacking in your life? (1)

(N4_123-129)

Content-oriented functions

Students often reveal a real interest in the target they compliment. This content orientation especially becomes obvious when speakers refer to the assessable repeatedly in the course of the conversation and/or require further information on how the compliment target can be obtained. This is the case in conversation (60), in which speaker AGf compliments on a song she heard the Tanzanian students sing. AGf emphasizes her love for the East African song by help of intensifying adverbs ("very much", l. 194) and a reiteration of her compliment in other words ("yeah it's great", l. 198). ATf orients to this interest and provides a lot of background information on the origin and lyrics of the song (ll. 199–205). The German student finally reinforces her interest by asking for the lyrics, explaining that she wants to learn the song, too (l. 222).

(60) 194 **AGf:** [. . .] i like very much the song you sing
195 **ATf:** @
196 **AGf:** @@@ [and]
197 **ATf:** [erm]
198 **AGf:** yeah [it's great]
199 **ATf:** [the song is] (1) kenyan?
200 **AGf:** okay?=
201 **ATf:** =they this the singers are kenyans it's a group of like [five guys]
202 **AGf:** [okay?]
203 **ATf:** they sing (.) very nice i just like their songs? but their song is about jesus?
204 **AGf:** oh okay.
205 **ATf:** yes it says erm:: jesus love me more today than you loved me yesterday
206 **AGf:** oh [okay.]

207 **ATf:** [yeah.] <sing> <L1sw> kuliko jana: {than yesterday} </L1sw> </sing>
208 **AGf:** ah.
209 **ATf:** <sing> 'more than yesterday' </sing>. yeah. so that's why i love this song because (.) it has such a nice meaning [a nice]
210 **AGf:** [yah.]
211 **ATf:** message behind it?
[. . .]
222 **AGf:** and can you maybe write down the text later? i want to learn it. but (.) i think it doesn't work but maybe @@@

(A3_194-222)

Interactional functions

Complimenting, however, does not always trigger elaborate exchanges on the compliment target of this kind, as the focus is not always on content. Instead, TeenELF compliments often serve interactional functions primarily, such as to start a conversation, keep it smooth or signal the end of a sequence.

Extract (61), for example, shows a short compliment to open the conversation in group C on Day 4. Even before the students look at their tasks for the day (l. 003), CTf positively comments on an accessory her interlocutor is wearing (l. 001). CGm accepts this compliment and shortly provides some background information on the compliment target, which he received the previous day as a present (l. 002). Using few words only, this compliment turn serves to open the conversation positively and establish a link to the previous day, before the students move on to work on their given tasks.

(61) 001 **CTf:** nice bracelet
002 **CGm:** thank you. (.) it's a present from (.) erm (1) i think it's (.) from [ATf/first name] (0.5) because we visited her home
003 **CTf:** oh okay (1.5) okay (.) erm (1) today it's:: (1) asking you on your present situation and your thoughts about the future.
004 **CGm:** o:kay.

(C4_001-004)

Compliments which are employed to smoothen a conversation are often reduced to single-word adjectives, such as *great*, *nice*, or in the given corpus also *cool*.

Used as backchannel items, these "minimal compliments" add positive value and appreciation to the signalling of attentiveness without interrupting the flow of the interaction. In (62), *cool* combines with laughter to produce backchannels of this kind (ll. 010; 014). Although *cool* can be understood to compliment QTf's leisure behavior, the interpretation of *cool* as an interactional backchannel rather than the significant first pair part of a compliment turn is suggested by the subsequent talk: a reaction to the compliment (acceptance, evidence, rejection; see Section 8.4) is neither provided nor does it seem to be expected. Instead, an overlap of speech prevents the compliment from coming into its own (l. 011). The conversation moves on without further notice of the "compliment" taken.[83]

(62) 009 **OTf:** °in my free time i just love chatting (with) my friends because that is the most (.) good thing?° (.) a::nd (.) after tha:t sometimes i usually try to play (.) basketball. @
010 **OGf:** @@ [cool.]
011 **OTf:** [although] i don't know. but i just do (it) for fun.
012 **OGf:** @@@=
013 **OTf:** =yeah. because i love running and jumpi(@)ng.
014 **OGf:** @@@ coo(@)l. (.) a:nd with your friends? [. . .]
(O3_009-014)

In similar ways, compliments can be used to prevent abrupt interactional standstills, as illustrated in (63). FTf signals attention to FGf's talk on friendships throughout by cooperative utterance completion (l. 145), reactive laughing-along (l. 147; see Section 9.2) and backchanneling (l. 149). When the conversation threatens to come to an awkward standstill, FTf adds a compliment ("it's nice", l. 151) to postpone the end of the sequence. Drawing on universal items such as the pronoun *it* and the adjective *nice*, the compliment remains vague in its assessable, thus exposing its function in not trying to elicit further information on the topic, but to wrap the sequence up in a positive way. In spite of this attempt to smoothen the passage from one topic to the next, the transition remains somewhat clumsy on this first day of the encounter, which shows in pauses, overlaps and the reading out of passages from the supportive task sheet (ll. 153–157).

83 On interactional functions of free-standing adjectives in ELF conversations, see also Thompson 2022: 156–158.

(63) 144 **FGf:** [. . .] the most of my friends i know from school? i think? but there are some i know from: from the village i lived 17 years? i just moved in the city? er:m (.) bu:t erm they are (.) w- we know each other since we ar:e=
145 **FTf:** =young?
146 **FGf:** yeah. very very (1) little so we where in kindergarten and (.) all these (.) ye(@)ars [(@@) primary school so]
147 **FTf:** [@@@@@@]
148 **FGf:** oh: yeah. a:nd erm er but the most (.) of my friends i know from school i am (.) no:w
149 **FTf:** mh:
150 **FGf:** yes.
151 **FTf:** it's ni:ce. (1)
152 **FGf:** yeah. (1)
153 **FTf:** ah: [another question]
154 **FGf:** [okay:?] okay {reading} how old are you? we we already checked it?
155 **FTf:** yes. (1)
156 **FGf:** {reading} where is your home? is it far from here?
157 **FTf:** ye:s it's far.

(F1_144-157)

Speech-act-supportive functions

TeenELF compliments often show a close affiliation to and indeed overlap with other expressive speech acts, such as thanking, expressing appreciation, joy and also sympathy.

In (64), for example, HGf asks her fellow student for help with pulling a sheet of paper out of an envelope. It is the accomplishment of this action that HGf refers to with her compliments "that's perfect" (l. 329) and "goo@d" (l. 331). Compliments on achievements are used in this way to express gratitude, with or without further direct expressions of thanks.

Speaker IGf in (65) employs compliments in an attempt to console her partner on the loss of an important person. Expressions of sympathy have preceded the short extract, in which IGf combines compliments ("you're a very good girl") and direct expressions of compassion ("i'm sorry") to comfort her interlocutor.

The positive force of complimenting may also be used to mitigate face-threatening acts such as criticism. In example (66), DTf feels safe to place a note of criticism after having first complimented on the German tradition of colouring Easter eggs. The formal realization of the compliment – the lack of intensifiers in "what i liked" and the choice of very moderate adverbs and adjectives in "it's pretty interesting" – already adumbrates a certain degree of reserve, which is confirmed in the subsequent act of criticizing the subjectively experienced irrelevance of the respective custom in the face of larger problems.

(64) 327 **HGf:** °@° (2) hm:: (.) okay. (don't) want to destroy it. whe- (.) when i pull it up (.) and you just take it out?
328 **HTf:** °okay?°
329 **HGf:** that's perfect.
330 **HTf:** @@@=
331 **HGf:** =goo(@)d @
332 **HTf:** yeah. [@@]

(H1_327-332)

(65) 026 **IGf:** he would be proud of you you're a very good girl (.) i'm [sorry]

(I4_026)

(66) 026 **DTf:** well: what i liked about german is (.) when i heard that you: (.) colour your eggs? it's pretty interesting. er but (in here?) there's (stuffs that are) kind of like (.) more important?

(D2_026)

Identificatory functions

Complimenting can also convey signals of identity, as has been shown on the example of the adjective *cool* and the particle *wow* to mark the young age of speakers (see Section 8.2). The design of compliments and compliment responses will also be suggested to reveal influences of cultural identity (see Section 8.4). At the same time, complimenting with plural addressees can attribute sociocultural membership categories such as national belongings to compliment receivers (see Section 8.1).

8.4 Compliment responding

The primary function of a compliment also affects compliment responding: previous research has found that "compliment recipients are sensitive to the function that compliments are performing, in that their responses are oriented to the *action* a complimenting turn is performing [italics in original]" (Golato 2005: 206). Action-orientation in compliment responding will be worked out in some examples to follow.

For a general classification of compliment responses, a continuum from compliment acceptance on the one hand to rejection on the other hand has been suggested (see Trosborg 2010a: 5–6). The scale features three major regions with acceptance (A) at one end, rejection (R) at the other end, and evasion (E) in the middle (see Figure 20). The present data suggest the existence of a further *zero response* category Z. Although silence as a response may also be interpreted as an expression of unease and evasion, the zero response is considered fundamentally different from evasion strategies in so far as a compliment response is neither given nor expected.[84] This is regularly the case for compliments in sequence closing functions used as second pair parts in adjacency pairs (see Section 3.1), especially for compliments expressing gratitude or agreement or serving as backchannel items, or for *WE*-compliments expressing satisfaction with a commonly achieved result. In (67), DGf asks for assistance with an entry into the dia|log|book, which DTf answers with a suggestion that she marks as tentative through rising intonation (l. 163). Her second and alternative suggestion, which DTf puts forward with falling intonation, thus expressing more confidence, is not only happily accepted with a confirmative "yeah", but also responded to by a compliment ("that's good", l. 166), which gains further force through repetition. Employing this compliment, DGf expresses her thanks towards DTf for providing a fitting wording and her satisfaction about the commonly achieved result. The short pause to follow is owed to DGf's writing down of the word in question. As this final compliment functions as an expression of gratitude and appreciation, no response seems to be expected here.

(67) 162 **DGf:** [. . .] what what shall i write down? develo:ping @@@@
163 **DTf:** developing: sports? (1)
164 **DGf:** {writing} developing (.) sports.
165 **DTf:** we could just say (.) activities.
166 **DGf:** yeah that's good. that's good. @@@@ (1) {writing} <activities>

(D3_162-166)

84 Non-verbal manifestations of evasion strategies, such as laughing or looking down, are also absent in zero responses.

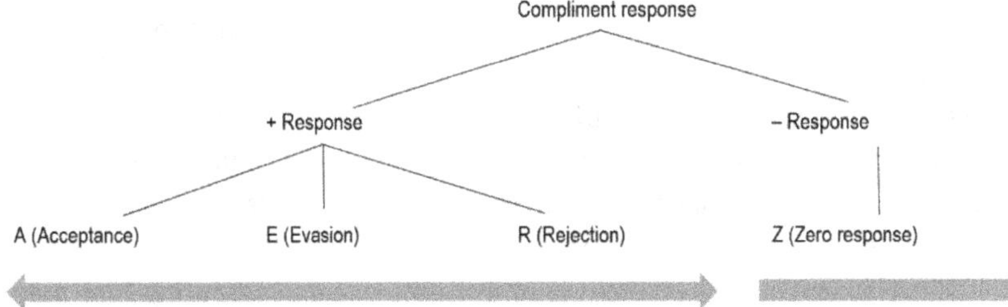

Figure 20: Taxonomy of compliment responses (partly based on Trosborg 2010a: 5–6).

In many cases, however, some sort of response to a compliment is expected. While compliment responses in the present data cover the full continuum between A and R strategies, there is a striking scarcity of compliment rejections in TeenELF, with students being roughly five times more likely to accept than to reject a compliment. Compliment responses have generally been found to cluster around particular areas of the continuum depending on linguacultural influences: speakers of varieties of English, and also of German to a slightly minor degree,[85] tend to accept rather than reject compliments (see Golato 2005). The preference for compliment acceptance may also be influenced by the speakers' age, as young people have been attested to communicate more directly than their adult counterparts (see Palacios-Martínez 2018: 365). It also appears likely that the clear dominance of accepting responses is at least partly due to the lingua franca situation, in which speakers may occasionally draw on short affirmative answers rather than engaging in complicated acts of rejection. Especially the functionally versatile and in TeenELF highly frequent particle *yeah* may often be employed as a rather neutral reaction signal in compliment responses rather than expressing a high degree of acceptance.

When responding to compliments, speakers generally find themselves in a politeness quandary, confronted with two conflicting constraints (see Danesi & Rocci 2009: 133), which Golato (2005: 206) delineates as follows:

> On the one hand, a compliment is a form of an assessment; as such, the preferred next pair part is an agreement with the assessment. On the other hand, engaging in self-praise is a dispreferred activity which is routinely sanctioned.

85 Although compliment and compliment responding has been studied for a number of languages (for an overview see Dingemanse & Floyd (2014)), there are, to my best knowledge, no studies so far on complimenting and compliment responding in Swahili or other Bantu languages. Of those languages studied, Arabic exerts the most direct linguacultural influence on Swahili. Speakers of Arabic also tend to accept rather than reject compliments (see Nelson et al. 1996: 411).

Evading a polar response through evasive laughter or the introduction of a topic shift (E strategy), for example, is just one of several strategies that compliment recipients employ to counter this conflict (see Pomerantz 1978; Golato 2005).

Students are also found to explicitly address both needs in just one response, combining agreeing and disagreeing features, as (68) illustrates in a prototypical way. CGm starts off his compliment response (l. 232) with the hesitation marker "erm", a short pause and the stretching of a sound ("yeah:"), granting him more time to prepare his answer. He immediately scales back his first acceptance ("yeah: a bit") and consequently offers both acceptance and rejection, which finds expression both syntactically ("yeah [. . .] but") and lexically ("terrible [. . .] good"). Quoting third party persons ("some people say"), CGm further refrains from self-assessment and leaves the judgement of his abilities to other people.[86]

(68) 231 **CTf:** `s- i heard you £can sing£. [LGf/first name] told me you can sing.`
232 **CGm:** `erm (0.5) yeah: a bit (.) but (.) m- some people say (.) my (.) singing is terrible and some say it's good`
(C1_231-232)

In their endeavour to combine supportive second-pair parts and self-praise avoidance, students also make use of referent shifts and evaluation shifts (see Pomerantz 1978). Referent shifts see "recipients of praise proffer subsequent praises of other-than-self referents" (Pomerantz 1978: 107), with return compliments representing a subclass. Extract (69) shows speaker NGf responding to a compliment by first accepting and immediately returning it ("thank you. you ↑too", l. 049). In agreeing with the previous speaker and re-projecting praise on her, the returning of the compliment here further increases solidarity between interlocutors.

(69) 048 **NTf:** `so (.) you have a special name.`
049 **NGf:** `@ thank you. you ↑too.`
(N1_048-049)

In evaluation shifts, in contrast, compliment recipients "praise the same referents as are praised in the priors, incorporating evaluative descriptors which are less positive than the prior" (Pomerantz 1978: 106). Speaker ITf in (70) accepts the

86 The indirect nature of the compliment in this extract – CTf passes somebody else's compliment – allows a functional interpretation of the compliment turn as a request. The further interactional process ratifies this interpretation, as CTf directly asks in turn 233: "can i hear?" and CGm, after some further hesitation, answers her request and sings to her (turn 234).

compliment on her proficiency in English, but relegates it by the use of a diminishing adverb of modality ("maybe") and a downgrading adverb of frequency ("sometimes", l. 265). IGf as the originator of the compliment, however, promptly reacts with a reverse upgrading of the time adverb ("a@lwa@ys", l. 266), which she utters laughingly so as to unmask ITf's understatement as a politeness strategy and signal that ITf's linguistic superiority does not threaten their relationship. ITf finally resorts to evasive laughter (l. 267). The shared laughter closing this sequence, however, also indicates that the students have maneuvered well through the potential pitfalls of complimenting and compliment responding and emerge from this sequence with their solidarity strengthened.

(70) 264 **IGf:** `yeah you are better than (.) me in english`
265 **ITf:** `@@ maybe sometimes`
266 **IGf:** `yeah@ a@lwa@ys [@@]`
267 **ITf:** `                  [@@]`

(I4_264-267)

(71) 292 **ITf:** `yeah you have a good handwriting @`
293 **IGf:** `really?`
294 **ITf:** `yeah`
295 **IGf:** `oh i don't like it but @@ thank you @@`

(I1_292-295)

Even when openly rejecting compliments, TeenELF students are still found to pay respect to the conflicting needs outlined above. In (71), IGf rejects the compliment on her handwriting in a plain statement of self-criticism ("oh i don't like it", l. 295), but weakens the offensive force of her disagreement by placing an evasive pseudo-question first ("really?", l. 293) and providing a word of thanks and hence appreciation for the compliment afterwards ("thank you", l. 295). The consideration of the two conflicting forces at work finds linguistic expression in the coordinator "but" (l. 295), which indicates a contrast (see Quirk 2012: 268).[87]

---

87 Complimenting and self-criticizing are found to be closely linked and can also work the other way round, as the following extract demonstrates, which evolves around the same assessable as (71):

OTf: `ah i don't have a good handwriti(@)ng.`
OGf: `@@ i like it?`
OTf: `@ (1) oh::. my mum says i have a bad handwriting. [@ @@]`
OGf: `[oh no that's not] right. (1)`

(O1_401-404)

8.5 Sociocultural aspects of complimenting and compliment responding

A quantitative perspective on complimenting in TeenELF may provide some further insights into the relevance of sociocultural factors such as gender or national backgrounds. Table 16 provides a detailed view of compliment frequencies, which allows for synchronic and micro-diachronic analyses. It shows that the average normalized frequency of complimenting remains stable over all four days of recording.

Table 16: Frequency of compliment turns (in compliment turns per minute; recte: dialogues between female speakers only; italics: dialogues between male and female speakers).

Day	1	2	3	4	Average
A	0.20	0.09	0.13	0.09	**0.13**
B	*0.00*	*na*	*na*	*na*	***0.00***
C	*0.37*	*0.19*	*0.10*	*0.14*	***0.20***
D	0.20	0.34	0.30	na	**0.28**
E	0.40	0.18	0.09	0.40	**0.27**
F	0.04	0.28	0.13	0.21	**0.17**
G	0.08	0.12	0.13	0.24	**0.14**
H	0.38	na	0.28	0.55	**0.40**
I	0.15	0.31	0.28	0.32	**0.27**
J	*0.15*	*0.10*	*0.21*	*0.14*	***0.15***
K	0.81	na	na	na	**0.81**
L	0.03	0.11	0.47	0.00	**0.15**
M	0.14	0.35	0.26	0.09	**0.21**
N	0.29	0.11	0.18	0.31	**0.22**
O	0.37	0.41	0.43	0.27	**0.37**
Average	**0.24**	**0.22**	**0.23**	**0.23**	0.23

Gender

Previous research on complimenting in different languages has suggested significant gender differences, which Trosborg (2010a: 5) summarizes as follows: "Women have been found to pay and receive more compliments than men; they are complimented more on appearances than men are, and their compliments, which are more geared towards building harmony and solidarity, are less likely to be responded to than men's (American English, French, Spanish and Greek)" (see also Herbert 1990). These findings can only weakly be confirmed in the TeenELF data. Peak values in the frequency of complimenting are indeed reached in female only dialogue pairs (see Table 16, H4; K1; L3), and frequencies of complimenting in dialogue pairs involving male students (groups B, C and J; marked in italics) only surpass the average once (C1). The complimenting behaviour in mixed groups is in general, however, not found to considerably differ from complimenting in female only pairs, neither qualitatively nor quantitatively. The data rather show a wide scattering of compliment frequencies: while the mixed group B, for instance, gets by without any compliments at all on the first day, mixed group C employs an abundance of compliments on that same day going far beyond the average. Larger data sets, however, especially data involving more teenage male speakers, would be necessary to make more generally valid propositions on potential gender differences in teenage and/or ELF complimenting.

Familiarity

Wolfson (1986: 75) has found links between the familiarity of speakers and the frequencies of complimenting in so far as most compliments are exchanged between people of moderate acquaintance, whereas total strangers on the one hand and very intimate people on the other hand compliment less. While the overall abundance of complimenting in TeenELF corresponds to Wolfson's findings of high frequencies for moderately familiar interlocutors, changes would have to be expected in the course of the week with students becoming more familiar. Mean values for all groups show no significant change over time, however (see Table 16), so that Wolfson's findings cannot be corroborated quantitatively here.

National backgrounds and roles

Striking differences with regard to complimenting in TeenELF, however, can be found when looking at national groups individually: the German students pass compliments about four times as often as their Tanzanian counterparts. This imbalance may be explained against the backdrop of the different roles as well as dominant targets and functions of compliments as outlined above: students often compliment on the local surroundings and on different ways of living. As the German visitors are surrounded by a new environment and immerse in the Tanzanian society, it comes naturally that they comment and compliment more on their experiences. The German dominance in complimenting may also partly be attributed to the fact that many compliments function as expressions of gratitude. It is again not surprising that guests should find more reasons for expressing thanks than hosts do. In addition, perceived differences in affluence may also contribute to the numerical imbalance of compliments. Whether or not pragmatic transfer is also at work, remains to be explored by further research. Significant differences concerning compliment response behaviour on the basis of national backgrounds, however, have not been found.

8.6 Summary of findings on complimenting

Within an overall appreciative and cooperative communicative behaviour, complimenting has been shown as a particularly useful instrument in the negotiation of rapport in TeenELF. TeenELF compliments are not primarily directed at appearance and material possessions, but often address a particular behaviour or accomplishment. Language-related compliments expose a heightened metalinguistic awareness in the given ELF setting. Complimenting with plural addressees invokes sociocultural membership categories, such as national or school-based group identities.

The previously described formulaic nature of complimenting has also been attested for TeenELF, both syntactically and lexically. TeenELF students, however, favour some formula otherwise rare, such as the structure *(ADV) ADJ (NP)!*, and the identity-marking lexemes *cool* and *wow*. As a preference for brevity marks ELF conversations and youth interactions alike, the frequent use of short utterances in TeenELF complimenting comes as little surprise.

Apart from interpersonal functions, TeenELF compliments may also serve content-oriented and interactional functions or support other speech acts, such as expressions of gratitude or sympathy. Compliment responses range from acceptance over evasion to denial strategies. An additional zero response category has been proposed, which comes into effect when no compliment response is expected in the first place, such as after compliments in interactional function. TeenELF students employ various strategies such as referent and evaluation shifts to deal with the politeness quandary evoked by complimenting. They frequently accept compliments, especially plural-oriented *WE*- and *YOU*-compliments, in which the conflicting force of self-praise inherent in compliment accepting responses is mitigated through the plural reference. The teenagers' overall preference for acceptance patterns in compliment responses has been suggested to be influenced by linguacultural backgrounds, which, however, needs to be investigated in further studies.

Previously described gender differences in complimenting behaviour cannot be confirmed either quantitatively or qualitatively in the present study. Larger studies including a higher percentage of male students would be needed to shed more light on this issue. The TeenELF data suggest a *reverse habitat factor* (see Section 10.3.1) at work in intercultural complimenting, with visitors paying more compliments than residents, expressing their gratitude and appreciation in the face of new experiences.

9 Laughter and humour in TeenELF

In addition to a context-sensitive realization of speech acts, the use of laughter and humour emerges from the present data as another central interactional means, employed for a management of rapport and further communicative functions. Interpersonal impacts of laughter have been shown to largely vary contextually: while laughter and humour often help to create a friendly atmosphere and express solidarity between interlocutors, they can also serve to confirm power constellations or alleviate interactionally difficult situations (see Schnurr 2010: 307; Glenn & Holt 2013: 17; Pullin 2018: 333–334). Könning (2018: 262–263) has pointed to the importance of laughter and humour in communicative practices of young people, particularly during breaks at school, and attests them a relaxing function. Although humour and laughter seem to be wide-spreadly used in ELF interactions (see e.g. Kalocsai 2014: 139–170; Walkinshaw 2022: 1; 3), they have not received much attention in ELF research so far (see Kaur 2022: 51).

This chapter will look into interactional functions of humour and laughter as "fundamentally social" phenomena (Glenn 2003: 53) in TeenELF (see also Beuter 2019a). It will start off from some overall quantitative insights (Section 9.1) pointing at functional aspects that will be analyzed qualitatively in the subsequent chapter (Section 9.2). The analysis will follow major stages in the relationship between students over the week of the student encounter: laughter and humour are analyzed in their interactional potential to contribute to building solidarity, dealing with problematic situations, celebrating newly established friendships, and bringing relations to a (preliminary) end. As examples from the TeenELF corpus will show, laughter is often closely intertwined with verbal means, illustrating the transmodal nature of ELF communication, where various semiotic resources are integrated and boundaries between different modes are transcended (see Hawkins 2018: 64; Ishikawa & Baker 2021: 26–27).

9.1 Frequency of laughter

In accordance with the VOICE transcription conventions (see VOICE Project 2007), laughter has been transcribed in the TeenELF corpus by help of the @ symbol, with the number of @ symbols representing the approximate number of syllables of laughter. Figure 21 shows the development of the frequency of laughter in TeenELF over time by plotting average syllables of laughter per minute for every day of the

https://doi.org/10.1515/9783110786576-009

encounter.[88] Analogous to a subjectively experienced intensification of relations in the course of the week as reported by students in interviews (see e.g. Int_FGf; Int_GrG), Figure 21 shows a clear overall tendency of increasing laughter for the period of investigation. This suggests a close interrelationship between laughter and rapport.[89]

The low value on day 2 can be attributed to factors both external and internal to the conversations: on the one hand, the Tanzanian students had to write exams both before and after their conversations with their German partners on that day and gave the impression of being exceptionally strained. On the other hand, students discussed particularly face-sensitive and difficult topics, such as culture-based stereotyping, questions concerning social justice and serious dangers students feel themselves confronted with. Some students, however, employ laughter precisely to deal with these troublesome topics, as the subsequent qualitative analysis illustrates.

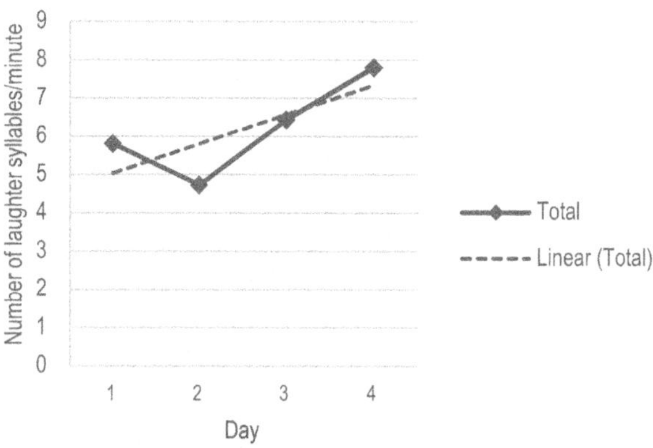

Figure 21: Frequency of laughter in TeenELF.

A more fine-grained quantitative analysis exposes considerable differences between groups and days as depicted in Table 17. For the functional analysis to follow, deviant cases will be drawn upon, as "[d]epartures from established patterns of interac-

88 Quantitative analyses have to be treated with special care in a comparatively small-sized corpus such as TeenELF, as idiosyncratic verbal and paraverbal behaviour may easily lead to distortions in average values. Nevertheless, frequency analyses can tentatively point towards some more general tendencies, which would have to be checked against the backdrop of larger data bases.

89 A comparative analysis to include further corpora appears rewarding, but almost impossible to realize in this respect for the gross intercorporal divergence in the coding of laughter. Transcriptions range from the coding of laughter as an event description over a syllable-sensitive sign-based coding to a sound- and syllable-sensitive orthographical coding.

tion are not treated as exceptions but as evidence for understanding the nature of the pattern" (Liddicoat 2011: 75). As primary communicative needs were found to change in the course of the encounter, extracts from different days will be analyzed in order to explore the range of functions laughter fulfils mainly with respect to interpersonal issues as they unfold during the week.

Table 17: Frequency of laughter in TeenELF (in number of laughter syllables per minute).

Day	1	2	3	4	Average
A	14.3	10.6	11.9	8.3	**11.3**
B	0.4	na	na	na	**0.4**
C	4.5	6.7	7.2	8.4	**6.7**
D	4.1	2.3	2.7	na	**3.0**
E	5.3	7.5	11.0	11.5	**8.8**
F	5.5	5.5	8.1	11.0	**7.5**
G	5.9	5.4	6.4	9.8	**6.9**
H	8.3	na	4.4	12.3	**8.3**
I	3.4	4.5	3.1	3.5	**3.6**
J	3.2	1.9	1	1.5	**1.9**
K	11.6	na	na	na	**11.6**
L	1.8	2.5	11.3	4.2	**5.0**
M	4.6	3.6	2.5	11.7	**5.6**
N	0.8	2.2	4.5	1.5	**2.2**
O	13.5	7.3	9.7	9.9	**10.1**
Average	**5.8**	**4.7**	**6.4**	**7.8**	6.2

9.2 Functions of laughter and humour

The functional analysis of laughter will draw on three elaborate extracts, in which students operate with an exceptionally high amount of laughter for various interpersonal purposes. Figure 22 provides a synopsis of the use of laughter in the dialogue pairs that produced the chosen extracts, compared to the overall results taken across all groups. The extracts chosen are taken from group A on Day 1 (A1), group C on Day 2 (C2), and group F on Day 4 (F4).

Building rapport through laughter and humour

As shown in Table 17 and Figure 22, students in dialogue pair A laugh exceptionally frequently. Especially their use of laughter on the very first day of their encounter strikes as outstanding, both compared to the Day 1 average of all groups and to sub-

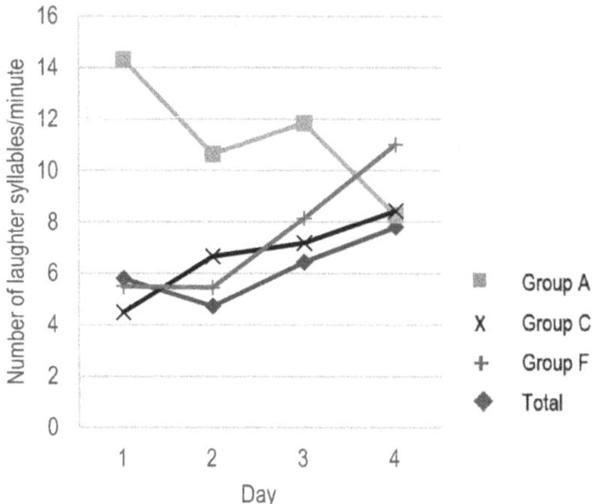

Figure 22: Frequency of laughter in select dialogue pairs.

sequent employments of laughter within group A. An extract from conversation A1 is given below (see (72)), in which students exchange personal information in order to get to know each other.

(72)
662 **ATf:** some facts that you can share like=
663 **AGf:** =erm:: [we (xxx)]
664 **ATf:** [‘bout you]
665 **AGf:** well: @@[@]
666 **ATf:** [@@]
667 **AGf:** @@
668 **ATf:** @@
669 **AGf:** i am not so@ a@ inter(@)esting@ per(@)son.
670 **ATf:** er::=
671 **AGf:** =erm:: i’m quite normal (.) i think (1)
672 **ATf:** yeah (.) you’re normal? erm:: i’m not normal
673 **AGf:** no?
674 **ATf:** @@@
675 **AGf:** @@
676 **ATf:** people say i’m funny? [well]
677 **AGf:** [yeah] yeah [@@@]
678 **ATf:** [@@@] people say i’m funny and they are l- in my class people always are laughing when i say something so it’s quite hard to make [people laugh in english]

679 **AGf:** [@@@@]
680 **ATf:** but (.) i'm really good in swa- and i like it when people
laugh or [i: i]
681 **AGf:** [yeah:]
682 **ATf:** hate it i hate grumpy people actually
683 **AGf:** yeah=
684 **ATf:** =you [know and i can]
685 **AGf:** [@@@]
686 **ATf:** spot a grumpy person from (.) very far i just like i'm
trying to make the person laugh and
[(xxx)]
687 **AGf:** [yah:=]
688 **ATf:** =like (.) "oh: (.) you're grumpy" you know?
689 **AGf:** @@[@]
690 **ATf:** [and] also:: (.) erm:: (1) er: what (.) in my class
people (.) @ make fun of my teeth (.) so: (.) i quite
use that as a comic thing to [make them laugh]
691 **AGf:** [@@@@@]
692 **ATf:** yeah [they all]
693 **AGf:** [well]
694 **ATf:** they say my teeth are milky li- like it's for childs
you know? (1) [yeah]
695 **AGf:** [yah] well som:e friends of me just (.)
well like my laugh [be(@)cau(@)se]
696 **ATf:** [@]
697 **AGf:** it sounds sometimes very strange @@
[@@@ hh they sometimes just]
698 **ATf:** [@@@ @ @ yeah true]
699 **AGf:** must laugh because i'm laughing @ [@]
700 **ATf:** [@@@] i know how they
are feeling you know when i laugh everybody laughs
[so]
701 **AGf:** [yah]=

(A1_662-701)

On this first day of their encounter, both students share the primary interactional goal to become acquainted to each other and put their relationship on a solid basis. Although laughter and humour do not necessarily co-occur, they are here combined in a multitude of ways for the sake of reaching these interpersonal goals.

Even before either of the two adolescents has revealed any personal information, AGf initiates laughter (l. 665), which is responded to by ATf's laughing along (l. 666). Continued laughter by both speakers creates a friendly atmosphere, which AGf builds her contribution on. A shy laughter intersperses her self-aware declaration "i am not so@ a@ inter(@)esting@ per(@)son" (l. 669), with which AGf follows Leech's maxim of modesty within his *Strategy of Politeness* model (see Figure 5 Section 3.2). ATf takes up this line and reacts with the ambiguous statement "i'm not normal" (l. 672). The German speaker doesn't seem to know how to interpret or evaluate this utterance and decides to confine herself to the neutral request "no?" (l. 673) as a reaction. The Tanzanian student now begins to laugh (l. 674), which she as the producer of the laughable, i.e. the utterance laughed about, may do without a fear of face loss. She thereby opens the field for her interlocutor, who joins in laughing (l. 675), signalling that she has now captured the ironic undercurrent.

ATf explains why she considers herself "not normal" and in doing so makes humour the subject of discussion. Using indirect speech ("people say i'm funny", l. 676–677) she turns the inherent self-praise into a compliment paid by others (see Section 8.1), again in accordance with Leech's model. Her interlocutor confirms the positive trait, thus further strengthening rapport between the two, which also finds expression in overlaps and renewed shared laughter (l. 677–678).

ATf now turns towards a metalinguistic level, mentioning that she does not find it easy to make people laugh in English (l. 678), which the girls have also chosen as their lingua franca; against this backdrop, ATf must interpret AGf's simultaneous laughter as a confirmative compliment further boosting solidarity and rapport.

People previously unknown to each other can also come closer through strategies of self-deprecation: conveying personal weaknesses with a wink can create openness and submit solidarity. In the present extract, the Tanzanian student ridicules her own teeth (see ll. 690; 694). ATf's preceding laughter marks this mockery as self-irony, which facilitates an interpretation of AGf's laughter as solidary laughing *with* rather than laughing *at* (see Glenn 2003: 112–114).

Providing advance input now pays off: the German speaker opens up as well and discloses personal information by picking up laughter and humour on a discourse level (l. 695). This is not only concomitant with a further boost of solidarity, but also with a gain in self-esteem for the speaker herself, who turns from a "not so@ [. . .] inter(@)esting@ per(@)son" (l. 669) to a personality with amiable and unique traits. It is the German speaker who initializes laughter this time, with the Tanzanian student joining in (ll. 695–696): a balance adequate to a vertical zero distance between the speakers has been restored. Towards the end of the given extract, both students confirm the success of their communicative relationship building by extensive shared laughter (ll. 697–700).

Both the interactional behaviour of the two teenagers in the given extract and the communicative content expose idiosyncratic components to also play a vital role in relationship building through laughter and humour: two funny individuals who love to laugh have found each other.

Steering through communicative crises using laughter and humour

Laughter and humour are not only employed in the service of building rapport, but also emerge as strategies to deal with difficult situations. This will be demonstrated by help of extract (73), which was recorded on Day 2 of the student encounter. As illustrated in Figure 22, the use of laughter in dialogue pair C on that day deviates in so far as the frequency of laughter does not only surpass the average for Day 2, but also exceeds the Day 1 value of the same group. The subsequent analysis will demonstrate how laughter and humour are here exploited to specifically address face-threatening situations.

(73) 134 **CTf:** you said people here are friendly?
135 **CGm:** yeah (.) people are friendly (4.5) do you have a stereotype that the germans are unfriendly? @@@
136 **CTf:** i don't find them unfriendly but (0.5) like
137 **CGm:** @
138 **CTf:** very hard to socialize [with.]
139 **CGm:** [mh?] (0.5) do you hear something ab- in the news about our country or europe? (2.5)
140 **CTf:** er: you guys are (0.5) too serious?
141 **CGm:** @@@@@
142 **CTf:** erm (.) you're not very social? (2) you:: (.) you don't £smile a lot.£
143 **CGm:** @@
144 **CTf:** @
145 **CGm:** tha@t's true. have you seen our <pvc> cancellor </pvc>? (0.5) angela merkel?
146 **CTf:** no
147 **CGm:** er she is always making a she's always standing (.) with (er) photos made like this. (1)
148 **CTf:** @@@@@
149 **CGm:** .hh @@ .hh it's not very@@ ni@@ce .hh (1)

150 **CTf:** @
151 **CGm:** and these movements if you put down your mouth like that a-[and]
152 **CTf:** [yeah]
153 **CGm:** your hands (0.5) it's called the (.) <pvc> merkel-movements. </pvc> @@
154 **CTf:** okay? (0.5) (say) <people> (4.5) people in tanzania. right? (2)
155 **CGm:** yeah w:well write it. (0.5) write what you think about it@ (1.5) i always think that these questions (0.5) oh wai- have to (.) glue (1) oh no. it's about society. (1) but i think i- (1) nearly everyone on the earth is nice.
156 **CTf:** yeah (6) everyone has their side.
157 **CGm:** mh? that's true. (4)
158 **CTf:** °has their (.) characters.° (2)
159 **CGm:** [yes a-]
160 **CTf:** [it's a really nice pen]
161 **CGm:** @ yeah (1.5)

(C2_134-161)

The extract starts off with a seemingly unproblematic compliment sequence, which the Tanzanian student elicits (l. 134) and her German counterpart, in line with Leech's maxim of agreement, operates (l. 135). A markedly long pause of 4.5 seconds is ended by a follow-up question ("do you have a stereotype that the germans are unfriendly?", l. 135), which CGm closes with a laughter, although no laughable is present. Instead, this nervous laughter reveals insecurity, possibly about the appropriateness of the question or a potentially face-threatening answer. Indeed, CTf operates a face-threatening act (FTA) in her response (l. 138), however only after following the politeness maxim of approbation first ("i don't find them unfriendly", l. 136). In this preceding statement, she draws on mitigating devices such as double negation ("i do**n't** find them **un**friendly", l. 136), hedging ("like"), procrastination and the choice of a third person pronoun ("them"), to lead up towards but take the edge off the FTA. In expectation of the FTA to come, which is syntactically announced through an adversative *but*-construction, the German student backchannels another nervous laughter (l. 137). The operation of the FTA ("very hard to socialize [with.]", l. 138) must put a strain on the interlocutors' relationship, especially since the accusation of Germans being "very hard to socialize with" implies general difficulties for a building of rapport.

CGm's next question receives a renewed and this time massive FTA as a response (ll. 140 and 142). Choosing a second person direct address this time ("you"), drawing on the intensifier "too" and building her accusation on three different arguments, CTf offends the maxim of approbation bald on record. She aggravates her final reproach ("you don't £smile a lot£") using a contrastive smiling voice, which, however, may also indicate that the speaker in fact wants her utterances to be understood as banter. Although irony can be employed in solid relationships to strengthen interpersonal bonds, it seems questionable whether the present relationship is sound enough from the perspective of both interlocutors for this strategy to work on Day 2.

Dealing with these face- and rapport-threatening utterances of his interlocutor, CGm draws on humour and laughter in various ways. He first employs prolonged and repeated laughter as a non-committal universal response (ll. 141; 143), granting himself planning time for an appropriate reaction. Instead of defending himself against the accusations put forward, the German student confirms the previous assessments, thus following the maxim of agreement. In his subsequent humorous explanations, CGm substantiates the stereotypes about Germans on a content level, while at the same time deconstructing them by means of his own way of communicating as a member of the national group in question: in accepting CTf's criticism, he unfolds a command of self-mockery, he laughs a lot and also makes his interlocutor laugh, drawing on strategies from the non-verbal domain amongst others (l. 148). Mocking an absent third person, the German teenager tries to ally with his Tanzanian counterpart through shared laughter (ll. 143–144; 148–150).

At the end of the sequence, both students seek to re-establish a previous balance: CGm by praising (almost) all human beings, regardless of national belongings (l. 155), CTf by an equally encompassing general criticism (l. 156; 158), which puts her statements against Germans into perspective. Both speakers accept these reconciliation attempts in affirmative reactions (ll. 156–157). With an explicit and adverbially intensified compliment (l. 160), the Tanzanian student finally changes the topic. In spite of the obvious weakness of this compliment in comparison to her earlier FTA, she thus shows her willingness to pay esteem in their further interaction.

Expressing happiness, ease and gratitude through laughter

Having mastered some relationally challenging situations especially on the second day of their encounter, which participants mainly put down to external factors such as examination stress and serious discussion topics, many students are seen to truly enjoy their interactions in the second half of the week, which for example finds explicit expression in the short extract (74). HGf's statement "that was fun today" (l.

482) is confirmed (l. 483) and elaborated (l. 485) by her interlocutor. The resulting interpersonally constructed frame is filled with joint laughter (l. 483–484).

(74) 482 **HGf:** =that was fun today.
483 **HTf:** ye(@)- @@[@@]
484 **HGf:** [°@@°]
485 **HTf:** much (much) fun.

(H4_482-485)

On the one hand, the overall topics suggested for Days 3 and 4 contained a large potential for students to discover commonalities and to revel in shared likes, such as particular movies or songs. On the other hand, however, teenagers were now also able to reap the rewards of previously invested relational work and celebrate their working relationships.

This development is clearly reflected in the use of laughter in dialogue pair F, in which the frequency of laughing steadily rises from Day 2 and reaches a high level peak far beyond the average on the last day (see Figure 22). The following analysis of extract (75) will explore primary functions of laughter at this late stage of the student encounter.

(75) 027 **FTf:** £are you happy?£ (1)
028 **FGf:** @ [↑ye(@)::s @@@@]
029 **FTf:** [@@@ @@@]
030 **FGf:** £yes i am happy.£ (.) because i had a (.) really really (.) great week? (.) with erm: many new experiences (.) a:nd (.) i:: >got to know< £some new frie:nds?£=
031 **FTf:** =@@@ @[@]
032 **FGf:** [a:(@)nd] (.) ↑yeah it was (.) really great. (.) i (.) think i had a <pvc> wery wery <pvc> good time. (.) i felt <pvc> wery <pvc> welcomed here? so (1) ↑yeah £thank you£ [@]
033 **FTf:** [hm.] @
034 **FGf:** and you?
035 **FTf:** (er) i'm very <happy> @ [@@@ @]
036 **FGf:** [that's ↑goo:d]
037 **FTf:** i meet with new frie:nds=
038 **FGf:** =yeah
039 **FTf:** friend that i: never expect (.) to meet with [the:m?]
040 **FGf:** [mhm?] (1)

041 **FTf:** s- (1) i'm ↑so <happy> [@@@ @@]

042 **FGf:** [@@@ that's grea:t]

043 **FTf:** @

044 **FGf:** °yeah.° (1)

045 **FTf:** <so: different culture: different> types of foo:d

046 **FGf:** ye:s:. (2)

047 **FTf:** £<pvc> gifts <ipa> /ʤɪfts </ipa> </pvc> german <pvc> gifts </pvc>?£ [@@@ @]

048 **FGf:** [@@@@@]

049 **FTf:** @

050 **FGf:** @@

051 **FTf:** <a:nd german bracelets>

052 **FGf:** yes.

053 **FTf:** mh: i'm so happy.

054 **FGf:** that's grea:t hm (1) °yeah.° (1) i think we did a lot (.) this week.

055 **FTf:** ye:s.

056 **FGf:** we (.) we (.) were always tired in the evening? (.) but we were al- (.) £always smiling and we er (.) told the teachers we are so happy to be here£ and (it's) so (great) so (1) yes. (3)

057 **FTf:** is there anything lacking in your life (5)

058 **FGf:** right now:? i don't think so(@).

059 **FTf:** @@@@@=

060 **FGf:** =cause i'm here so. (.) everything is fine? (1)

061 **FTf:** ↑hm. (1) same to me:.

(F4_027-061)

Happiness characterizes this excerpt in various respects. It is made the explicit topic of the conversation at the beginning of the sequence (l. 027), and the adjective "happy" runs through the extract like a golden thread (ll. 030; 035; 041; 053; 056). It is backed up especially by further adjectives carrying positive semantic force such as "great" (ll. 030; 032; 042; 054; 056) or "good" (ll. 032; 036), which are often intensified ("so happy", l. 053; "really, really great", l. 030; "very, very good", l. 032).[90] In their final pair of turns in this sequence, the teenagers express the situated reason, extent and mutuality of their joy in a nutshell: "i'm here so. (.) everything is fine?" "↑hm. (1) same to me:." (ll. 060–061).

90 On the use of repetitions in TeenELF, see Chapter 6.

The happiness and ease expressed on a content level would remain a mere lip service were it not given substance by stylistic and paraverbal means. Smiling voice and laughter feature centrally in this excerpt. Using a smiling voice in her opening question (l. 027), the Tanzanian speaker sets the tone for the rest of the sequence. Both students carry the joyful atmosphere through their dialogue by employing a smiling voice repeatedly (ll. 030; 032; 047; 056).[91] The smile in their voice may be read as a harbinger of the outright laughter to follow.

In FTf's initial question concerning the happiness of her interlocutor (l. 027), the smiling voice also gives away the speaker's expectation of a positive answer, which is provided indeed in the response (l. 028).[92] FGf prepares her affirmative "yes" by a short laughter as the first audible reaction, which serves as a cohesive device in taking up and moving forward the happy mood prepared in the previous turn. The laughter interspersing and following the verbal response intensifies the message: the teenager draws on laughter along with a high pitch voice and a sound stretch as easily available paraverbal means to emphasize that she feels really happy. Intensifying laughter of this kind is employed repeatedly by both students throughout the sequence (ll. 037; 041; 058) and mostly taken up by the interlocutor, expressing solidarity through an overlapping production of laughter (ll. 029; 042; 059). The social nature of laughter becomes particularly well observable in a mid-sequence row of turns (ll. 047–050).

At this final day of their encounter, students occasionally resort to an indirect and teasing diction, building on the common relational ground that they have established throughout the week. It is the smile in FGf's voice which makes her interlocutor decode the semantically neutral utterance "i:: >got to know< £some new frie:nds£" (l. 030) as a relationally relevant inclusive statement. FTf responds with a salvo of knowing laughter (l. 031). Similar mechanisms seem to be at work when FTf talks about "german <pvc> gifts </pvc>", or more precisely "german bracelets" she received (l. 047; 051). FTf's smiling voice and initiation of laughter may be inter-

91 FGf claims that this finding extends beyond this sequence to the whole week, noting that "we were al- (.) £always smiling and we er (.) told the teachers we are so happy to be here£" (F4_056).

92 The one-second pause in between question and answer may suggest indecisiveness on behalf of FGf concerning her answer. Judging from the further proceeding of the conversation and from additional information gained from the participant's information sheet and her comments conveyed in an interview, however, it seems more likely that the pause is owed to a cognitive planning process: as FGf finished her formal education in English two years before, she reports to need some time to get back into the swing of English (Int_FGf). Although the present conversation was conducted towards the end of the week, the extract analyzed comprises a very early sequence on that day. Cognitive planning will here have been needed for an adequate expression of affection rather than for lexico-semantic planning. It is likely that the pause will moreover have been filled with non-verbal facial expressions, especially the spread of a smile on FGf's face, as well.

preted as an expression of gratitude to the alleged donor FGf, who immediately joins in to produce joint knowing laughter. The reciprocal continuation of laughter here (ll. 047–050) exposes the social and contagious nature of happy laughter.

9.3 Summary of findings on laughter and humour

Humour and laughter are employed as functionally versatile and frequently used instruments in TeenELF, not only for dealing with interpersonal issues, but also for an organization of discourse (see Meierkord 2012: 189) and for an expression of individual or shared identities (see also Kalocsai 2014: 170). The analyses have revealed that both the quantity and the quality of laughter change during the course of the week through complex adaptation processes, with the use of laughter being contextually adapted to situational needs. Shy laughter employed as an ice-breaker to build rapport gives way to nervous laughter in interpersonally critical situations, which again is displaced towards the end of the week by joyful laughter, when students reap the fruits of their previously accomplished relational work. Multimodal research designs and analyses would be able to render even more illuminating insights, not only into the particular mechanisms of laughter and humour in ELF interactions, but into relational aspects of interactions more generally.

Laughter has been found to often co-occur with code-switching in ELF (see Brunner & Diemer 2018: 83), where it is for instance used as polite laughter to make up for potential mismatches in understanding. The following chapter will investigate code-switching and other translanguaging phenomena in ELF in their forms and communicative potentials.

10 Translanguaging in TeenELF

ELF is inextricably linked with multilingualism by definition (see Kramsch 2016: 184; Seidlhofer 2017; Mauranen 2018a). Recent theorizing has foregrounded the multilingual framework of ELF and has phrased a clear desideratum for more empirical work into the nature of translanguaging (i.e. multilingual practices in which language boundaries are blurred) in ELF (see e.g. Jenkins 2015; Cogo 2016a; Hülmbauer 2016; Cogo 2018a; on a detailed introduction of the concept of translanguaging, see Section 2.2.4). Conversation analysis reveals translanguaging indeed as one of the most striking characteristics in the present data. The following chapter will therefore shed a close look at translanguaging as "the creative exploitation of multilingual resources according to users' needs and circumstances" (Cogo 2018b) in the highly multilingual setting of the present TeenELF study.

Taking into account the plurilinguacultural, hybrid background of most young people participating in the study (see Section 4.1), the encounters analyzed here constitute a "contact between hybrids" (Mauranen 2012: 29). Students find themselves in a complex "second-order language contact" situation (Mauranen 2012: 29), in which different similects[93] of English, influenced themselves by first-order contact between English and various home languages, are brought together. In the need to find a common code for communication, the students draw on English as a shared lingua franca, but also bring in their individual multilingual repertoires (IMRs; see Pitzl 2018b: 33). Background languages of participants appear to be "lying just underneath the surface and come into view whenever something is making waves" (Mauranen 2013: 233). Forms and functions of this "language leakage" (Jenkins 2015: 75) in TeenELF will be analyzed in the following sections.

10.1 Metadiscourse on multilingualism and ELF

While intercultural communication research has often marginalized linguistic aspects (see Section 2.2.3), intercultural agents themselves appear to consider language and multilingualism central issues, bringing them up as discourse topics repeatedly (see also Mauranen 2013: 233). Not only do students exhibit a distinct interest in each other's home languages and thrive in common experiences as language learners, they also explore the nature of their commonly chosen medium

93 Mauranen uses the term *similects* to refer to "parallel idiolects of speakers with similar language backgrounds" (Mauranen 2018a: 19).

https://doi.org/10.1515/9783110786576-010

English with regard to forms and functions, and set English in relation to other languages.

In all of this, the interlocutors are aware of – and, as they say, "fascinat[ed]" by – the globally integrative function of English as a Lingua Franca, as illustrated in (76). Both students shortly and hesitantly (see pauses, l. 158; rising pitch, l. 159) take French into account as an additional global medium of communication, but finally ascribe the dominant position to English.

(76) 158 **CGm:** `[. . .] for me if (0.5) it's fascinating? (2.5) that people from all over the world can (0.5) communicate each other with (.) one language because everyone nearly everyone is learning english (1.5) or french (1.5)`

159 **CTf:** `↑fre:nch (1.5) maybe english @`

(C1II_158-159)

The intercultural setting, however, does not only make students aware of the need for and the benefits of a shared lingua franca, but also seems to account for a general interest in questions of languages, nations and cultures, in the framework of which English is allocated one place among several other languages, including the interlocutors' home languages. In (77), students explore English as well as their own languages as part of the African linguistic landscape and – overtly or covertly – draw connections between language, history and culture.

(77) 374 **CTf:** `i have been to kenya.`

375 **CGm:** `erm do they speak er kiswahili too?`

376 **CTf:** `yah: they do`

377 **CGm:** `is the culture very similar to here? (.) or is [it different.]`

378 **CTf:** `[no] (.) it's different? (.) ke- kenyan (.) for example their school system is different.`

379 **CGm:** `yeah. o[kay.]`

380 **CTf:** `[it's] follows the cambridge system. (1) and they do speak swahili but it's not (0.5) it's not as good as (0.5) the tanzanian. (0.5) cause they speak english. (0.5) [most of it]`

381 **CGm:** `[okay.]`

382 **CTf:** yeah (0.5) speak english (2.5) °yeah° (0.5) even erm ruanda burundi:: those countries they also speak swahili. (.) congo (1) they (de[mocratic)]
383 **CGm:** [don't they in] congo speak french?
384 **CTf:** they DO
385 **CGm:** @[@@@ .hh]
386 **CTf:** [it's their national language]
387 **CGm:** why@@ .hh if i would (0.5) come to congo i (1)
388 **CTf:** @
389 **CGm:** i: (.) would have a big problem. because my french is not a@s goo@@d
390 **CTf:** M
391 **CGm:** so good (.) [so]
392 **CTf:** [it's their] national language.
393 **CGm:** mh? (2) in namibia ↑german is (the) national language too next to english and afrikaans
394 **CTf:** ↑german
395 **CGm:** ↑yeah (.) really
396 **CTf:** £namibia?£
397 **CGm:** yeah (0.5)
398 **CTf:** [wow]
399 **CGm:** [thei:r] erm capital is called windhoek (0.5) and their erm (1) they call their cities german £names it's really funny.£ (.) [like]
400 **CTf:** [↑oh]
401 **CGm:** <L1de> lüderitz </L1de> (1) or something yes it's. (1) it's a really fun fact. (1)
402 **CTf:** very fascinating.

(C3_374-402)

Various aspects of and perspectives on multilingualism, some seemingly contradictory, are talked into relevance here: while students draw on essentialist notions when comparing and contrasting the use of languages in a number of African countries, they deconstruct the myth of linguaculturally homogeneous nation-states at the same time, observing that one language can be used across boundaries (e.g. Swahili in Kenya, Tanzania, Ruanda, ll. 383–387) and one country can use several languages (e.g. German, English and Afrikaans in Namibia, l. 398). The speakers create "docking stations for identification" by including their own home languages Swahili, English and German into the language spectrum discussed, but create a distance between themselves and the people they talk about by mostly using the third person plural pronoun *they*. When speaker CGm in a thought experiment re-introduces a first person perspective (l. 392), he does so by activating an interlanguage learner identity. This interlanguage perspective comes along with a normative view ("my french is not [. . .] so good", l. 394–396), tying in with normative statements on language competence previously conveyed by CTf ("they do speak Swahili [i.e. the Kenyans], but it's not [. . .] as good as the Tanzanian", l. 385).

Students assess multilingualism in its fascinating richness as a resource rather than a problem. Speaker HTf in (78) considers it a "bless[ing]" to be able and express oneself in different languages, here Arabic, English, Swahili and further vernacular languages.

(78) 269 **HTf:** `of different kinds because (.) a::s (.) i can say tanzanians we have been blessed. (we) can sing er: (1) arabic? we can sing er: engli:sh? in er (.) in any language. @`
270 **HGf:** `yeah.`
`[. . .]`
277 **HTf:** `=@@ yes? (.) yeah and er: (.) arabic english and swahili. (.) and the l- (.) n:ative songs in: tanzania=`
(H3_269-270; 277)

Among the many languages discussed, English stands out as a language topicalized especially frequently in TeenELF. A cross-corpus comparison illustrates the popularity of English as a topic in ELF (see high frequencies in TeenELF and VOICE in Figure 23 and Table C.2 in Appendix C). In accordance with their everyday life experiences and addressing the tasks provided, students in TeenELF mainly talk about English in school contexts, particularly as a school subject. In (79), it is listed among further language subjects such as German, Latin, French and Spanish. Sometimes, English is also explored in its (non-)use as a medium of instruction. In her depiction of de-facto bilingual practices, speaker LTf in (80) at the same time expounds potential problems connected with English as a medium of instruction.[94]

94 In Tanzania, these problems have given rise to widespread discussions (see Mohr & Ochieng 2017), culminating in recent changes in the language policy with a proposed strengthening of Swahili as the medium of instruction at secondary schools.

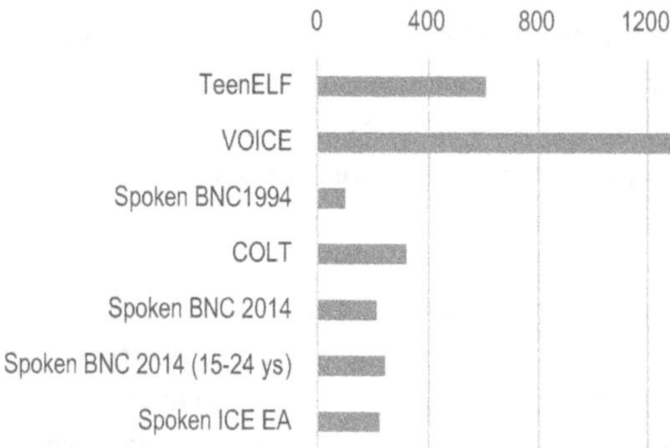

Figure 23: Frequency of the lexeme *English* in select corpora (hits per million).

(79) 036 **EGf:** [. . .] okay so we have (.) a lot of subjects i would say? we ha:ve erm: (.) the: major subjects are mathemati:cs (.) german (.) english (1) er:: (.) latin (1) or french or spanish (.) then we have geography or economics (1) er:m: then we hav:e music (.) or musician (.) sports (1) er::m: hm hmhm hmhm: er politics? (1) a:nd (.) something else? er: biology. (1)

(E3_036)

(80) 234 **LTf:** since the subjects are taught in english (.) we can translate in order t- for us to understand better. (.) we can translate them in (.) swahi- in in (.) swahili. (.) but erm: (1) we we (.) mainly (0.5) when perhaps we are (0.5) d-she:'s trying to explain to me something which i don't understand we can use swahili. (.) but er th- for things which are understandable (.) we use english.

235 **LGf:** use english.

236 **LTf:** yah.

(L1_234-236)

Talking a lot about English in school contexts supports the students in co-constructing their shared identity as learners of English, while at the same time they experience themselves as competent users of English in a multilingual setting. Their shared multilingual learner identity helps to create an open space in which interlocutors feel free to seek support (see Chapter 7) and to explore multilingual resources (see below) in order to co-construct meaning as effectively as possible.

Students also draw on explicit references to English when they either search for words or pronunciations in English (see (81)), or provide a translation of an item introduced in a different code (see (82)).[95] Against the multilingual backdrop that becomes discernible in these contexts, students explicitly draw on their shared code to activate a common pool (see Mauranen 2013: 239) and ensure intersubjectivity.

(81) 061 **OGf:** i: al-ways said yeah i wanna: (.) study: erm: (1) psy- (.) psy- (.) °er ps-° (.) don't know how to say in english. in german you sa:y (.) <L1de> psychologie? {psychology} </L1de> (1)

(O4_061)

(82) 070 **DTf:** <L1sw> simba </L1sw> in in english it means lion?

(D2_070)

While students thus use English as a linguacultural bridge, they also realize and discuss the plurality of this language system itself, which arises from the influence of other languages. Diversity within English becomes most noticeable for the students in phonological differences, as mentioned repeatedly in interviews and illustrated in (83):

(83) 452 **CTf:** =your accent is fascinating.
453 **CGm:** why (0.5) be[cause it (.) sounds]
454 **CTf:** [because it's]
455 **CGm:** so german? @@@@
456 **CTf:** no: that's really (.) you know (.) like among all of you. your accents are different. (0.5)
457 **CGm:** i think er every (.) accent who l- is learning english is different for example the indian accent (0.5)
458 **CTf:** [yeah]
459 **CGm:** [l-] (.) it sounds (.) [also (different)]
460 **CTf:** [but among you] like the ger[man stud]ents.
461 **CGm:** [yeah]
462 **CTf:** [(it's all so different there)].

95 See Section 10.3.4 for a detailed analysis of the functions of code-switching.

463 **CGm:** [also the am↑erican english] is so different to a british english
464 **CTf:** yeah (1) the british have the (1.5)
465 **CGm:** yeah that's a [good point]

(C3_452-465)

This excerpt also reveals a paradigmatic difference between speakers in the conceptualization of the relationship between language and nation (see Chapter 2): while the Tanzanian student repeatedly points to intranational variation, her German partner uses categories of nations to distinguish between varieties. It seems reasonable to attribute these differences to the distinct linguacultural situations and paradigms in Tanzania and Germany as described above (see Section 4.1). In a retrospective group interview (Int_GrG) on the one but last day of the encounter, however, one of the German participants also draws attention to intranational variation with regard to Tanzanian English pronunciation, which suggests that an intercultural exchange can contribute to an increase of language awareness and a deconstruction of closed language-nation-culture concepts in general.

The omnipresent discourse on languages and cultures from the very first day illustrates that participants already enter their intercultural encounters with a heightened linguacultural awareness, which they further sharpen through communication in ELF during the course of the week. Participants, however, do not only talk *about* multilingualism and ELF, but draw on their individual multilingual repertoires (IMRs) as a resource, practising translanguaging in various ways (see Sections 2.2.4 and 10.2), so that ELF emerges as a translingual and transcultural phenomenon to the core. The influence of various linguacultures on ELF is not restricted to a few perturbances through transfer phenomena here and there. Instead, multilingualism is part of the very nature of ELF, which is thoroughly permeated by a diversity of linguacultures dependent on context. Clear-cut and well-established boundaries between languages and cultures are re-constructed in the discourse as depicted above, but become blurry in the linguacultural practices performed. English serves as a matrix and a cloak for formal and conceptual linguacultural influences of various kinds, which render the language semantically enriched and structurally transformed.

In subsequent sections, translanguaging will first be approached from a theory-building perspective, which will then be applied in detailed analyses of the most salient types of translanguaging in the present data.

10.2 Transparency in translanguaging

While in their conversations students tend to reconstruct clear-cut boundaries between individual languages and nations as depicted in Section 10.1, they practice the transgression of linguacultural boundaries – in other words, translanguaging – at the same time. Their use of ELF is found to be influenced by various home, vernacular and formally acquired languages alike (see Section 4.1) in multifaceted ways.

Some of these 'border crossings' follow well-trodden paths, for instance in the use of loan words, which have already found permanent entry into the English lexicon. In the present data, this can clearly be illustrated on the Swahili loan *safari* (literally: 'journey') or the German loan *kindergarten* (literally: 'children's garden'), which are used naturally by speakers across languages (e.g. *safari* by IGf in I2_171; *kindergarten* by MTf in M2_563 and by NGf in N3_87). Employing these loans, participants can build on common ground, but engage in identity work and strengthen their cross-linguacultural relationships at the same time – albeit mostly without conscious awareness on behalf of the speaker.

In most instances, however, translanguaging follows far less consolidated routes, but is rather employed as an ad-hoc, context-sensitive practice. While influences from other languages often slip in unconsciously, interlocutors may also employ translanguaging practices deliberately and in very creative ways, as the subsequent sections will illustrate. Translanguaging turns out to be a functionally versatile tool in an emerging transcultural space.

10.2.1 The transparency continuum of translanguaging

The forms of translanguaging found in my data vary especially in their degree of overtness or formal transparency. While some influences from background languages leak through to the surface of ELF and become clearly perceptible as chunks from other languages embedded into English, others remain more opaque, permeating English on cognitive sub-surface levels. In a similar way, Cogo (2016a: 84) differentiates between overt multilingual phenomena in ELF, which "clearly show the use of two or more languages in discourse", and covert phenomena, concerning "the influence of the user's multilingual resources on their communication, which nonetheless remains in English". Rather than conceptualizing a clear-cut opposition between covert and overt phenomena (see Cogo 2016b: 63–65) and restricting translanguaging to the latter category (see Cogo 2021: 43), this study assumes a continuum from *intransparent* (also *opaque* or *covert*) over *semi-transparent* to *trans-*

parent (also *overt*) translanguaging practices, based on the criterion of linguistic or *formal transparency* (*F-transparency*) (see Figure 24).

Along this continuum, cultural conceptualizing takes a position at the very covert end as the semantic transfer taking place here is not reflected in linguistic forms (see Section 10.4.4). The realization of speech acts as one kind of pragmatic transfer also constitutes a rather intransparent form of translanguaging, mainly finding expression in sequential and syntactic forms. In calques or loan translations, conceptualizations find formal entry into new words, which, however, still make use of regular English linguistic units, so that calquing is also allocated towards the more covert side of translanguaging (see Section 10.4.3). The creation of formally hybrid protologisms, which combine two or more morphemes from different codes, is considered a semi-transparent practice, with full morphemes from donor languages leaking through (see Section 10.4.2). Small-scale foreign-language elements become perceptible in phonological transfer (see Section 10.4.1), which in their sum are highly perceptible as accents, as participants in the present study repeatedly report. Code-switching shows the most overt formal manifestation of translanguaging in integrating words, phrases and even full sentences from background languages into ELF, mostly with a retaining of the embedded languages' phonology (see Section 10.3).[96]

Whether these practices can unfold their full potential in supporting intersubjective meaning-making processes or not also depends on whether the translanguager him- or herself is or becomes conscious of the processes and enriches them accordingly. I introduce the subjective concept of *speaker transparency* (*S-transparency*) to denote the degree of awareness a speaker demonstrates of his or her translanguaging practices (see also Pitzl 2018a: 221). Although the full continuum of translanguaging phenomena as depicted above can be practiced against a backdrop of zero S-transparency, it is most likely for phenomena with a low formal transparency to go undetected, not only by the speaker him- or herself, but also by his or her interlocutor. However, translanguaging of any given degree of F-transparency can enter the speaker's consciousness,[97] which is often triggered by interactional cues. Speakers who are or have become aware of translanguaging then often use metalinguistic strategies, such as flagging and explanations, to make multilingual

96 Note that these processes are not restricted to ELF contexts, but can be observed wherever language contact takes place. This includes language learning in school contexts, where learners' hybrid use of languages tends to be devalued as interference, non-conformist to 'native' speaker norms. The underlying processes and resulting linguistic phenomena as depicted in Figure 24, however, are the same for ELF and EFL contexts, arising from the speakers' pragmatic use of their full linguistic repertoire for effective communication (see Seidlhofer & Widdowson 2020: 327–328).
97 On the conscious and unconscious use of multilingual resources in ELF, see also Pitzl 2022: 65.

	Intransparent			**Semi-transparent**			**Transparent**
Category of transfer	Semantics	Pragmatics		Morpho-syntax		Phonology	Lexicology
Phenomenon	Linguacultural conceptualizations	Realization of speech acts	Syntactic transfer	Calquing	Formally hybrid protologisms	Phonological transfer	Code-switching
Examples from TeenELF[98]	Divergent concepts of *family*, *book*, *boyfriend*	Greeting, giving thanks, complimenting	*we know us since ten years* (from German 'Wir kennen uns seit zehn Jahren') *it's nice cool* (from German 'Es ist schön kühl')	*social livings* ('council house' from German 'Sozialwohnungen') *nice-writing pen* ('calligraphy pen', from German 'Schönschreibstift')	***hoop**ing* ('honking'; from German 'hupen') *mo**shee**s* ('mosques'; from German 'Moschee')	*fan* [f**a**n] *tax* [t**ɛ**ks] *sports* [**ʃ**pɔ:ts]	*eating* Lebkuchen ('gingerbread') *like yesterday*
Further references	Section 10.4.4	Section 8.5		Section 10.4.3	Section 10.4.2	Section 10.4.1	Section 10.3

Figure 24: The transparency continuum of translanguaging.

98 Examples listed show a strong bias for transfer from German due to the researcher's own German L1 background.

assets accessible to everyone present (see Section 10.2.2). The hearer's reaction allows a glimpse on the degree to which the act of translanguaging has also entered the hearer's consciousness (i.e. *hearer transparency* or *H-transparency*). Speaker NGf in excerpt (84), for example, hears and becomes aware of her dialogue partner NTf's code-switching between Swahili and English when greeting a bypassing teacher (XTx).[99] NTf first indicates H-transparency by a short high pitch interjection ("↑ah:", l. 118), corroborating her conscious perception and processing of the code-switched item in more explicit words lateron when she also repeats the item in question ("oh i heard l:ike you said <L1'sw> shikamoo </L1'sw>", l. 122).

(84) 116 **NTf:** <L1sw> shikamoo </L1sw>
117 **XTx:** <L1sw> maharaba. </L1sw> ah
118 **NGf:** ↑ah:
119 **XTx:** this is your friend
120 **NGf:** @ hello
121 **NTf:** (xx)
122 **NGf:** oh i heard l:ike you said <L1'sw> shikamoo </L1'sw>
(N4_116-122)

In his or her reaction, the hearer may also lay bare potential difficulties in the processing of some previous talk containing translanguaging, using again explicit strategies such as repair initiators or metalinguistic checks for understanding. He or she can further contribute to an enhancement of overtness through working with contrastive concepts in order to negotiate understanding.

In contrast to the linguistic category of formal transparency, both speaker and hearer transparency constitute cognitive categories, which can only be inferred from interlocutors' contributions through the next-turn-proof procedure (see Section 4.4). Translanguaging hence emerges as another truly socio-linguistic phenomenon, which is interactionally enacted in various forms to perform communicative functions. Excerpt (85) illustrates the interplay between S- and H-transparency in the social negotiation of understanding. Aware of her additional conceptual knowledge regarding the Swahili name *simba* ('lion') of a Tanzanian football team, speaker DTf translates the term in question (l. 071). S-transparency is thus employed to enhance H-transparency, which DGf signals by repeating the English translation in question ("lion", l. 072). While DTf has already started to continue her former narrative ("they have", l. 071), she interrupts herself as a reaction to her interlocutor's signal of processing.

99 The code-switching applied in this extract will be taken up, explained and further elaborated on in Section 10.3.

DTf's contrastive explanations containing explicit references to the linguacultural systems at play (ll. 073 and 075) serve to further enhance the overall transparency in the present sequence. DGf closes the sequence by endorsing her understanding with a final affirmative discourse marker and falling intonation ("okay.", l. 076).

(85) 069 **DTf:** [there are kind of like these] two national teams? there is one called simba?
070 **DGf:** mhm?
071 **DTf:** <L1sw> simba </L1sw> in in english it means lion? [they have (.) yes]
072 **DGf:** [lion (.) okay?]
073 **DTf:** lion: (.) lion is in english?
074 **DGf:** yah?
075 **DTf:** <L1sw> simba </L1sw> is in (.) swahili?
076 **DGf:** okay.

(D2_068-075)

Transparency is suggested to play a vital role in the achievement of communicative goals through translanguaging. It is expected that the less transparently translanguaging is performed overall, the more likely influences from embedded languages will pass unnoticed by both producer and receiver. If the speaker's and hearer's cultural conceptualizations or schemas do not match, for example, these covert acts of translanguaging may lead to communicative problems, the reasons for which will then be hard to detect. On the other hand, mis- or non-understanding can also occur on formally more overt levels if there is a lack of S- and H-transparency.

Examples found in the present data, however, repeatedly show heightened explicitness in the face of all sorts of translanguaging, which reveals metalinguistic and metacultural awareness on the part of the interlocutors. In order to illustrate the relationship between translanguaging, transparency and communicative success, Figure 25 projects formal, speaker and hearer transparency into a three-dimensional room, as the overall transparency of any act of translanguaging emerges from a dynamic interplay of all three dimensions.

10.2.2 Transparency and communicative effectiveness

Transparency turns out to be a decisive factor when it comes to the communicative success of code-switching, for example. This will be illustrated by help of two examples, in which code-switching is used for conceptual reasons (see Section 10.3.4).

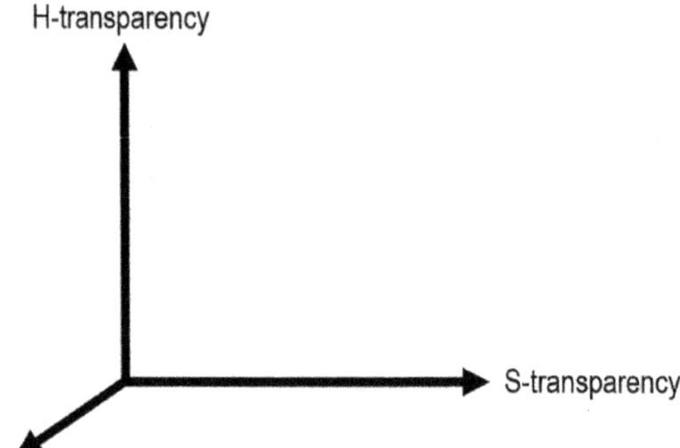

F-transparency: formal transparency; S-transparency: speaker transparency; H-transparency: hearer transparency

Figure 25: The three interrelated axes of transparency in translanguaging.

Extract (86) shows an example in which code-switching is made highly transparent so as to increase the chance for a successful negotiation of meanings. The sequence evolves around a tree growing on the school yard, the English name of which (*neem tree*) is unknown to either student. LTf provides the Swahili label "mwarobaini" (l. 352). She increases the transparency of her code-switch through a number of what I will call *transparency enhancing devices* (TEDs), such as flagging, also mentioning the language used ("ah in Swahili we call them", l. 352), repetition (l. 354) and a conceptual extension of the item in question ("you can use it to (.) cure malaria", l. 356) so as to render it as concrete as possible for her interlocutor. The hearer appropriates the word by trying to repeat it herself (l. 353).

(86) 351 **LGf:** `and how (.) do you call this tree?`
352 **LTf:** `ah in swahili we call them <L1sw> mwarobaini {neem tree} </L1sw>`
353 **LGf:** `<L1'sw> mworobai </L1'sw>`
354 **LTf:** `yeah. (0.5) i don't know in english (0.5) but in swahili we call it <L1sw> mwarobaini </L1sw> (1) yah. (0.5)`
355 **LGf:** `[@]`
356 **LTf:** `[so you can use it] to (.) cure malaria. [. . .]`
(L1_351-354)

Code-switching is made less transparent in example (87). ETf here tries to explain a Tanzanian ball game to her German interlocutor, for which she employs the Swahili label *rede* as a conceptually motivated switch (l. 353). The Swahili term is introduced without flagging and with little repetition only (l. 353), but is enriched by an elaborate conceptual explanation (l. 355). EGf's rare and non-committal backchannels "mhm?" (ll. 354; 356) leave the level of understanding open, but suggest a low degree of H-transparency. Three minutes further on in the conversation, it becomes apparent that intersubjective understanding has not been achieved. ETf returns to her formerly introduced concept of *rede*, using the Swahili term again unflagged (l. 395). The hearer has obvious problems in processing this code-switch – which may not be perceivable as a switch to her at all – and in retrieving the belonging concept, which she expresses by repeated questions, now also including repetitions of the noun in question (ll. 396; 398; 400; 402). ETf on the other hand is clearly frustrated about the lack of success in the face of her previous elaborate explanations (l. 401; 403). H-transparency could here have been enhanced through the use of TEDs surrounding the code-switch.

(87) 353 **ETf:** we have a game called <L1sw> mdako </L1sw> [. . .] (1) we have <L1sw> rede </L1sw> (.) the <L1sw> rede </L1sw> (.) first of all you have to play ↑it (.) you have to choose an area open area. after all it has to be a track- (.) triangle.

354 **EGf:** mhm?

355 **ETf:** no triangle (xxx) you can say an re- rectangle rectangle. (1) the:n (.) you have to have two teams. (1) (for example) (.) the other team they can be (.) two? or more than two but (.) the min::- (.) the minimum va:lue it is has to be two. (1) going up. then: (.) the two? (1) for example are going to start on our side (xx). so are going to play at (.) you are going to start (.) playing inside. you're (xx) inside. (xx) walk (.) you have to <pvc> excape </pvc> the ball. so the (.) other team they'll ↑be (2) they'll be on the other side of the (angle). there (are the xx) the other side. then they're going to throw the ball?

356 **EGf:** mhm?

[. . .]

395 **ETf:** do you like my <L1sw> rede </L1sw> game? @@@

396 **EGf:** which game?

397 **ETf:** <L1sw> rede </L1sw>

398 **EGf:** rede?

399 **ETf:** <L1sw> rede </L1sw>

400 **EGf:** what is [it?]

401 **ETf:** [i] explained for you <L1sw> rede </L1sw>. (2) the game of <L1sw> rede </L1sw> (1)

402 **EGf:** rede?
403 **ETf** ya:h. i told you that you have to have two teams.
404 **EGf:** <L1de> ach so {oh i see} </L1de> this game okay. yeah. sorry.
405 **ETf:** @@@
406 **EGf:** er:m yes it sounds interesting. but i'm so bad in sports really @.

(E2_353-356; 395-406)

Whether or not conceptually motivated code-switching leads to intersubjective understanding, however, also depends on further contextual and personal factors. The given examples illustrate the importance of motivational factors for communicative success, for example. The German speaker in extract (86) expresses her interest in the discourse matter by help of a question, which triggers the code-switch in the first place ("and how do you call this tree?", l. 351). EGf in example (87), in contrast, concedes her own unathletic nature at the end of the sequence (l. 406), which serves as a mitigating device, but may also hint at a more general lack of interest in sports, counteracting EGF's immediately preceding polite reaction "it sounds interesting". Motivation both triggers and is in turn positively affected by an active interactional involvement, which shows in short alternate turns in extract (86), contrasting with monologues in extract (87) (ll. 535; 355). These insights into the interplay between interactional features, understanding and motivation bear an important pedagogical potential to be unlocked and made transparent by teachers with regard to their own as well as their students' interactional behaviour.

If interlocutors want to fully exploit the communicative potential of translanguaging, they need to strive for a maximization of transparency on the basis of a given F-transparency. A high degree of metalinguistic awareness can positively influence both S- and H-transparency. Speakers who are or have become aware of translanguaging at work can then employ TEDs in order to increase H-transparency. Hearers conscious of translanguaging on the other hand can increase S-transparency through questions or contrastive contributions. In these ways, S- and H-transparency can positively influence each other, contributing to an overall increasement of transparency in their interactional interplay. The transparency cube of communicative effectiveness (Figure 26) provides an abstracted model of how the overall transparency of translanguaging in a particular sequence of speech depends on the interdependent factors of F-, S- and H-transparency. This model bears important implications for ELT that will further be explored in Section 12.2.3.

A fourth and final dimension of transparency which becomes important in the researching of translanguaging is the subjective degree of transparency for the researcher (R-transparency), which necessarily differs from both S- and H-trans-

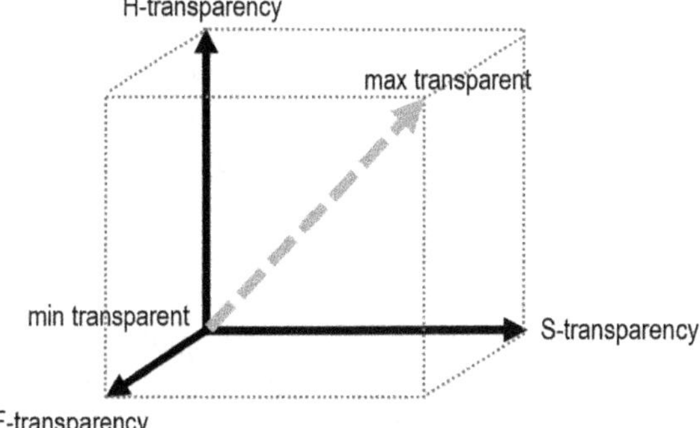

Figure 26: The transparency cube of communicative effectiveness.

parency due to the particular linguacultural background the researcher comes equipped with.[100] The more overtly translanguaging is performed in the data, the more accessible it becomes to the analyst. Formally covert translanguaging phenomena can be detected indirectly through a conversation analysis of the interlocutors' surrounding talk. The analyses in the following sections commence with code-switching as a particularly accessible phenomenon of translanguaging: not only does code-switching range on the formally overt end of the translanguaging transparency continuum (see Figure 24); it is also often employed consciously by the speakers and made highly transparent through further transparency enhancing strategies, such as flagging, repetitions and paraphrasing. The resulting high overall transparency makes code-switching a very accessible research phenomenon.

10.3 Focus on code-switching

> or <L1de> einf- {jus-} </L1de> or just @@ i'm just (.) switching into german. (DGf in D1_202)

Translanguaging becomes formally most transparent in code-switching (CS), which is the "visible marker" of transformation (Bhatt 2008: 196), situated at the crossroads between "the concept of language as finished product" and "globalized post-modern concepts of blurred boundaries and dynamic and progressive evolution in situations of intense contact" (Ehrhart 2015: 305). While translanguaging and code-switching have sometimes been conceptualized as two complementary viewpoints on one and the same phenomenon, with translanguaging implying a

100 Ideally, research on translanguaging in intercultural groups is carried out by researchers with various linguacultural backgrounds, some of which similar to those of the interlocutors, so that a broad range of translanguaging phenomena can be detected and analyzed.

more "flexible and dynamic view of multilingual resources and, compared to code-switching, a less clearly marked change or switch into 'another language' and an emphasis on the permeability of languages" (Cogo 2018a: 362), the lines between the two are increasingly blurred. Crystal's revised definition of code-switching as "the process in which people *rely* simultaneously on two or more languages to communicate with each other [emphasis mine]" (Crystal 2012a: 164), for instance, has moved closer to translanguaging definitions as introduced in Section 2.2.4. The problem of notional overlap is confirmed on a larger scale by Pietikäinen (2014: 7). Building on García's proposition that "[t]ranslanguaging [. . .] goes beyond what has been termed code-switching, although it includes it" (García 2009: 140), I will here use *translanguaging* to denote the overall practice of multilinguacultural permeation, and code-switching as its most overt manifestation.

In Myers-Scotton's (1993: 75–119) influential *Matrix Language Frame Model* for CS, a dominant *matrix language* or variety is joined by one or more *embedded languages* or varieties. Switches between languages can take place within sentences (*intrasentential CS*) or between sentences (*intersentential CS*). In intrasentential CS, the matrix language provides the overall morphosyntactic frame (Myers-Scotton 1993: 3–4). Any discussion of code-switching, however, also gives vivid expression to the conceptual and terminological problems discussed in Chapter 2: while the term *code-switching* itself presupposes the existence of clear-cut linguistic codes, its practice exposes languages as hybrid and fluid entities (see also Horner & Weber 2018: 110).

In TeenELF, variously sized chunks of languages other than English are embedded into speech, reaching from word fragments, words and phrases to sentences and parallel discourses permeating the main line of talk. The following analysis will look into formal, semantic and pragmatic-functional aspects of code-switching in the TeenELF data.

10.3.1 Frequency of code-switching

In the present data, more than 600 instances of code-switching were recorded in 26 hours of speaking time. As far as embedded languages are concerned, participants switch into their L1 in 86% of all cases, while "cross-over switches" (Brunner & Diemer 2018: 69) into the respective interlocutor's L1 (L1') amount to 9%, and switches into other languages (Ln) to 5% (see Figure 27).

The more detailed picture in Table 18 shows that within the sector of L1 as the embedded language switches into German outnumber those into Swahili by far, while the reverse is true for the L1' sector, which means that German students switch codes significantly more often than their Tanzanian counterparts. Considering the location of the exchange, this finding comes about unexpectedly.

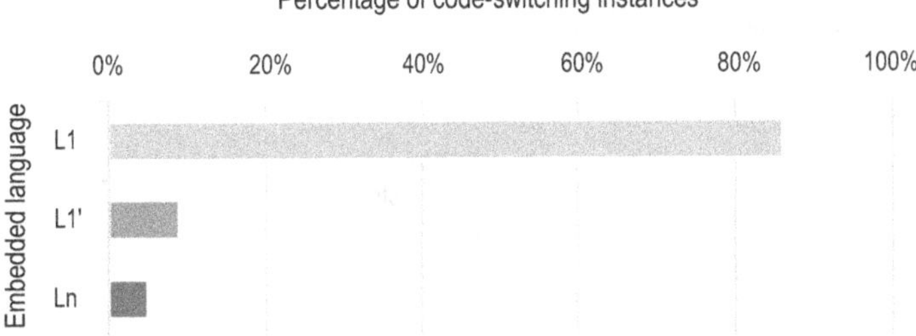

Figure 27: Embedded language categories in TeenELF code-switching.

Table 18: Embedded languages in TeenELF code-switching.

Embedded language		**Absolute numbers**		**Percentages**
L1		**625**		**86%**
	L1de		342	
	L1sw		195	
L1’		**57**		**9%**
	L1’de		13	
	L1’sw		44	
Ln		**31**		**5%**
Total		**625**		**100%**

The asymmetrical distribution as far as embedded languages are concerned calls for an exploration of variables that influence the employment and frequency of code-switching. It is presumed that the composition of the group, the years of formal education in English, ideological aspects, the typological distance between matrix language and embedded language, content aspects as well as the linguacultural setting may have an impact on the frequency of code-switching (see Figure 28).

Some of these hypotheses can be corroborated in the present data through a synopsis between conversational data and data obtained from the participant information sheet. Table 19 provides a detailed insight into the code-switching behaviour in individual conversations, which help understand the factors influencing the frequency of code-switching. Normalized values are listed in code-switching events per 1000 words.

Group size and composition

The group size and composition of a group are found to have a very distinct influence on the frequency of code-switching (see Cogo & House 2018: 218). Code-switching

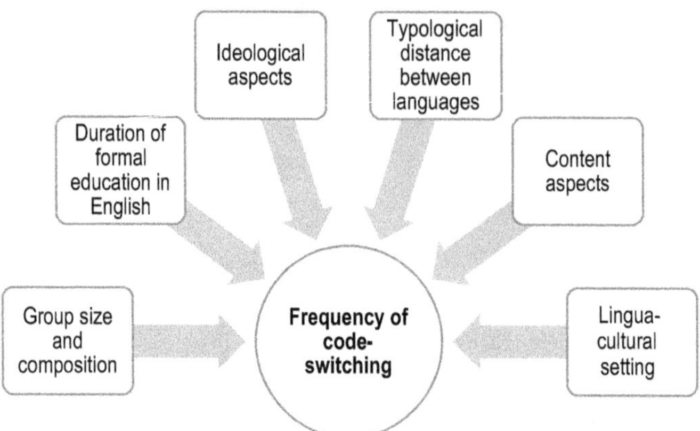

Figure 28: Potential factors influencing the frequency of code-switching in ELF.

Table 19: Frequency of code-switching in TeenELF (in code-switching events per 1000 words).

	Day 1	Day 2	Day 3	Day 4	Average
A	2.64	2.06	1.20	1.44	**1.84**
B	0.74	na	na	na	**0.74**
C	1.78	1.85	2.03	1.41	**1.77**
D	1.09	2.23	1.23	na	**1.52**
E	0.85	11.83	0.58	4.11	**4.34**
F	1.88	6.68	3.82	2.93	**3.83**
G	2.73	4.79	5.59	2.16	**3.82**
H	0.99	na	2.04	5.98	**3.00**
I	5.43	13.78	4.93	2.00	**6.53**
J	1.78	2.22	1.37	3.68	**2.26**
K	0.00	na	na	na	**0.00**
L	3.31	2.66	0.00	0.53	**1.62**
M	7.15	3.91	0.29	27.86	**9.80**
N	0.71	1.18	0.33	0.76	**0.74**
O	4.82	0.54	0.42	0.52	**1.58**
Average	**2.39**	**4.48**	**1.83**	**4.45**	**2.89**

takes place most frequently in groups of three, with Table 19 showing code-switching frequencies above the average for all conversations in which three students were present (F2, I2, I3, M4). While only four out of 52 or 7.7% of all conversations recorded were produced in groups of three students, these four conversations account for a total of almost one third of all code-switches. The overall dominance of switches into German can be explained by the fact that in all groups of three there were two German speakers present. Students sharing an L1 often switch into this mode when they face communicative difficulties, hoping for support from their own classmate as in (88), or, in an exclusive practice, in order to discuss discursive threads not considered relevant for the third person present, who has no command of the embedded language. This is the case in (89), where the Tanzanian speaker FTf explains a game to her German interlocutors (l. 373), while HGf deploys a short pause for reflection in FTf's turn to introduce a parallel discourse in German (l. 374). Drawing on German and speaking in a markedly quiet voice, she allows the matrix discourse to simply continue after her interjection (l. 375).

(88) 126 **FGf:** `@@@ <L1de> wa(@)s hei(@)ßt spießer auf englisch? {wha@t i@s spießer {stuffed shirt} in english?} </L1de> (.) erm we are like (.) the german s- stereotype is like (1) very (3) erm: very (.) organized? (2) but (1) i think (.) too orga(@)ni(@)sed. so(@) (.) everything <pvc> haves {has} </pvc> to be f- perfect and on ti:me and (.) we don't have this (.) relaxing (1) atmosphere?`

(F2_126)

(89) 373 **FTf:** `and another (1) another play ↓no:: i forgot what it's called er: (1) it's use five coins like these? (.) °(xxx)° (.)`

374 **HGf:** `(<L1de> mich hat ne ameise gebissen {i was bitten by an ant} @@ (.) hasse die viecher {hate these creatures} </L1de>° (1) okay.`

375 **FTf:** `it's simple but i think it's hard (.) for you to understand.`

(F2_373-375)

Formal education in English

The Tanzanian students' less frequent switches into their L1 might also be ascribed to their overall longer and more intense exposure to formal education in English (see Section 4.1, Table 6). Tanzanian students received 11 years of schooling in English as a subject and 7.5 years in English as a medium of instruction (EMI) on average, while their German counterparts average out to 8.7 years and 1.8 years respectively. Smaller-scale intranational deviation in the frequency of code-switching, however, cannot primarily be explained in terms of the years of formal education in English in the present data. In dialogue pair H, for instance, codes are switched slightly more often than average (3.00 CS/1000 words vs. 2.89 CS/1000 words; see Table 19) although both speakers have received formal education in English as a subject longer than the average. This finding, albeit eclectic in nature, also supports the claim (see e.g. Klimpfinger 2009: 350) that former deficiency conceptualizations of code-switching, employed by speakers who allegedly lack competence in at least one of the codes employed, fall short of a communicative reality in which code-switching fulfils a range of functions, which will further be explored below (Section 10.3.4). Larger scale quantitative studies are needed to shed further light on potential relationships between code-switching and the length of formal language education.

Ideological aspects

Up until recently, official language policies, in line with the Tanzanian population majority's preferences (see Mohr & Ochieng 2017), promoted English as the only medium of instruction in Tanzanian secondary schools (see Figure 29). While in fact code-switching between English and Swahili has always been a common practice, the official language policy, upon educationalists' advice, is now also in the process of changing in favour of multilingual approaches which include African languages in higher education. The legacy of the previously strictly monolingual language policy is likely, however, to still influence the students' language behaviour and to bear an influence on the comparatively infrequent use of code-switching by Tanzanian teenagers in the TeenELF data.

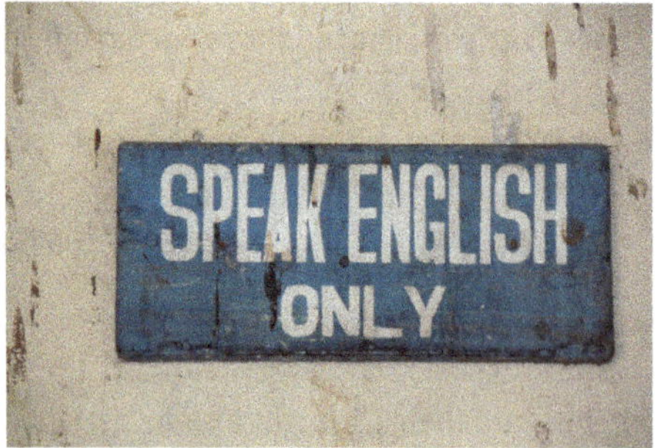

Figure 29: Promoting the monolingual use of English at a Tanzanian secondary school (own photograph).

Typological factors

Whether or not the typological distance of languages contributes to the frequency of code-switching is open to discussion and needs further exploration through larger scale comparative studies. It is expected that a typological closeness between two languages makes an integration of the two codes easier on a structural level. The present observation that German students switch into German about 1.75 times as often as Tanzanian students change into Swahili might also be ascribed to the typological closeness between English and German, both West-Germanic languages of the Indo-European language family, and the comparative typological distance between English and Swahili, the latter one a noun-class Bantu language of the Niger-Congo language family. Examples (90) and (91) demonstrate two linguistic surroundings in which TeenELF code-switching into German takes place, but where switches into Swahili are very unlikely for typological reasons. In the first example, a code-switch occurs between the subject pronoun *you* and the main verb *write*. In Swahili as an agglutinative language, verbs are composed of a lexical stem with prefixed subject and potential object concords plus one or more affixed TAM (tense-aspect-mood) marker(s). (*Maybe*) *you write* correspondingly translates into one single Swahili word ('uandike'). A switch between the English subject pronoun and the verb is therefore highly unlikely in Swahili. In the second example, a German lexical morpheme is used to compose the first part of a hybrid compound (see Section 10.4.2). While compound nouns are common in both English and German (here: *school life*, 'Schulleben'), Swahili prefers phrasal realizations of semantic combinations (here: 'maisha ya shule', i.e. *life of school*), so that nominal compounds consisting of one Swahili and one English part are again unlikely to occur.

(90) 132 **CGm:** `maybe you <L1de> schrei- {writ-} </L1de>`
(C1_132)

(91) 007 **CGm:** `<L1de> schul- {school} </L1de> -life`
(C3_007)

Most code-switches, however, constitute isolate nouns, which are syntactically easy to integrate and can be incorporated into ELF regardless of typological proximity or distance between embedded and matrix language.[101]

---

101 Typological closeness also opens the door for false friends. There is a wide range of false friends influenced by L1 German found in the present data (e.g. floor – Flur ('corridor', F1_326), internet – Internat ('boarding school', G1_196; often – offen ('open', I2_157); equal – egal ('indifferent', C2_205)). On the potential of false friends to become 'true friends' in ELF conversations, see Hülmbauer (2009: 341).

Content aspects

Another factor influencing the frequency of code-switching is the discourse topic. In the present data, code-switching peaks on the second day (see Table 19), when students discuss aspects of nature and society. The semantic analysis in Section 10.3.3 will demonstrate that code-switched items very often refer to specific natural and cultural phenomena that either do not have linguistic-conceptual equivalents in English or the translation of which is unknown to the speakers. Among the code-switched items to be found on the second day, there are concepts such as *rede* (a Tanzanian ball game), *ugali* (a traditional East African cornmeal mush) or *Erntedank* (a German festivity celebrated during harvest season), for which English translations are hard to find. Day 3 in contrast, on which students mainly address aspects of school and leisure, shows remarkably few code-switches. This may be ascribed to the finding that many students on that day discover their shared knowledge of and enthusiasm for international youth culture phenomena such as films and music that are often expressed in English as a global language anyway.

Linguacultural setting

Last but not least the linguacultural setting or what Pölzl & Seidlhofer (2006: 155) call the "habitat factor" has distinct influences on code-switching behaviour as well. With the exchange taking place in Tanzania, German students are found to use Swahili items more than three times as often as Tanzanian students employ German expressions. In their conversations with their Tanzanian hosts, German students address bits and pieces of Swahili talk they encounter day to day when discovering their linguaculturally new surroundings, while Tanzanian students teach their German guests words and idioms to make them familiar with meanings and behavioural codes of their home. The following two extracts show how German students become familiar with the concept of greeting persons of respect with the Swahili term *shikamoo*. This is brought about through explicit code-switching ("shikamoo"), which in (92) comes along with flagging ("we say") and pragmatic explanations ("when you find a person older than you") by the Tanzanian speaker. In (93), the same expression is used in its natural surrounding by a Tanzanian student greeting her teacher, and is then reflected and metalinguistically commented on by the German speaker ("oh i heard like you said <L1'sw> shikamoo </L1'sw>", l. 122), who displays a high degree of H-transparency here as shown in Section 10.2.1.

(92) 568 **LTf:** [for here] the (.) morals. morals are maintained. (1) yah. so when perhaps when you find a person older than you? (1) in swahili we say <L1sw> shikamoo {i hold your feet; *greeting to an elder or superior person*} </L1sw>. (1) yah. that's swahili you say <L1sw> shikamoo </L1sw> that means (.) giving respect (.) to that person.
(L1_568)

(93) 116 **NTf:** <L1sw> shikamoo </L1sw>
117 **XTx:** <L1sw> marahaba. {*response to shikamoo*} </L1sw> ah
118 **NGf:** ↑ah:
119 **XTx:** this is your friend
120 **NGf:** @ hello
121 **NTf:** (xx)
122 **NGf:** oh i heard l:ike you said <L1'sw> shikamoo </L1'sw> (.)
(N4_116-122)

10.3.2 Forms of code-switching

Code-switches may involve any length of items from word-fragments over words and phrases to clauses, sentences and whole passages (see Klimpfinger 2009: 350). Table 20 illustrates forms of code-switching with examples from the present data.

Table 20: Forms of code-switching in TeenELF.

Code-switched unit	Examples from TeenELF		
Word fragment	**DGf:**	<L1de> **fragez-** {question ma-} </L1de> er er: sorry @ @@ question mark	(D1_200)
Word	**ETf:**	a game called <L1sw> **mdako** </L1sw>	(E2_339)
Phrase	**IGf:**	and they're very have a (.) good living (1) erm: (.) <L1de> **so ne gute lebeneinstellung?** {a good attitude to life somehow} </L1de> (.)	(I2_155)
	ITf:	it's around about </L1sw> **saa tatu** {clock three} </L1sw> so the i meant nine	(I1_168)
Clause	**GGf:**	(.) i miss the word erm° (3) <L1de> zufall: {chance} </L1de> (.) uh <L1de> **bin ich blöd**. {am i stupid} </L1de> (3)	(G1_140)

Table 20 (continued)

Sentence	**IGf:**	what do you li- er [do you like s-]	
	ITf:	[what do you like]	
	IGf:	erm summer i think. you like [summer at most]	
	KGf:	[no] [nein wie das]	
	IGf:	[no?]=	
	KGf:	=<L1de> **wie des wie des klima is soll'n wir sagen** {we're supposed to say what the climate is like} </L1de>	(I2_281-286)
Discourse (side sequences)	**ETf:**	[. . .] how do you distribute money? (1) [. . .]	
	EGf:	mhm. (5) hm: (4) [JGm/first]? (2) <L1/de> **was hast du bei (1) was hast du bei der geldfrage gesagt?** {what did you say on (1) what did you say on the question on money?} </L1de>	
	JGm:	<L1de> **geld?** {money} </L1de>	
	EGf:	<L1de> **ja:** {yes} </L1de> (2)	
	JGm:	<L1de> **er:: (2) ja dass zum beispiel die leute ohne jobs unterstützt werden wie hartz vier oder** {er:: (2) well that people without jobs are supported like hartz vier[102] or} </L1de>	
	EGf:	okay.	(E2_429-438)

Passages of code-switching sometimes develop discontinuously, with particular items or more complex discourse topics being taken up in the L1 repeatedly within a stretch of talk in the matrix language. The phenomenon of what I call *discontinuous code-switching* is illustrated by means of an example from a group of three students on the last day of the encounter (excerpt (94)). While the Tanzanian and the two German interlocutors jointly develop their ELF talk on that day's overall topic *Present and future*, the two Germans follow a second discontinuous line of a different discourse – namely on dreaded insect bites – in German, subdued in volume. This parallel discourse develops further with every new bite discovered.

102 Hartz IV is the name of a German unemployment benefit programme.

(94) 328 **MGf:** [. . .] that's (.) different from germany.
329 **MTf:** okay:? (6)
330 **MGf:** °<L1de> ich hab n stich {i've got a bite} </L1de>° (1)
[. . .]
330 **MGf:** °<L1de> ah ich hab sogar zwei stiche. {ah i've even got two bites} </L1de>°
[. . .]
333 **MTf:** kay?
334 **DGf:** °(erm::)°
335 **MGf:** erm:: (3)
336 **DGf:** i don't know if (.) [(x)]
337 **MTf:** [also::]
338 **DGf:** yeah?
339 **MTf:** we wear a uniform. (1)
340 **MGf:** yeah. (.) ↑yeah.
[. . .]
530 **MGf:** okay. great. (2) [°(very good.)°]
531 **DGf:** °<L1de> [ich hab hier] auch nen neuen stich [. . .]° {i've also got a new bite here} </L1de>
532 **MGf:** oka:y.
533 **MTf:** °(ka:y?)° (1) when you arrive at germany? (.) you have to cook (.) cassava for them.
534 **MGf:** oh:. (woa) (<L1de> aber {but} </L1de>) i don't know (.) if we have (.) er: (.) this (fruit.)
[. . .]
634 **MGf:** <L1de> oh mann:. (.) ich hab sogar [vier stiche:.] {gosh (.) i've even got four bites} </L1de>
635 **DGf:** <L1de> [ja ich hab] (.) ich (hab) vorhin {yes i have (.) i (have) only just} </L1de> (1)
636 **MTf:** what? (3) <L1sw> mimi ni [MGf/first]. {i am [MGf/first]} </L1sw>
637 **MGf:** <L3sw> mimi ni [MGf/first]. {i am [MGf/first]} </L3sw>
638 **MTf:** my name is [MGf/first].

(M4_328-638)

After the final mention of insect bites in German, the Tanzanian speaker leads the talk back to ELF by help of an unspecific question word ("what", l. 636) – just in order to switch codes immediately again, this time to Swahili. She here takes up another discontinuous sequence, in which the Tanzanian student tries to teach her two German interlocutors how to introduce themselves in Swahili. Three different lines of discourse can thus be performed simultaneously in a complex way, which is made possible by an assignment of different codes to individual topics.

Speakers use code-switching consciously or unconsciously (i. e. with varying S-transparency). Conscious code-switching is often accompanied and openly marked by TEDs (i.e. transparency enhancing devices; see Section 10.2.2), employed by the speaker to help the receiver process the message. In (95), speaker CGm points towards his consciously employed code-switch ("ohrwurm", l. 328) in advance by not only exposing the linguistic limits at play through a metalinguistic comment ("how do you call it", l. 324), but also by flagging his switch with a direct mentioning of the linguaculture of reference ("in germany we've got the word", l. 328). Repetitions (ll. 324-326) and paraphrases ("you (.) always hear a so- (.) a song in your mind.", l. 324; "it's erm (.) that y- (0.5) a: animal is in your ear and always (.) sings it", l. 328) are further used to increase the chance of a successful negotiation of meaning surrounding the code-switch.

(95) 324 **CGm:** [. . .] how do you call it (.) if you (.) always hear a so- (.) a song in your mind. (3)
325 **CTf:** i always hear a song [in my mind.]
326 **CGm:** [if you] always hear a song in your mind and you always want to sing it. and you always have to think about it. (2)
327 **CTf:** mm i don't know maybe (.) passion? (1)
328 **CGm:** i don't know in germany we've got the word <L1de> ohrwurm {earworm} </L1de> (.) for that. it's erm (.) that y- (0.5) a: animal is in your ear and always (.) sings it. @@@
329 **CTf:** i don't think we have a word for tha@t [@@]

C2_324-329

Speakers, however, do not always consciously plan to switch codes but often produce lapses or unconscious switches as in (96). These slips may enter the speaker's consciousness in the course of speaking, which then often results in self-interruptions ("fragez-", l. 200), post-hoc translations ("question mark", l. 200), laughter (ll. 200; 201), apologies ("sorry", l. 200) and metalinguistic comments ("i'm just (.) switching into german", l. 202). Awareness-raising and transparency enhancing processes surrounding switches employed unconsciously in the first place can also be triggered by a (non-)reaction on behalf of the hearer as an expression of non-understanding.

(96) 200 **DGf:** erm: (1) when we just (.) female erm: and (.) male friends <L1de> fragez- {question m-} </L1de> er: sorry @ @@ question mark a(@)nd [@]

201 **DTf:** [@@@]
202 **DGf:** a:nd erm: a point erm: (1) well (.) examination:? point
(.) or <L1de> einf- {jus-} </L1de> or just @@ i'm just
(.) switching into german. so: erm: just (.) male and
(.) female friends (1) have a point and then we just (.)
i don't know (.) write something down. (2)
(D1II_200-202)

While longer L1 stretches are almost only employed in the presence of an additional speaker of the embedded language (e.g. random bypassers on the school premises, students from other groups sitting close enough to be contacted, the researcher handing out material, etc.), code-switches within the dialogue pairs proper consist of single words or word fragments mainly. The majority of these words and word fragments are discourse markers, particularly interjections, and nouns (see also Klimpfinger 2009: 359), which will be subject to a semantic analysis in the following section.

10.3.3 Semantics of code-switches

The majority of German and Swahili words switched into ELF in the present German-Tanzanian dialogue pairs are found to fall into four large semantic categories, namely cultural concepts and artefacts, natural phenomena, greetings, and interjections. Table 21 gives an overview of semantic categories with examples from the TeenELF corpus.

While words for natural and cultural phenomena feed into dialogues from German and Swahili alike with participants sharing their respective worlds with each other, the large majority of greetings originates from Swahili, which in comparison to German greetings are used about five times as often. It is again the habitat factor (see Section 10.3.1) which can provide an explanation here, as Swahili greetings are more prevalent and relevant in the East African setting.

German adolescents, on the other hand, use L1 discourse markers in great abundance, with *also* featuring topmost, followed by *oder*, *genau* and *ach (so)*. The present data suggest that the frequency of code-switched discourse markers, which normally slip in unconsciously, seems to be interrelated with the extent to which a speaker employs English in his or her everyday life (data obtained from participant information sheets). This very tentative finding would need to be tested against a larger data base, just as any other more detailed semantic analysis of code-switching would have to build on a larger corpus. This seems all the more advisable as individual code-switched items are used disproportionally often by particular individual speakers, or are repeated over and over again in processes of

Table 21: Semantic categories of code-switches in TeenELF.

	Donor language	Example	Meaning	
Cultural phenomena (e.g. clothing, food, festivals, inventions)	German	*Erntedank*	harvest festival	(C1_266)
		Lebkuchen	'gingerbread'	(F2_227)
	Swahili	*bajaji*	three-wheeled motorized vehicle	(M4_409)
		posa	letter of proposal	(L1_510)
Natural phenomena (e.g. animals, plants)	German	*Tanne*	'fir tree'	(N2_124)
		Erdbeben	'earthquake'	(I2_508)
	Swahili	*nyati*	'buffalo'	(N2_339)
		mwarobaini	'neemtree'	(L1_352)
Greetings and thanks	German	*Morgen*	'morning'	(F3_437)
		hallo	'hello'	(G3_527)
	Swahili	*mambo*	Informal greeting ('Hey!' 'What's up?')	(A1_51)
		karibu	'welcome'	(I4_303)
Discourse markers	German	*also*	'well'	(G2_309)
		ach	'oh'	(C4_189)
	Swahili	*eh*	universal discourse marker (affirmative, interrogative, expressive)	
Miscellaneous	German	*Zufall*	'coincidence'	(G1_140)
		Ohrwurm	'catchy tune'	(C2_328)
	Swahili	*saa*	'hour'	(I1_168)

meaning negotiation (see Chapter 6), which further distorts quantitative results in this comparatively small data set.

Against the backdrop of these caveats, Figure 30 provides an overview of the distribution of semantic categories for single-word code-switches from German as they turn up in the TeenELF corpus. Participants draw particularly often on function words in their L1 in the present data, but also switch codes to refer to cultural and natural phenomena or to express greetings and thanks. These major semantic categories of code-switching are directly linked to communicative functions of switching, which will be explored next.

10.3.4 Functions of code-switching

As has been shown, many code-switched words refer to natural or cultural phenomena specific to the interlocutors' different home regions. Drawing on expressions from their primary linguistic codes such as German *Gymnasium* (H3_82; an

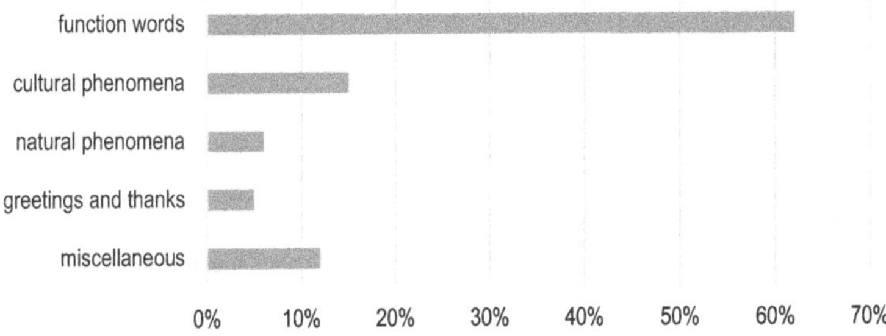

Figure 30: Semantics of single-word code-switches for L1de.

academically oriented form of secondary school in Germany) or Swahili *maharage* (M1_298; a bean dish common in East Africa), students introduce cultural concepts at the same time, which may not have English equivalents.

Conceptual functions, however, often overlap with further functions of code-switching. Three major functional categories can be distilled from a synopsis of previous research on code-switching in ELF (see Table 22), namely conceptual functions, affective functions, and addressee specification. In addition, code-switching can be used for interactional and cognitive functions, particularly the latter ones of which have received little attention in ELF research so far. In a close analysis of sequences that contain instances of code-switching, this section will examine the functions of code-switching in the present data. All functional categories listed here can be attested in the TeenELF corpus.

Conceptual functions

In the present data, code-switching is prominently employed for conceptual reasons. In about a quarter of all 529 coded instances (24.8%), interlocutors switch codes in order to introduce new concepts, often natural or cultural phenomena specific of the participants' home regions, which are hard or impossible to translate into English.[103]

Extract (97) illustrates an example of conceptual code-switching, in which the Swahili term *ugali* (l. 225) is used for a mush of sweet corn which is very common in East Africa, but does not have an English equivalent. Assuming her German interlocutor's unfamiliarity with *ugali*, the Tanzanian speaker OTf prepares her switch

103 As functions of code-switching often overlap as will further be illustrated in this section, an overall contrastive numerical distribution of functional categories appears impossible.

Table 22: Functions of code-switching in ELF (based on Klimpfinger 2009: 359–366; Mauranen 2013: 242–243; Vettorel 2013: 159–162; Pietikäinen 2014: 6–7; Brunner & Diemer 2018: 70–82; Cogo & House 2018: 2018–220).

Functional category	Subcategory
Conceptual function	Filling lexical gaps, introducing new concepts
Affective function	Exploring and signalling cultural identity and membership
	Promoting solidarity, creating rapport
	Displaying a flexible and appreciative orientation towards multilingualism, linguistic variation & hybridity
Addressee specification	Including and excluding interlocutors
Interactional function	Structuring discourse
	Continuing conversation
	Emphasizing message
	Searching for words, appealing for assistance
	Conducting management talk
Cognitive function	Supporting cognitive processing

by flagging it ("'s called", l. 225). OGf acknowledges the reception of the term and asserts her unfamiliarity with it straight away, asking for an explanation (l. 226). OTf repeats the term in question and searches for an explanation, which she finds hard to generate, as becomes visible in the use of hesitation markers, prolongations, hedges, rising intonation and softly muttered, hardly understandable, probably self-directed inserts (l. 227). However, she finally comes up with the English quasi-translation "porridge", later specified further by the attributive "strong" (l. 229), which does help her German interlocutor understand the concept, as is signalled in OGf's affirmative response (l. 228). OTf, however, dissociates herself from her own translation, using a third person indefinite pronoun ("others", l. 229) and explicitly emphasizing that she does not know the "proper" English term, implying that *ugali* encompasses an untranslatable concept of its own.

(97) 225 **OTf:** ah:. what i cook. (.) i can cook. (.) first thing's called <L1sw> ugali {stiff porridge} </L1sw>?
226 **OGf:** okay. what's that?
227 **OTf:** <L1sw> ugali </L1sw> it's li:ke (.) erm: they say what's:: (.) long::? (.) it's likes? (.) (xxxx) (.) porridge they say:?=
228 **OGf:** =okay yeah?=
229 **OTf:** =er:: the strong porridges (.) others say that
230 **OGf:** @@

231 **OTf:** i(@) don't know its (.) name in english? (.) and i can keep (.) i can cook (.) rice?

(O1_225-231)

Conceptual switching can go beyond the semantically rather clear-cut grammatical category of nouns. In (98) the adjective *hitzefrei* is used as a code-switch for conceptual reasons. Hesitations, self-interruption and hedges (l. 121) all indicate that MGf experiences troubles in conveying this particular concept in ELF. She flags her intended switch and culturally grounds the concept to be introduced ("in Germany we have", l. 121). Transparency is further increased by an immediately following paraphrase of the term introduced ("when it's (.) very hot (.) then:: (.) there's no school", l. 121). MTf's expression of surprise in the subsequent turn ("oh:", l. 122) shows that the concept is new to the Tanzanian student indeed (l. 122). Lines 123-125 see the students elaborate on the differences ("you", "here", "for us") that become visible through the introduction of this culture-sensitive concept. Laughter has been shown to frequently accompany code-switching as an interpersonal means to communicate humour or reduce awkwardness (see Brunner & Diemer 2018: 83) and may here be understood as another expression of surprise in the face of a new concept that has been transported linguistically to a different world, in which it is unimaginable.

(98) 121 **MGf:** do you have like (.) erm: (.) so in germany we have (.) er <L1de> hitzefrei? </L1de> (.) that means (.) that when it's (.) very hot (.) then:: (.) there's no school.
122 **MTf:** oh:.
123 **MGf:** you don't have that here don't you(@)? (.) [°(x x)°]
124 **MTf:** [for us (have)] everyday we co(@)me to(@) [school. @]
125 **MGf:** [yea(@)h @@]

(M2_121-125)

Conceptual switches often start off as word searches, with speakers assuming an English translation to the term to exist, which they just cannot think of. Extract (99), however, demonstrates that due to diverging linguacultural semantic categorizations clear-cut conceptual equivalents are often hard to find or to negotiate in ELF. German-English dictionaries (see PONS n.y.; Langenscheidt n.y.) provide the translation 'cereal', 'grain', or 'corn' for the German word *Getreide*, with 'grain' and 'corn' denoting harvested crop only. LGf, however, seems to exclude *Getreide* from her semantic field of polysemantic 'corn', as she introduces *Getreide* as an additional concept (see l. 344). She offers an explanation to convey her intended meaning, upon which LTf suggests the English hyponym *wheat* (l. 347), which the German speaker accepts as a synonym. Pronunciation deviation further complicates the search for conceptual clarity: possibly influenced by LTf's phonological realization of *wheat* as [wid], AGf enters the written form "wheed" [*sic*] into the dia | log | book, which suggests a potential further conceptual influence of *weed*.

(99) 341 **LTf:** `[. . .] what crops do you grow in germany. (2.5)`
342 **LGf:** `m:: (.) a lot of corn?`
343 **LTf:** `corn? aha?`
344 **LGf:** `corn? (.) a:nd (.) hh. <L1de> getreide. {cereal} </L1de> (2) mm: (3) yeah (witt) (.) something (.) you can (2) °mm:° (.) use (0.5)`
345 **LTf:** `mm`
346 **LGf:** `for bread?`
347 **LTf:** `ah that is <pvc> wheat </pvc>`
348 **LGf:** `yeah. <pvc> wheed {wheat} <ipa> wi:d </ipa> </pvc>`
(L2_341-348)

While code-switching is often employed for conceptual reasons, this example also shows that even in the face of prolonged negotiation strategies, some concepts remain vague. Communicative problems in this sequence do not only, and maybe not even mainly, arise from code-switching as such, but from differences in the semantic knowledge about English lexemes and from pronunciation variation as illustrated above – issues urgently to be addressed in English language teaching if communicative effectiveness in intercultural communication through ELF is to be enhanced.

Conceptual code-switching turns out to be particularly effective whenever cognates or internationalisms are involved (see Hülmbauer 2011). In excerpt (100), for instance, the code-switched item "kemia" does not seem to pose any trouble to the German hearers, both of whom react with an immediate confirmative backchannel. They can easily infer the meaning of the Swahili word from the interplay between context (science, physics) and the closeness of the item in question to English *chemistry* and German *Chemie*.

A word search causes speaker OGf in (101) to employ a distinctly flagged code-switch ("what do you sa::y how do you say in english. (.) er in german it c- it's called <L1de> schiff {ship} </L1de>", l. 136), which she further enriches with an example ("titanic") to help her interlocutor understand. As the code-switched item has an English cognate, speaker OTf has an easy job in providing the English lexeme in question (l. 137).

Speakers of closely related languages such as English and German, however, are sometimes also tempted to rely on alleged cognates or internationalisms where they do not exist. In (102), speaker GGf lends an English pronunciation and intonation (['ɪntənet]) to the German lexeme *Internat* ([ɪntɐ'na:t]; 'boarding school'), making it sound like the English word 'internet' (l. 196), in an expectation of her interlocutor to understand. When any reaction fails to come even after a second attempt, GGf realizes that her strategy does not work here and resorts to a different word ("hostel", l. 196). In her reaction ("ah okay", l. 197), GTf finally signals that her problems with the previous concept have now been overcome and mutual understanding has been achieved.

(100) 138 **ITf:** at (.) maybe? right now (i'm doing science) right? (.) i'm only taking physics <L1sw> kemia {chemistry} </L1sw> and and [those]
139 **KGf:** [yeah]
140 **IGf:** [mmh]
141 **ITf:** [other] subjects

(I3_138-141)

(101) 134 **OGf:** yeah yeah. (.) i am also scared about (.) huge
135 **OTf:** @ @@
136 **OGf:** yeah. (.) huge erm: (2) what do you sa::y how do you say in english. (.) er in german it c- it's called <L1de> schiff {ship} </L1de>? (.) erm the titanic?
137 **OTf:** in titanic? (.) [ship?]
138 **OGf:** [yeah.] (.) YEAH yeah. (.) @@=
139 **OTf:** =@@@@=
140 **OGf:** =sure @@ (.)

(O3_134-140)

(102) 196 **GGf:** okay. (.) (yeah) some of my friends are: in: (.) an <pvc> internat {boarding school} <ipa> 'ɪntənet </ipa> </pvc> too. (.) °intern-° (.) °erm° (1) yeah they are at a hostel too?
197 **GTf:** ah okay.

(G1_196-197)

Affective functions

Code-switching, however, is not only employed for conceptual reasons, but, often at the same time, serves various interpersonal functions, too. Interlocutors for instance explore and express their sense of linguacultural belonging by drawing on their L1, but also communicate interest and promote solidarity by employing crossover code-switching and using words from their interlocutor's L1 (L1'). At the same time, speakers construct a third space through code-switching in which they position themselves as hybrid individuals (cf. Bhatt 2008: 177; 193), and thrive in linguistic plurality and shared multilingualism using further languages (Ln). Examples (103) to (106) illustrate correspondent manifestations of interpersonal functions of code-switching, which will be analyzed below.

(103) 351 **LGf:** and how (.) do you call this tree?
352 **LTf:** ah in swahili we call them <L1sw> mwarobaini {neem tree} </L1sw>
353 **LGf:** <L3sw> mworobai </L3sw>
354 **LTf:** yeah. (0.5) i don't know in english (0.5) but in swahili we call it <L1sw> mwarobaini </L1sw> (1) yah. (0.5)
(L1_351-354)

(104) 600 **MTf:** [december] only. (1)
601 **MGf:** <L1de> ach so {oh i see} </L1de> only december.
602 **MTf:** yeah.=
(M1_600-602)

(105) 496 **NGf:** [. . .] it's really windy? oh. (.) you have you have to tell me one more time the word for wind.
497 **NTf:** <L1sw> upepo </L1sw>
498 **NGf:** <L3sw> upepo </L3sw> (1.5) okay i have to wr@ite this d@own (x)? (1) will (1) remember this [. . .]
(N3_496-498)

(106) 413 **HTf:** °yeah in er:° (2) you know spanish? (1)
414 **HGf:** yeah. (.) but i learn it in school. so a lot of us do.
415 **HTf:** (ah./o:-) (.) -kay? °(that sounds nice)°
416 **HGf:** do you want to learn a word?
417 **HTf:** yea:h.
418 **HGf:** whi- one. which one.
419 **HTf:** maybe (okay) (.) i can try this. i think i know some words?
420 **HGf:** ↑yeah? (.) tell me.

421 **HTf:** (<L4sp> grashn (.) gracia </L4sp>) (2)
422 **HGf:** what does it mean? °(i can't tell)°
423 **HTf:** °thank you?° (1)
424 **HGf:** °ah° <L4sp> gracias. </L4sp>
425 **HTf:** <L4sp> gracias. </L4sp> yes. (1) °<L4sp> gracias </L4sp> an:d (1) (i know) (.) <L4sp> papa? </L4sp> (1)
426 **HGf:** <L4sp> la papa </L4sp>
427 **HTf:** <L4sp> papa </L4sp> (2) dad
428 **HGf:** ah yea:h. yeah of course.
429 **HTf:** it's <L4sp> papa? </L4sp> (1)
430 **HGf:** yeah. (3)
431 **HTf:** °(i)° (.) °(i'm not) so° sure [@@]
432 **HGf:** [°@@°]
433 **HTf:** °ye:s° (.) so (.) erm: (.) can you tell us more? (.) °(s- maybe)° (1)
434 **HGf:** what do you want to know? i'll tell you.
435 **HTf:** hello? (.) [(ha)]
436 **HGf:** [<L4sp> hola </L4sp>]
437 **HTf:** <L4sp> hola </L4sp>
438 **HGf:** <L4sp> hola </L4sp>
439 **HTf:** °(-kay?)° (.) °yeah?° (.) °(and)° (2) how are you?
440 **HGf:** <L4sp> que tal? </L4sp>
441 **HTf:** <L4sp> qui tal? </L4sp>
442 **HGf:** <L4sp> que (.) tal. </L4sp>

(H4_413-442)

In the previously quoted extract (103), the Tanzanian speaker uses the Swahili word *mwarobaini* to refer to a particular tree that grows in her school yard (ll. 352; 354). Explicitly contrasting her knowledge gap in English ("i don't know in english", l. 354) with her linguistic expertise in Swahili, and choosing the first person pronoun *we* in combination with an active voice construction ("in swahili we call it", l.354), LTf makes a clear statement on her linguacultural belonging.

Linguacultural identity can also find expression without conscious planning or explicit purpose on behalf of the speaker. Although MGf's German reaction "ach so" ('oh, i see') in (104) (l. 601) comes about unplanned,[104] it will contribute to MTf's other-identification of MGf as a member of a particular linguacultural group.

104 As a prototypical example of an emblematic switch, this slip occurs at an utterance juncture, which poses a cognitively demanding situation (see Mauranen 2013: 238). The cognitive functions of code-switching will further be explored below.

Speaker transparency may leap up post-hoc, with speakers becoming aware of their switches, which often shows in self-interruptions or post-hoc comments. So, while I agree with Pietikäinen (2014: 19) in considering intent as a general prerequisite of active signalling (of culture or any other object), I would still grant emblematic switches or lapses the function of passive expressions of linguacultural belongings in accordance with Klimpfinger's (2009: 360) general line of argumentation.[105] Even in the face of low speaker transparency at the moment of switching, formal and hearer transparency (and eventually also speaker transparency) may be high,[106] contributing to perceived identities.

Identity work is also at play in crossover code-switches as in excerpt (105). By first explicitly asking for the Swahili word for *wind* and then repeating it herself, NGf expresses her interest in her interlocutor's language as a representative part of NTf's identity. The code-switched lexeme *upepo* becomes a 'lexical souvenir' that the German speaker pins down on paper and takes home with her as a symbol of her bonds with her Tanzanian friend.

In (106) finally, both speakers display some knowledge of Spanish, a language foreign to both of them alike. The students' switching into this language reveals for once their pride of their linguistic knowledge ("do you want to learn a word?", l. 416; "i think i know some words", l. 419), which includes the possibility of teaching and learning from each other, but also their fascination with plurilingualism and their joy in exploring new linguacultural territory together. This interpretation is supported by HGf's statement earlier in the same conversation "i guess i'm interested in languages" (H4_152). In contrast to the often demarcating functions of L1 use, the employment of a language foreign to all interlocutors from a "shared multilingual resources pool" (Pitzl 2018a: 194–196) strengthens an inclusive identity of competent multilingual speakers.

---

105 It is in the same line of thinking that I include initially unconsciously used informative signals alongside intentional communicative signals (see Yule 2017: 13) in this study on pragmatics. While it may be argued that pragmatics is interested in the purposeful use of language in communicative contexts, it often seems impossible to decide when exactly the borderline between unconscious and conscious use of language is crossed. Any originally unplanned use of language may not only pass communicatively relevant information, but may also be reflected and taken up by interlocutors and may thus insert influence on a subsequent monitored and purpose-driven use of language.

106 On the different perspectives between analyst, speaker and listener in code-switching, see also Ehrhart (2015: 308).

Addressee specification

Code-switching is sometimes also used to address a particular speaker in the TeenELF corpus (17%), which happens especially in groups of three. This function will be illustrated by help of examples (107) to (109).

(107) 091 **KGf:** [so] you can choose (.) if. (.) you have (.) two (.) languages? (2) or (.) and one (.) yeah (.) erm (.) scientific? (.) erm: (.) subject? (1) for example (.) latin english? (.) or (.) latin spanish [english spanish? (.) >do you know what i mean<]

092 **IGf:** [<L1de> ich glaub das is zu konst- das ist zu- das is zu kompliziert {i think this is too cons- this is too - this is too complicated} </L1de>]

093 **ITf:** yeah

094 **KGf:** or: (.) <L1de> und dann {and then} </L1de> one of (.) biology chemistry <L1de>od- </L1de> or physics? (.) one of them (.) or you have (.) two scientific subjects (.) for example biology and chemistry? (.) and only ONE (.) erm language?

095 **IGf:** the system is VERY [complicated >you have<]

(I3_091-093)

(108) 479 **LTf:** [. . .] global warming yeah. (5.5) <L1sw> shikamoo mwalimu {respectful greeting to teacher} </L1sw>

480 **XTf:** <L1sw> maharaba {response to shikamoo} </L1sw> [. . .]

(L2_479-480)

(109) 399 **JTf:** °okay.° (.) let me take another (chair) for writing.

400 **JGm:** yeah. (8) <L1de> sie geht einen stuhl holen. {she's gone to get a chair} </L1de> (12) °perfect.°

(J2_399-400)

In (107), recorded in a group of one Tanzanian and two German participants, different addressees are clearly allocated on the basis of different codes. KGf tries to give ITf an overview of the German students' options in their choice of subjects. IGf interrupts her mid-turn, addressing her German classmate in German, suggesting that her elaborations might be too complicated (l. 092). Code-switching that specifies a particular addressee normally excludes other participants at the same time.

In the present example, this exclusion can be regarded a face-saving strategy, as the face-threatening act of criticizing is understandable only to the immediate person criticized (KGf), and not to the Tanzanian interlocutor (ITf). KGf therefore can and indeed does neglect IGf's advice and keeps on explaining in English, although she inserts occasional slips from German, potentially influenced by being addressed in German (l. 094). When IGf realizes her advice is being ignored, she changes the code and the addressee to make her message heard (l. 095).[107]

Addressees specified by code-switching may also originally be external to the group. Participating students sometimes address classmates discussing in pairs nearby to ask for advice or discuss organizational matters in their common L1 (see (111)), or to address random bypassers with a greeting in Swahili, as is the case in (108) where a student greets her *mwalimu*, her teacher, in Swahili.

Going to extremes, a speaker may switch codes to address a person not even present at all, who only exists as an imagined user of the embedded language. In (109), the German speaker fills the temporary absence of his Tanzanian interlocutor with a German comment on the action silently taking place ("<L1de> sie geht einen stuhl holen. {she's gone to get a chair} </L1de>", l. 400). This meta-level remark is potentially addressed at the German speaking researcher, whom the speaker may picture listening to his audio-recording subsequently.

Interactional functions

In many of the given examples, code-switching fulfils interactional functions at the same time. Code-switching employed for addressee specification, for example, often introduces alternative discourse threads. In (108), speaker LTf interrupts her pondering on global warming to greet a Tanzanian bypasser in Swahili, for instance. This strategy can be taken to extremes as illustrated in extract (94) (Section 10.3.2), where in a group of three two German speakers lead a discontinuous discourse in German on insect bites parallel to their English main discourse, marking the alternative discourse threads by the use of different languages. Similar to the common phenomenon of code-switching used for classroom management talk in language classrooms (see Cogo & House 2018: 219), students often employ code-switching to organize their discussing and recording sessions, as extracts (110) to (112) illustrate.

107 Note the little but – from a politeness perspective – decisive change of the adverb from excessive *zu* ('too') to intensifying *very*: with a change of addressee, this adjustment becomes necessary to save the hearer's face, as *too* might imply the limits of KTf's understanding capacities whereas *very* redirects the focus to the complicated issue under discussion.

(110) 180 **MGf:** okay. <L1de> ich muss das mal irgendwo abstellen. {i need to put this down somewhere} </L1de> (1) okay. (1) {clearing her throat} (4) present and future.

(M4_180)

(111) 456 **EGf:** <L1de> seid ihr fertig? (1) okay ja wir kommen auch gleich {have you finished? (1) alright we'll also be back soon} </L1de> erm: i think (.) it's e- (.) kind of sad [. . .]

(E2_456)

(112) 690 **KGf:** yeah (5) <L1de> haste auf stop gedrückt? {have you pressed the stop button?} </L1de>

(I2_690)

Interactional functions often go hand in hand with cognitive aspects of code-switching, which will further be explored in the final paragraph of this section. Speakers often automatically employ their L1 in cognitively demanding positions such as utterance junctures as illustrated in extract (113) (also see Mauranen 2013: 238), or resort to code-switching as a strategy to keep a troubled conversation going as illustrated in (114).

(113) 262 **NTf:** you do group works [(yeah)]
263 **NGf:** <L1de> [ja] genau {yes exactly} </L1de> and (.) er ye-@ yes. @ and erm sometimes erm we are meeting in the evening? (.) and then: sometimes e:rm (.) we watch a movie

(N1_262-263)

Cognitive functions

Code-switching can also be employed to support cognitive processes, which will be illustrated by help of example (114). ITf here talks about the time she normally gets home at night. The code-switched phrases ("saa mbili usiku", l. 166; "saa tatu", l. 168) open a window to the speaker's mind: ITf voices her thoughts aloud so as to prevent the conversation from coming to a standstill while she is thinking. The cognitive task ITf has to fulfil is a somewhat demanding one indeed: the Swahili time concept differs from the English one in so far as the Swahili counting of hours of the day starts with dawn, whereas the English counting begins at midnight. 7 o'clock in the morning consequently equals 1 o'clock in Swahili terms. When talking about time in ELF, L1 Swahili speakers therefore do not only have to translate, but calculate and transform at the same time. Code-switching supports this cognitive process and grants the speaker enough time for processing. In uttering her words aloud, the speaker holds the floor and continues the conversation.

(114) 166 **ITf:** [. . .] maybe our teacher will be finishing at ee (2) at <L1sw> saa mbili usiku {hour two night} </L1sw> it's be night that will be (.) eight in night but=
167 **IGf:** =oh okay=
168 **ITf:** =yeah so when i when i'll be at home? (.) it's around about <L1sw> °saa tatu° {hour three} </L1sw> so (.) i meant nine

(I1_166-168)

While code-switching for conceptual reasons may hamper cognitive processing on behalf of the receiver (see "rede" example (87) in Section 10.2.2), self-directed code-switching may on the other hand promote cognitive processing on behalf of the speaker. The interplay between cognition and code-switching, which has been demonstrated in the present data, seems to have otherwise received little attention in research so far (for exceptions, see e.g. Mauranen 2013; García & Li 2014) and is in need of further exploration.

10.4 Other translanguaging phenomena

While code-switching may represent the most overt form of translanguaging (see Section 10.2.1), plurilingual influences leak through into the matrix language in many other ways. Transfer may affect all linguistic levels from phonology to morphology and syntax to semantics and pragmatics (see Danesi & Rocci 2009). Although ELF speakers' plurilingual repertoire enriches their overall communicative potential, linguacultural interference may also lead to misunderstandings (see Jenkins 2000). While Danesi & Rocci (2009: 22) suggest that in intercultural communication "semantic interferences tend to produce more deleterious effects on the interpretation of messages than do phonological, morphological or syntactic interferences" as the former often remain intransparent, TeenELF speakers report more overt phonological interferences to particularly hamper mutual understanding (see Int_ETf; Int_FGf; Int_GrG). The first part of this chapter accordingly explores the omnipresent phenomenon of phonological transfer in its interplay with aspects of communication and identity. The chapter further explores the semi-transparent phenomena of hybrid word formation and calquing, before it moves on to investigate covert influences of linguacultural conceptualizations in TeenELF. In all that, transparency is once more worked out as a decisive factor for a maximization of the communicative potential of translanguaging.

10.4.1 Phonological transfer

Languages also leak into ELF, thereby becoming part of ELF, via phonological transfer, which has been a central object of interest from the early days of ELF research (see Jenkins 2000). Although research here will not focus on this well-explored area, any work on multilingual ELF excluding the ubiquitous phenomenon of phonological transfer in ELF would remain incomplete. Jenkins (2007) has explored the relationship between ELF accents and identity in detail. She speaks of a situation of "linguistic schizophrenia" (Jenkins 2007: 216), with ELF interlocutors seeking to express both inclusive global and exclusive local aspects of their identity at the same time. Many ELF speakers do so by drawing on English as a global language while using "a locally-influenced English accent" out of a "desire (perhaps subconscious) to maintain and project [their local] identity" (Jenkins 2007: 202).

While accents play an important role in the constitution of identities on the one hand, they have also been found to influence the negotiation of meaning through their potential of hampering mutual understanding (see Jenkins 2007; Ishamina & Deterding 2018). Tanzanian and German students participating in the present study alike foreground each others' accents as the primary source for difficulties in this respect. Extracts (115) to (117) will serve to illustrate how phonological transfer can impede mutual understanding.

Misunderstandings in extracts (115) and (116) both arise from a variation in the TRAP vowel /æ/. While in East African varieties of English, the TRAP vowel is realized as [a] (see Schmied 2010: 161), many German speakers of English resort to the phoneme [ɛ] instead (see Eckert & Barry 2005: 19–24; Schmitt 2016: 104–112; Sönning 2020: 53–86). The misunderstanding in the previously quoted example (115) (see Section 7.2), in which two students talk about their prospective jobs, arises from this raising of the vowel [æ] to [ɛ] as influenced by the German phoneme system. As a consequence, *tax* is mistaken for *text* (ll. 542-543), which triggers an other-initiated repair sequence, in which the misunderstanding is first exposed and finally resolved as presented in Chapter 7.

(115) 542 **LGf:** i want to (.) go to the <pvc> tex {tax} </pvc> office.
543 **LTf:** text office?
544 **LGf:** <pvc> tex {tax} </pvc> office.
545 **LTf:** you want to become a (messenger)? (1)

546 **LGf:** er:m: ts (.) i work at a <pvc> tex {tax} </pvc> office so (.) i: (.) look (.) that (.) all the people?
547 **LTf:** mh?
548 **LGf:** pay their <pvc> texes {taxes} </pvc> [in the right way.]
549 **LTf:** [↑oh:]y-(.) so you want to become a: (0.5) in charge of taxes. (0.5) ↑i like it.

(L2_542-549)

While the very vowel in question here, /æ/, is not part of the Swahili phoneme inventory either, East Africans tend to lower this phoneme to [a] rather than raise it, which can again lead to misunderstandings, as illustrated in extract (116), in which students talk about the FIFA World Cup 2014. The first utterance of the word *fan* [fan], which causes the misunderstanding, is followed by significant silence (l. 526). The lack of a verbal reaction on the part of the German speaker indicates difficulties in processing the received message. The Tanzanian speaker, upon realizing the communicative problem, repeats her utterance to help her partner understand. By taking up only the complement noun phrase with rising intonation ("fun", l. 527), the German speaker now pinpoints the exact trouble source. Neither of the two interlocutors seem to perceive the slight difference in vowel qualities, as the Tanzanian speaker confirms the German understanding check ("yeah", l. 528), but repeats her slightly different version of the word in question (l. 528). Whether understanding is finally achieved because the German speaker has truly become conscious of the phonological difference, or through contextual inference mainly, remains unclear. It is interesting to note in any case that in signalling understanding the German speaker again practices translanguaging through unconscious code-switching (l. 529). This emblematic switch may have cognitive reasons, as mental capacities are occupied by the negotiating process so that a switch to cognitively less demanding linguistic productions become more likely.

(116) 520 **MTf:** [. . .] i remember (.) on erm:: (1) twenty fourteen (1) there was erm:: (1) the world (.) cup.
521 **MGf:** mhm?
522 **MTf:** °yeah.° (.) germany won it.=
523 **MGf:** =germany won [yeah.]
524 **MTf:** [°yeah°] (.) [i remember]=
525 **MGf:** [that (was) great.]
526 **MTf:** =that i was your <pvc> faan. {fan} </pvc> (1) i was your <pvc> faan. {fan} </pvc>

527 **MGf:** a fun?
528 **MTf:** yeah. i was your <pvc> faan {fan} </pvc>
529 **MGf:** <L1de> ach ↑so {oh i see} </L1de> you you ↑ah.
530 **MTf:** °yeah.°=
531 **MGf:** =cool. (.) yeah.

(M1_520-531)

While the misunderstanding in the final example is based on a confounding of the two glides /r/ and /l/, which is regarded characteristic of East African Englishes (see Schmied 2010: 159) influenced by alveolar realizations of <r> in Bantu languages, the strategy of dealing with this phonological transfer for the sake of mutual understanding resembles previously described actions. The meaning-making process surrounding this non-understanding, which is based on phonological transfer again, includes silence to follow the problematic item *role model* (ll. 336; 338), repetitions both on behalf of the producer (l. 339) and the receiver (l. 338), increasingly concrete questions to elicit support (ll. 337; 339; 341), a metalinguistic comment to openly express non-understanding (l. 343), and paraphrases (ll. 342; 344), which finally lead to communicative success.

(117) 336 **KTf:** and (.) who is your <pvc> role <ipa> ləʊl </ipa> model </pvc>? (.)
337 **KGf:** hm?
338 **KTf:** who is your <pvc> role model </pvc> (1) your <pvc> ROLE model. </pvc>
339 **KGf:** low model?
340 **KTf:** yeah.
341 **KGf:** what's that?
342 **KTf:** somebody you can er (.) you can (.) you are <pvc> impressed <ipa> ɪm'plest </ipa> </pvc> with? (2)
343 **KGf:** i didn't understand what you (.)
344 **KTf:** i mean somebody you can look and (.) follow what he or she does.
345 **KGf:** OH
346 **KTf:** yeah=
347 **KGf:** =okay=
348 **KTf:** =who <pvc> impresses </pvc> you. (1)
349 **KGf:** my mother and my father.=
350 **KTf:** =oh wow@

(K1_336-350)

In all three examples, the student interlocutors show a high degree of patience and persistence. This reveals a true desire to understand each other, and at the same time an underlying expectancy and acceptance of necessary negotiation work in a context of linguacultural plurality.

10.4.2 Hybrid word formation

Translanguaging is not only realized through code-switching of whole words or larger units, or expressed in clearly perceivable L1 accents, but also finds its manifestation in formally more subtle ways. Morphemes from English and other codes may, for instance, be merged in creative ways to render hybrid neologisms. Hybrid words are made up of lexical morphemes from different codes that are combined to form new compounds. In the aforementioned compound "schul-life" (C3_007), for instance, the German cognate of the English lexeme *school* is prefixed to *life*. Due to their similarity in form and meaning (see Cogo 2016a: 85), cognates seem especially prone to slip into constructions of this kind. In the given case, the processing of the hybrid compound *schul-life* is not expected to cause any difficulties on behalf of the hearer, all the more as the corresponding Swahili lexeme *shule* itself constitutes a permanent loan from German.

Lexical morphemes from embedded languages may also receive English functional affixes in creative bifurcative processes of hybridization, in which the matrix language English provides the morphosyntactic frame (see Myers-Scotton 1993: 3–4). This may affect words from different word classes as the following examples demonstrate. In (118), the German speaker NGf incorporates the German verb *hupen* ('to honk'). A salient pause before the item in question and the speaker's post-hoc metalinguistic comment "okay i do@n't know wh@at (.) what the word is for that" (l. 276) reveal the motivation for resorting to L1 resources. In order to render the verb phrase grammatically complete in the progressive aspect chosen, the speaker attaches the English progressive suffix *-ing* to the German stem, which results in the hybrid form *hooping*. Due to the comparatively close typological relationship between English and German and the resultant high number of cognates, the chosen strategy holds a certain probability to work. The further unfolding of turns, however, clearly indicates that intersubjective understanding is not achieved through translanguaging here, as the Tanzanian student mistakes the verb for *overtaking* (ll. 277; 279), which in turn is not denied but confirmed by the German speaker (ll. 278; 280).

(118) 276 **NGf:** [. . .] sometimes two cars erm (.) are driving a-(.) at one time and then they are both (1.5) <pvc> hooping </pvc> okay i do@n't know wh@at (.) what the word is for that erm (.)
277 **NTf:** overtaking each other. (.)
278 **NGf:** yeah maybe (.) i have=
279 **NTf:** =the one is driving and other is coming front of it (1.5)
280 **NGf:** yeah [. . .]

(N2_276-280)

The same strategy is employed by CGm, who resorts to the German noun *Moschee* ('mosque') in the face of lexical problems in (119). The English plural suffix *-s* is attached to the German stem, and the resulting word is transformed prosodically and phonetically ['mɔʃi:z] to adjust it to its English matrix. Hesitation phenomena such as short pauses, self-interruption, rising intonation and the hesitation marker "erm" (l. 076) again reveal the reason for the employment of L1 resources: the student cannot access the English lexeme in question. Aware of potential problems arising from this strategy, the speaker provides a paraphrase of the word in question ("where the muslims go in? (.) to pray?", l. 076). The further proceeding of the conversation reveals that transparent translanguaging has facilitated mutual understanding here: while CTf's neutral backchannel "mm" (l. 077) still allows for an interpretation of the let-it-pass strategy being employed here, her later active use of the word in question, "mosque" (l. 082), reveals a true understanding. Offering the word searched for by embedding it in natural talk somewhat distanced from the potential trouble source, the Tanzanian here also manages to initiate repair in a face-saving way. When CGm, however, reveals in the following term that he has not appropriated the English term yet (l. 083), CTf resorts to more direct other-repair (l. 084). She thus finally succeeds in teaching her German interlocutor the English term, which CGm then repeats (l. 085) and applies in a sentence so as to incorporate it into his active lexicon (l. 087).

(119) 076 **CGm:** but in germany it's forbidden for example erm (2) erm (1) that erm (.) mo- (.) the (.) <pvc> moshees? <ipa> 'mɔʃi:z </ipa> </pvc> so where the muslims go in? (.) to pray? erm (.) they do (.) they are not allowed to look typical. (.) erm <like they> do look. so (.) they have to look like normal houses. (0.5)
077 **CTf:** [mm]
078 **CGm:** [i don't] know why (.) but it's so (1.5)

080 **CTf:** hm (.) here you can design it any way you want. (0.5) if your [church is]
081 **CGm:** [yeah]
082 **CTf:** ten storeys high your mosque is (.) three storeys high
083 **CGm:** i think in germany we've got only two or three m- erm (1) musl- i s- (0.5) just call it now muslim churches (0.5) [erm]
084 **CTf:** [mosques]
085 **CGm:** mosques.
086 **CTf:** yeah=
087 **CGM:** =okay mosques. i try to remember it. erm (0.5) erm there (.) they look (0.5) erm which are really big and wh-ich are allowed to look (.) as we- (.) as real mosques. (.) [. . .]

(C2_076-86)

In a similar process to the ones encountered for hybrid verb and noun formation, adjectives and even complex prepositions may be affected by hybridization. The neologism *quirly* in (120), for example, combines the German adjective stem *quirl-* from *quirlig* ('lively, bubbly'), with the English adjective suffix *-y*. In (121), English *out* in the complex preposition *out of* is replaced by the German cognate *aus*.

(120) 542 **HGf:** =erm (.) what i find interesting that you are about fifty students in a class and can still °concentrate? because in our class it (was)° (.) °(would)° (.) °(x) just (be:)° (.) wouldn't be possible? becau:se (.) i guess students are too: (.) especially the younger ones are quite (.) <pvc> quirly? </pvc> and (1) er:? (.) yeah (.) always jump around?

(H3_542)

(121) 198 **CGm:** yeah (.) so (.) from the pigs erm (.) and also erm (.) cows and so (.) a:nd (.) we'll make sausages <L1de> aus </L1de> of it [. . .]

(C1_198)

10.4.3 Calquing

While code-switching, phonological transfer and hybrid word formation incorporate language material from languages other than English into ELF on a formally perceptible level, calquing is predominantly based on semantic and idiomatic transfer (see Danesi & Rocci 2009: 157–161). Calques, also termed loan translations, make use of English words and phonemes only and consequently look and sound English on the surface, but are idiomatically strongly influenced by source languages other than English and stand out as collocationally unusual in English. Table 23 lists some examples of calques in the present data and their English meanings.

Table 23: TeenELF calques.

Calque		Source (donor language)	Meaning in English
nice-writing-pen	(C2_111)	'Schönschreibstift' (German)	'calligraphy pen'
lovely song	(G3_460-461)	'wimbo kipendwa' (Swahili)	'favorite song'
social livings	(C1_47)	'Sozialwohnungen' (German)	'council housings'
real school	(H3_587)	'Realschule' (German)	secondary school leading up to grade 10

Again, a variety of conversational clues, such as flagging, hesitation markers and rising intonation, reveal various degrees of speaker transparency. Enrichment and explicitness strategies are employed to secure intersubjective understanding. In (122), CGm reveals a high degree of S-transparency around his use of the calque *social livings* (from German 'Sozialwohnungen', English 'council housing'). Not only does he use flagging to start with ("in Germany, we call these buildings", l. 047), but he also provides further explanations on the concept in question subsequently ("the community pays them", l. 047). CTf signals her understanding by providing the respective term which is used in her own linguacultural context ("national housing", l. 048).

(122) 047 **CGm:** `in germany we call these buildings erm <pvc> social livings </pvc> so. (.) the community pays (them) [so (.) you do not]`
048 **CTf:** `[ah (.) we call it] (.) national housings.`
(C1_021-026)

Calquing as one form of translanguaging also figures prominently in the use of pragmatic markers. The German question tag *oder*, for instance, permeates as a calque into ELF in form of the widespread universal question tag *or*, the use of which is illustrated in (123) (l. 037).[108]

(123) 034 **ETf:** `how old are you?`
035 **EGf:** `yeah 17.`
036 **ETf:** `17?`
037 **EGf:** `you're 18 or?`
038 **ETf:** `↑mm`

(E1_034-038)

TeenELF speakers also employ the sequence-final *or so* (mainly German participants)[109] and *or what* (mainly Tanzanian participants) as well as *okay* as frequent discourse markers.[110] A cross-corpus comparison may once more shed light on the question whether translanguaging, youth languaging or none of the two is at work here. In addition to the overall problematic nature of cross-corpus comparisons as outlined in Section 8.2, comparisons here seem all the more problematic as for *or so* and *or what* sequential and prosodic factors are at play (falling intonation for sequence-final uses), which are not coded in all corpora. FOLK was searched for the German equivalents ('oder so', 'oder was'), which adds the problem of conceptual and pragmatic divergence.[111] Findings are accordingly presented as tentative in the appendix (Appendix C) and have to be treated with adequate caution. Figures C.1 and C.2, however, strongly suggest cross-linguacultural influences in the form of calquing for both *or so* and *or what*, as frequencies particularly in the FOLK corpus, but also in ICE EA outnumber frequencies in the British corpus. The case is less clear for the discourse marker *okay*, which arises from the findings as a discourse marker highly characteristic of TeenELF interaction. Figure C.3 depicts the popularity of this discourse marker in ELF interactions in general (highest frequencies in TeenELF and VOICE), which may be ascribed to its functional versatility (e.g. affirmative, interrogative). At the same time, the frequency of *okay* as an English loan in the German corpus even surpasses corresponding frequencies in the British based corpora. Indirect cross-linguistic influences may consequently be suggested

108 On the use of *or* as an invariable question tag in ELF, see also Hülmbauer (2007: 21–22).
109 On the high frequency of discourse markers in youth languages in general, and the frequent use of *und so* ('and so') and *oder so* ('or so') in particular as attested through German youth language research, see Androutsopoulos 1998: 7–8.
110 Cogo & House (2018: 215–218) provide a summary of salient discourse markers as used in ELF. Another discourse marker highly salient in TeenELF for pragmatic and phonological reasons is *yeah*, which calls for further explorations in follow-up studies.
111 On further matters of disambiguation, see also comment on Table C.2 in the appendix.

for German speakers of ELF. Data also propose an age factor at work, as frequencies for *okay* are higher for young speakers in both lingua franca and BNC2014 corpora respectively.

10.4.4 Linguacultural conceptualizations

At a very opaque level, translanguaging involves a transfer of cultural conceptualizations inherent in the languages at play. The conversations analyzed feature examples of varying and at times contrasting cultural schemas, categorizations and metaphors (see Section 2.2.2). When conceptualizations of different provenance clash, they may or may not become conscious to the interlocutors. In those cases where diverging conceptualizations are made more overt or even openly discussed, they also become accessible to the analyst. The following examples show instances in which different linguacultural conceptualizations are made transparent.

Cultural schemas

Extract (124) discloses different primary schemas at work for the lexeme *book*: while the Tanzanian speaker refers to books as constituting a "basic need" (l. 060), activating a schema of books as important instruments of studying, the German student links a book primarily with the realm of hobbies and pleasure ("do you love reading?", l. 073). The clash of these competing primary schemas accounts for a prolonged negotiation sequence, which contains several repetitions (ll. 066-071) and checks for understanding (ll. 069; 071).[112]

(124)
058	**GTf:**	is there anything (.) lacking in your life?_
059	**GGf:**	erm: lacking? (3) erm: (2) <health> (.) and you? (.) oh (.) sorry. (3)
060	**GTf:**	er: er like (1) some basic needs.
061	**GGf:**	basic needs. okay. (5) <basic> (1) nee:ds? (.) [sorry]=
062	**GTf:**	[li:ke]
063	**GGf:**	= i changed it
064	**GTf:**	maybe i specify like (1)
065	**GGf:**	li::ke oh::
066	**GTf:**	(1) boo:ks? (1)
067	**GGf:**	what?

112 The explicitness exhibited is, however, partly also due to the fact that the German student is taking notes for the dia | log | book at the same time as discussing the topic.

068 **GTf:** books.
069 **GGf:** books?
070 **GTf:** yeah.
071 **GGf:** boo:ks?
072 **GTf:** (wa@)
073 **GGf:** do you love reading?
074 **GTf:** yea:h [@]
075 **GGf:**   [↑oh:. @] (1)
076 **GTf:** °er books (for)°
077 **GGf:** if i would have known that i could have bring o(@)- some (xx)=
078 **GTf:** =↑ah::=
079 **GGf:** =i didn't knew:.@
080 **GTf:** er:
081 **GGf:** @=
082 **GTf:** =books of (.) study in the class.
083 **GGf:** okay.
084 **GTf:** °yeah.° (1)
085 **GGf:** <studying> (1)
086 **GTf:** study in the class. (1)
087 **GGf:** °class° okay. (3)

(G4_058-087)

Another divergence of primary schemas, this time with regard to *children*, is brought to light in sequence (125). The clash of interpretations between "children as a burden" on the one hand and "children as a blessing" on the other hand is laid bare in GTf's resistance to accept a schema of "children as a problem" as outlined in GGf's introductory statement (l. 551). Although GGf makes the underlying schema very explicit by stating that "there are lots of families (who) don't wanna get any children"(l. 551), GTf rejects this conception and reinterprets her interlocutor's statement by giving an alternative explanation for people not having many kids in line with her own schema ("so it's not allowed to have many kids", l. 552). When her German conversation partner reaffirms the first-mentioned schema of children in more drastic terms ("it's allowed to (have children) [. . .], but nobody wants to", ll. 553; 555), GTf meets the unexpected qualification of her own schema with an expression of surprise, which shows in a high pitch, rising intonation and the employment of laughter (l. 556).

(125) 551 **GGf:** it's big (.) problem in germany (.) tha:t (.) er there are lots of families (who) don't wanna get any children? (1) so: (1) there are (.) lots of families °(who)° (.) who don't ha:ve kids? (1) an:d (.) most of them who have kids have (.) two kids? (1) some of them just one kid? (.) [and]
552 **GTf:** [so] it's not (.) allowed to have many kids.
553 **GGf:** it's allowed to.
554 **GTf:** it's allo[wed.]
555 **GGf:** [but] nobody wants to.
556 **GTf:** a@o-↑kay?

(G3_551-556)

Cultural categorizations

Diverging underlying cultural categories become apparent when it comes to concepts of *family*, for example. Various instances confirm the possibility of the category *family* to include pets on the German side, which is often met with critical surprise on the part of the Tanzanian interlocutors. Excerpt (126) illustrates divergences between cultural categories around *family* and *cats*. While for the German student her cat represents her beloved "baby" (l. 093), the Tanzanian speaker categorizes cats not as cuddly pets but as useful control agents to keep plagues at bay (l. 098). This categorical difference has behavioural consequences as outlined by the Tanzanian student: no Tanzanian would think of sharing a bed with a cat (l. 100). The Tanzanian speaker prefers to cuddle with her baby brother instead (ll. 096; 104-108).

The categorical difference between concepts of *cats* as outlined above is corroborated and depicted in its affective dimension in (127): while the German speaker BGm draws a picture of cats as beloved pets in his home (l. 187), the Tanzanian speaker BTf conceptualizes cats as straying animals nobody really wants (l. 188).

(126) 091 **IGf:** mm. (.) erm i think (2) my family's (.) mm: (.) as i sa-family i see my erm cats@
092 **ITf:** @@[@]
093 **IGf:** [so] so it is like i have a cat and it's like my baby my own baby and i [love her]
094 **ITf:** [ah so] you love cats no
095 **IGf:** yeah

096 **ITf:** actually i have nothing (home) apart i i meant my pet is my young brother because
097 **IGf:** mh
098 **ITf:** you know in africa (.) all of us <pvc> cuts </pvc> cats are using to eat to catch the rats in the [house]
099 **IGf:** ahh okay [ohh]
100 **ITf:** [yeah] so there h- the cats is there but h- he has al- he has (.) he do he does something else not just like we can sleep with him with [that]
101 **IGf:** [ah okay]
102 **ITf:** not like that.
103 **IGf:** ahh okay
104 **ITf:** yeah especially y' know in africa a- a- you know in in africa er the young ones er they the young the young children like re- the (very) young i have a young brother (xx) brother's (like my pet) sometimes=
105 **IGf:** =ahh
106 **ITf:** when i'm bored so it's there
107 **IGf:** @@@@=
108 **ITf:** =there for me.
109 **IGf:** that's cute.

(I1_091-103)

(127) 187 **BGm:** [in germany] [. . .] many people like (.) cats (xx) and (.) take them home and (.) use [them as pets.]
188 **BTf:** [ah::?] ah:: okay (1) here they're just roaming around (.) nobody want them (1)

(B1_187-188)

Cultural metaphors

Cultural conceptualizations also become part of ELF in the form of transferred metaphors (see Pitzl 2018a), as excerpt (128) demonstrates. The German proverb *Geld wächst nicht auf Bäumen* ('money does not grow on trees') has been the source of inspiration for the German speaker ("nothing is growing on plants or trees", l. 294). Proverbs display "a major form of influence culture exerts on language" (Meierkord 2002: 114). The particular saying used here expresses the cultural belief of having to work hard for something deeply aspired. In pre-empting this meaning (l. 292), the German speaker here does not run a risk of losing his Tanzanian interlocutor through the use of culturally inspired metaphorical speech. His self-repair at the very end of the sequence ("or trees", l. 294), which he operates to bring the saying closer to the German original, reveals a high degree of speaker transparency at this point.

(128) 292 **CGm:** yeah? (1.5) but (.) i think you h- (0.5) everyone who wants to do something. (2) has to work hard for it. (.) [and then]
293 **CTf:** [yeah] (.) very
294 **CGm:** mh (0.5) we also do have work hard for it so in germany nothing (.) is growing on (.) plants @ (.) or trees
(C2_292-294)

In extract (129), the German speaker IGf employs the L1 influenced metaphor and simile of a *scissor* (ll. 431; 433; 435) to refer to the social gap between rich and poor. A micropause before the first mention of the metaphor ("it is a (.)", l. 431) indicates insecurity concerning the appropriateness of the chosen term on part of the speaker. She consequently interrupts herself ("s-") and starts the sentence anew, this time enriched with flagging ("we say") and constructed as an explicit simile ("like"), which both reveal local S-transparency, and serve to raise H-transparency to facilitate intersubjective understanding. After hearer understanding of the basic meaning of the metaphor is enquired ("do you know what a scissor is?", l. 431) and confirmed ("yah", l. 432), IGf carries on to contextually explain and elaborate the metaphor (ll. 433; 435). Finally, the second German speaker present here in a group of three steps in as a mediator, providing an idiomatic English expression for the German L1 influenced metaphor in question ("[i would] say the gap [between] [. . .] rich and poor people (.) will get bigger?", l. 436; 438). A sociocultural identity and sense of belonging is here expressed through an interplay between content (description of society in home country), explicit language use (1st person pronouns "in **our** (.) society", "**we** say", l. 431; "**we** have a middle (.) erm rich society", l. 433) and covert translanguaging.

(129) 431 **IGf:** i think (.) erm (.) it is a (.) s- erm (.) we say it is like a scissor? in our (.) society? (.) do you know what a scissor is? (2) a scissor yeah=
432 **ITf:** =yah.
433 **IGf:** erm (.) it is a scissor between poor people and very rich people? (.) so we have a middle (.) erm rich society what is (.) not that much. it is (.) [erm]

```
434 KGf:                                                  [mmh]=
435 IGf:  =sometimes it is (.) very much poor and very much
           rich? (.) for example in america it is very often? and
           in (.) germany there is a developing to (.) go to the
           scissors (.) so it's (.) not that (2) [that]
436 KGf:                                          [i would] say
           the gap [between]
437 IGf:   [(yes)]
438 KGf:   rich and poor people (.) will get bigger?
```

(I2_431-438)

10.5 Summary of findings on translanguaging

Starting off from an exploration of the metadiscourse on multilingualism in the present data, this chapter has explored forms and functions of translanguaging in TeenELF. It has proposed a transparency continuum of translanguaging phenomena to overcome the previously suggested binary distinction between covert and overt phenomena and do justice to semi-transparent phenomena such as calquing and hybrid word formation. In addition to the more objective category of formal transparency (F-transparency), the subjective and alterable concepts of speaker and hearer awareness or transparency (S- and H-transparency) have been proposed, which are presumed to correlate particularly towards the more transparent end of the scale. All three strands of transparency individually contribute to the overall transparency in a given context and can further influence each other as depicted by help of examples. The resulting overall transparency of translanguaging in a particular context influences the communicative effectiveness. This very link unfolds the pedagogical potential of the transparency model: multilingual learners can employ translanguaging as an effective tool when they monitor the various aspects of interactional transparency.

On the basis of examples from the TeenELF corpus, translanguaging phenomena covering the whole continuum of formal transparency have been investigated, reaching from code-switching on the overt end to phonological transfer, hybrid word formation and calquing as semi-transparent phenomena to linguacultural conceptualizations on the covert end of the spectrum. A particular focus was placed on code-switching, which is best accessible to the analyst for its high formal transparency.

The frequency of code-switching has been shown to vary according to group size and composition, discourse topic and setting. Potential links between the years of formal education in English and active English use in everyday life on the one hand, and the frequency of code-switching or translanguaging more generally on the other have been suggested, but need further exploration on the basis of larger data sets. In line with previous findings, discourse markers and nouns, referring mostly to natural or cultural phenomena, constitute the majority of one-word switches in TeenELF. It has been argued that linguacultural identity is not only expressed through conscious switches of content words, but also through code-switched discourse markers, mostly slipping in as emblematic switches. These lapses often occur at cognitively demanding points in conversation, such as turn changes, and fulfil important interactional functions in structuring the discourse. Especially in cognitively challenging situations, speakers also employ code-switching to gain more planning and processing time while holding the floor and securing that the conversation does not come to a standstill. Discontinuous code-switching has been described as a further formal means to fulfil important interactional functions, as it allows the parallel negotiation of two or more discourse strands within one line of conversation. While both interactional and cognitive functions of code-switching – unlike more prominent conceptual or interpersonal functions – have received little attention in previous research, the present study has highlighted their significance in TeenELF.

Insights have further been gained on more covert yet communicative influential practices of translanguaging, such as hybrid word formation, calquing and inferences based on diverging linguacultural conceptualizations. The importance of transparency enhancing devices for a securing of communicative success particularly in the context of more covert practices of translanguaging has been emphasized.

Part III: **Discussion**

11 Summary and critical reflection

English as a Lingua Franca as used by adolescents from Tanzania and Germany in intercultural interactions has emerged from the present analyses as an encompassing transcultural negotiation space. Drawing on a broad range of interactional means from their full linguacultural repertoires, students do not only negotiate meanings and manage rapport in this space, but also co-construct their identities, which has been exposed as pivotal in, though not restricted to, teenage communication. As depicted in the Venn diagram of Figure 31, negotiations in all three areas often take place at the same time, though in a specific situation one particular aspect may be foregrounded. The present analyses have revealed adolescent interlocutors as competent communicators in ELF, who effectively employ a variety of interactional means in the service of these goals. This chapter provides a critical methodological reflection and a synopsis of linguistic findings in order to pave the way for a final discussion of theoretical implications, from which suggestions for language teaching will be derived (see Chapter 12).

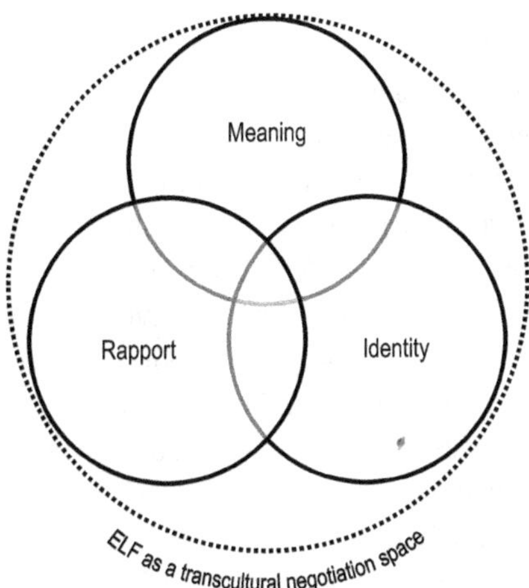

Figure 31: The transcultural negotiation space of ELF.

11.1 Methodological reflection

The overall research design applied allowed for a fine-grained qualitative analysis of teenagers' use of ELF in the given setting and the sketching out of cross-sectional trends and micro-diachronic developments. Due to the relatively small

https://doi.org/10.1515/9783110786576-011

corpus size, findings from quantitative analyses of TeenELF corpus data, however, must be treated with much care and read as tentative tendencies only, in need of back-up studies based on larger databases (see Schlüter 2019: 198). Sociolinguistic statements on the influence of gender on TeenELF interaction in particular seem problematic against the backdrop of the low number of male participants in the present study. Larger scale, more balanced follow-up studies are needed to gain more informative insights into this area.

As communication comprises more than words, research on intercultural pragmatics can gain informative insights from multimodal analyses as conducted through video-analysis in a growing number of studies (e.g. Schröder 2014; Huensch 2017; Brunner et al. 2017). Video-recordings, however, were not deemed feasible in the given context: in addition to the fact that some participants were hesitant to agree on being video-recorded while not objecting to audio-recordings, the equipment would not have allowed for the recording of the given number of parallel conversations. In order to also gain some insights into the non-verbal communication of teenagers in the given ELF context, two sequences from group works were video-recorded, which, however, turned out to be of little relevance for a context-sensitive analysis of conversations in dialogues. A rewarding and pragmatically feasible compromise would have been to complement the audio-recordings by a given number of video-recordings taken in the same settings.

Some passages within the retrospective interviews are found to show social desirability effects along the line of Spencer-Oatey's (2007: 654) arguing "that such post-event comments may be unreliable reconstructions, or may themselves be enactments of face with the researcher" (see also Krug & Sell 2013: 75). Potential distortive effects, however, are minimized by placing the actual conversational data and conversation analysis first. Altogether, interviews grant important retrospective insights into the participants' experiences and metalinguistic awareness. It would therefore have been helpful in the analysis to be able to resort to a broader base of interview data, the compilation of which did not founder on a lack of interview partners, but rather on the restrictions of a densely packed timetable.

The task of pragmatic data annotation turned out to be demanding for reasons which Weisser (2015: 84) further explicates. He observes that "[a]ny type of linguistic annotation is a highly complex and interpretive process, but none more so than pragmatic annotation" and ascribes the particular complexity here to "the fact that this type of annotation, unlike, for example, POS (part-of-speech) or semantic tagging/annotation, almost always needs to take into account levels above the individual word and may even need to refer to contextual information beyond those textual units that are commonly referred to as a 'sentence' or 'utterance'". In a kind of vicious circle, the annotation process itself requires a previous analysis of context, which on the other hand is to be accomplished in the subsequent analysis of annotated items. While adjustments are possible in the process of fine-grained qualitative analysis (see Liddicoat 2011: 74), larger-scale quantitative analyses often arrive at findings without another closer look on context. This problem has to be kept in mind with regard to quantitative analyses applied to the TeenELF corpus data, which further strengthens a conceptualization of the findings as tendencies rather than monolithic truths.

A different kind of problem arises when it comes to an analysis of the communicative means of translanguaging as conducted in the present study (see Chapter 10), as the researcher's bias will bear an undeniable influence on findings. Any researcher will (or will not) be able to detect and interpret translanguaging, particularly when it comes to more covert phenomena, against the backdrop of his or her own linguacultural background. While in the present study the researcher as an L1 speaker of German with a sound basic knowledge of Swahili tried to counter the given bias to some degree by consulting a Tanzanian Swahili speaker, a gross analytical imbalance in favour of German influenced translanguaging cannot be denied. Ideally, researchers from different linguacultural backgrounds should equitably work together to arrive at understandings of translanguaging as deep as possible.

The overall research design, however, turned out to meet the various demands introduced at the beginning of the chapter very well. Students vividly engaged in meaningful ELF interactions, in which they exchanged ideas and information, negotiated relationships and reflected their identities. The participants felt to benefit from the dialogues so much that they expressed the urgent wish to implement the format as a regular element of the annual student encounters, which has meanwhile been put into practice by accompanying teachers. The design developed in the framework of the present research has thus not only proven a sustainable format participants have felt to profit from, but has, exactly because of its beneficial nature, also provided the researcher with rich natural data for linguistic analyses.

11.2 Summary of central findings

In response to the overall research question of the present study, fine-grained conversation analyses have disclosed how teenagers participating in a German-Tanzanian student exchange employ linguistic and paralinguistic resources in ELF to reach their primary communicative aims: the negotiation of meaning, rapport, and identity. Key strategies have been exemplified by the use of repetition and repair, the realization of the speech act of complimenting, the use of humour and laughter, and the employment of translanguaging as major interactional devices.

Supporting previous findings from ELF research (see e.g. Cogo 2016a: 83), repetition and repair have been found to constitute central means to increase explicitness and secure intersubjective understanding. Framing, or distant self-repetition, has been worked out and described as a pervasive strategy used abundantly in the TeenELF corpus, not only to enhance explicitness, but also to provide cognitive support and structure the discourse by creating cohesion. While the omnipresence of repair, particularly of self-initiated self-repair, further corroborates earlier discoveries, the present data exhibit a relative abundance of other-involvement in repair. Learner identities and interpersonal peer factors appear to play major roles contributing to the given frequency of this phenomenon.

In favour of rapport building, an overall positive parlance is employed, with complimenting standing out as a commonly used speech act. The present findings suggest that complimenting in intercultural teenage communication shows distinctive features with regard to objects and forms. Deviating from findings in English L1 settings, complimenting in TeenELF does not primarily attend to appearance or possessions, but rather addresses non-material targets such as behaviour, ways of living, abilities or achievements, which, however, will also partly be due to the communicative tasks and topics in the given setting. Short structures of the syntactic pattern *(ADV) ADJ (NP)* enjoy great popularity in TeenELF, which can be ascribed to their versatility and easy comprehensibility. Lexical preferences such as *cool* and *wow* serve as identity markers, showing clear influences of youth languages. Compliment responses suggest cross-linguacultural influences, with compliment acceptance forming the overall strategy of choice in the present data.

Students further employ laughter and humour as versatile means for their management of rapport, but also as markers of identity. Depending on the context, laughter may contribute to relationship building, be employed to deal with interpersonally difficult situations, or give expression to shared joy and happiness. The micro-longitudinal design of the present study has made both quantitative and qualitative changes in the students' use of laughter observable. Against the backdrop of a growing acquaintance of participants, the present data show an overall rising tendency in the frequency of laughter, with shy laughter giving way to happy laughter, interspersed with nervous laughter to accompany communicatively difficult situations where necessary. As a paraverbal means, laughter proves particularly useful in ELF as it continues to exert communicative functions even where verbal communication reaches its boundaries.

These same limits are also overcome by practices of translanguaging, which have been disclosed as pervasive in the present corpus. Drawing on their full linguacultural repertoires, students expose ELF as a fluid and hybrid phenomenon, deconstructing essentialist conceptualizations of clear-cut community-language-culture units, which have dominated scientific and public discourse for a long time (see also

Piller 2007: 211–214; Seidlhofer 2010: 64; Baker 2018a: 30–31). Translanguaging has been shown to work along various degrees of transparency, which has been thrown into relief as a central feature when it comes to communicative effectiveness. A transparency model for translanguaging has been proposed to both facilitate a categorization of translanguaging phenomena, and to provide a framework for a better understanding of the relationship between different modes of translanguaging and communicative effectiveness (see Section 10.2.2). The suggested continuum of formal transparency in translanguaging ranges from culturally influenced conceptualizations at the covert end to calquing and other semi-transparent phenomena to code-switching on the overt end of the scale. Formal transparency affects the perceptibility of translanguaging for both speaker and hearer, which can further be enhanced through the use of TEDs (i.e. transparency enhancing devices). The three interrelated dimensions of transparency in translanguaging (i.e. formal, speaker, and hearer transparency) have been suggested to project into a three-dimensional space, in which any interactional instance of translanguaging can be located on the basis of its context-dependent overall transparency. As it postulates communicative success to rise with an increase of the overall transparency, the model unfolds its pedagogical potential, promoting the striving for a maximization of transparency as a major learning objective in language teaching.

The following section explores some pedagogical implications of the findings presented here, revealing the high relevance of empirical linguistic research for advancements in language teaching.

12 Implications of linguistic findings for language teaching

As teaching never takes place in a sociocultural vacuum, the same global developments which have instigated ELF research must also influence English language teaching (ELT) (see Seidlhofer & Widdowson 2020: 325). Pedagogical implications of ELF research have indeed been considered from the onset of investigations into ELF (see e.g. Beneke 1991; Jenkins 2000: 123–232). Debates on how to prepare students best for using English as a Lingua Franca in most various settings have gained force in recent years (see e.g. Bowles & Cogo 2015; Bayyurt & Akcan 2015; Tatsioka et al. 2018). While a number of suggestions have been put forward with regard to conceptual implications and new approaches in teacher education so as to work on teachers' sets of knowledge, attitudes and beliefs (see e.g. Seidlhofer & Widdowson 2020; Choi & Liu 2020; Dewey 2021), only few changes in classroom practices seem to have been realized so far (see Bayyurt & Dewey 2020: 370). This theory-practice gap has on the one hand been put down to conservative testing practices mostly orienting towards traditional standards of English (on current developments concerning ELF-oriented testing practices, see Jenkins 2020), and a lack of concrete classroom suggestions on the other (for notable exceptions, see e.g. Kordia 2020; Sifakis et al. 2020). It may be due to the fact that contextual language use lies at the very heart of any ELF paradigm that researchers have remained hesitant with recommending concrete actions for implementation in highly diverse teaching contexts. However, tangible examples of classroom practices appear decisive for encouraging teachers to put an ELF-orientation in ELT into effect.

Linking in with ongoing debates, this chapter will not only look at conceptual consequences, but will also explore more concrete classroom implications of the linguistic findings on ELF interactions among adolescents which have been portrayed in the present study. As theoretical and practical developments need to go hand in hand, it will start with conceptual implications to be fed into ELF-aware teacher education, and will continue to explore more tangible changes in classroom practices.

12.1 Conceptual implications

ELF research has called into question some well-established concepts lying at the very heart of ELT (see Seidlhofer 2011: 70–91; Widdowson 2012). The present section takes up this discussion and explores the central concepts of language and

https://doi.org/10.1515/9783110786576-012

culture, learner-users and linguistic correctness versus appropriateness on the basis of the linguistic findings from teenage ELF use as presented in previous chapters (Chapters 6 to 10).

12.1.1 Fluid and hybrid concepts of language and culture

While "essentialist national language and culture correlations are still prominent in language teaching, especially ELT" (Baker 2021: 11), many ELF studies, including the present one, have pointed to the inappropriateness of fixed language-culture concepts. In a post-structuralist perspective, most ELF scholars view languages and cultures as "non-finite, non-bounded, inherently dynamic, emergent, unstable and heterogeneous" entities (Pitzl 2022: 64; see also Baker 2011: 209; Cogo 2016a: 88).

A social-constructivist approach to language learning in Kohn's (2018) sense requires a conceptualization of language itself as an open, fluid and malleable system, which often runs counter not only to differentialist perspectives in language teaching, but also to teachers' normative mindsets and epistemic beliefs (see Illés 2016: 140; Blair 2017). It has hardly found entry into teacher education so far, either (see Dewey 2021: 618). In ELF interactions, which per definition involve speakers of different linguacultural backgrounds, however, this fluid nature of language becomes most obvious (see e.g. Hülmbauer 2016; Cogo 2018b). Students' ELF interactions as transcribed in the TeenELF corpus show an abundant use of translanguaging practices, in which interlocutors blur the boundaries between clear-cut languages on all linguistic levels, from phonetics to morpho-syntax to lexicology, semantics and pragmatics (see Section 10.2.1). ELF in particular, but also language in general emerge as complex adaptive systems (see Larsen-Freeman 2018, but also Baker 2015), with interlocutors adapting their language use to fit situational needs by drawing on their full linguistic repertoire.

The exploration of translanguaging practices in teenage ELF interactions also sheds further light on the nature of and relationship between culture and language. Covert and overt practices of translanguaging go hand in hand with practices of transculturing (see Section 2.2.3), with cultural concepts of various sources finding entry into and expression through ELF. On a semantic level, linguacultural conceptualizing, for example, allows a single English lexeme such as *family*, *book* or *boyfriend* to be loaded with various speaker-specific cultural concepts (see Section 10.4.4).

While the data illustrate a close relationship between language and culture, with language moulding culture and vice versa, they also demonstrate very clearly the dynamic nature of and relationship between both semiotic systems, which combine in multifarious and ever-changing ways. Western ideas of monolithic and clear-cut language-culture-nation units and stable boundaries hence seem inappropriate in ELT if it seeks to live up to the global reality of English as a Lingua Franca. They need to give way to more fluid and hybrid concepts of linguacultures (Risager 2012), appearing more apt in the face of local, regional and global diversity. When teachers and students get the chance to experience linguacultural relativity and complexity (see Ehrhart 2015: 309; Holmes & Dervin 2016: 17–18) and enact variability and hybridity in using ELF, essentialist conceptualizations of monolithic language-culture-nation units can be deconstructed in the classroom and beyond.

12.1.2 The concept of learner-users

The adolescent students in the present study display their identities as language learners, which also wield influence on their communicative behaviour, showing for instance in their noticeable openness to other-repair (see Section 7.4). At the same time, the conversational data clearly demonstrate how these learners build on their acquired proficiency in English and successfully employ interactional strategies in ELF – such as enhancing explicitness through repeating or rephrasing or exploiting their multilingual repertoires – to reach their communicative goals. In reflective interviews, several students participating in the exchange expressed their surprise and excitement about how easily they were able to communicate with each other (Int_Etf, Int_HTf, Int_GrG). Learners of English emerge as competent users of the language at the same time as they still acquire language knowledge, prompting a reconceptualization from a consecutive relationship between learners and users towards a more integrative and simultaneous view of *learner-users* (see Seidlhofer 2011: 189; Widdowson 2012: 5; see also Kohn's (2018: 5–14) concept of *speaker-learners*).

When learners are provided the chance to experience themselves as interactionally successful users of the target language in authentic contexts, this will boost their self-confidence and have positive motivational effects on their learning behaviour (see Seidlhofer 2004: 229; Vettorel 2013: 166–167). Using ELF in various settings can also go hand in hand with the insight that no single group of 'native' speakers "owns" the language (see Widdowson 1994: 382), but that English is a tool available for everyone to employ to his or her very own communicative needs in contextually different ways. While learner-users may not, for example, have the same range of lexical devices at their disposal as 'native' speakers do, they may as multilingual speakers benefit from an increased pragmatic and cultural awareness and can employ communicative strategies to accommodate their use of ELF to situation-specific needs. At the same time, authentic communicative contexts may also make learner-users aware of their individual linguistic shortcomings, such as insufficient lexical, structural or semantic knowledge, and promote their motivation to further engage in language learning.

While communicative strategies and corresponding linguistic phenomena such as repetition, repair and translanguaging, are basically the same for learners of English and ELF users, they tend to be judged very differently depending on the context: devalued as learner errors and interferences in prescriptive school settings, while praised as communicative resources offering the potential of adaptation to diverse contexts in ELF settings. An ELF-informed pedagogy needs to try and conciliate these two perspectives (see Seidlhofer & Widdowson 2020: 329), orienting ELT to the communicative needs that come along with the use of English as a global language. This implies a reconsideration of goals and assessment practices, in which the focus shifts from correctness to contextual appropriateness and a functional perspective on language in use.

12.1.3 From correctness to appropriateness

The TeenELF corpus data illustrate how communicative success does not necessarily depend on grammatical 'correctness' – often measured against disputable monolingual 'native' speaker standard norms (see Baker 2020: 258) – but emerges from situationally appropriate interactional behaviour (see also Widdowson 2015: 364). It is this concept of pragmatic appropriateness, which needs to receive more prominent weight in communicatively oriented language classes (see Seidlhofer 2011: 14; Cogo 2016a: 88). While normative learning contexts cannot and do not need to dispose of orientation-providing norms, the choice of contextually appropriate norms has to follow learners' needs and local realities (see Dewey 2012: 163). ELT in a paradigm of English as a Global Language needs to put any such norms into perspective and make learner-users familiar with diverse forms and functions of English step by step (see Rose & Galloway 2019: 16). At the same time, learner-users need to be encouraged to make the language their own[113] through social interaction and use it to their respective communicative needs, which goes along with a redistribution of power from 'native' speakers to *all* speakers of English. Seidlhofer (2011: 23) has called for more "detailed accounts of ELF inter-

113 Kohn (2018: 4) introduces the concept of *MY English* to emphasize the creative and social-constructivist process of language learning and speaking, and emphasizes the idiosyncratic nature of the target language (see also Widdowson 2012: 23).

actions [. . .] to counter the pervasive myth that adherence to ENL norms is necessary for effective intercultural communication", some of which are provided in the present study. Extract (130) illustrates on the one hand how ELF speakers orient their speech towards external norms ("is it the right word?", l. 533), but also how 'native' speaker norms may become irrelevant in ELF ("i(@)t doesn't matter", l. 534; 536) as they turn out unnecessary for intersubjective understanding ("it's fine", l. 536).

(130) 533 **ATf:** {writing} <friends> exploring the social media? is it the right word like "exploring"? exploring s-? (2)
534 **AGf:** well [i(@)t doesn't]
535 **ATf:** [@]
536 **AGf:** matter i think @ (.) it's fine @@

(A3_533-536)

The "aggressively promoted" (Holmes & Dervin 2016: 18) implicit or explicit prevalence of English as a 'native' language in ELT contexts has led many teachers, parents, linguists and especially lay people to regard 'non-native' speakers as somewhat "deficient" communicators (see Seidlhofer 2011: 41), a conceptualization which ELF research like the present study has substantially called into question. Interactional self-empowerment, which finds expression in ELF speakers' ability to use language towards their personal intentions (see also Alexander 2012: 2), needs to be complemented by discursive other-empowerment through an acknowledgment of ELF speakers as competent communicators.

Although a paradigmatic change from correctness to appropriateness, or from accuracy to communicative effectiveness (see Bayyurt & Dewey 2020: 371) has repeatedly been suggested in ELF-informed teaching approaches, 'standard'-oriented testing practices in particular have been pointed out as major obstacles when it comes to putting this change into effect.[114] It is not only in the area of testing that ELT practitioners would benefit from more concrete suggestions for classroom applications in order to translate an ELF-orientation into their teaching practices. In order to address this need, Section 12.2 will explore some more concrete classroom implications of ELF research, particularly as arising from the present study, hoping to provide ELT practitioners with further ideas.

---

114 For an overview of current debates on testing practices in an ELF-oriented framework, see Jenkins 2020.

12.1.4 The pivotal role of teacher education

Reconceptualizations along the lines outlined in this chapter can only gain ground in ELT through language teachers (see Bayyurt & Dewey 2020: 373), who serve as multipliers and role models at the same time. Pre- and in-service teacher education becomes the linchpin, which needs to provide space for critical reflection and discussion. In their prominent model of teachers' professional competence, Baumert & Kunter (2011:32) name four central aspects contributing to this professional competence, namely 1) motivational orientations, 2) self-regulation, 3) beliefs, values and goals and 4) professional knowledge. Two of these aspects appear of specific importance here: ELF-informed teacher education particularly needs to address teachers' values, beliefs and goals (see Illés 2016: 137; 140) as well as their content and pedagogical content knowledge as components of their professional knowledge.

While (future) teachers build their professional knowledge about English as a global language on adequate informational input, any explorations of and attempts to leave impacts on beliefs, values and goals must necessarily include dialogic and reflective approaches (see e.g. Dewey 2012: 141). Illés (2016: 143) emphasizes that "[d]oubts and criticism expressed by teachers can contribute to a fruitful and necessary dialogue between teachers and researchers which can have long-term effects on teachers and their teaching of English". Bayyurt & Dewey (2020: 373) propose action research and opportunities for critical reflection as central for raising teachers' awareness of ELF. Discussions in university classrooms, the conduction of interviews, cooperative research projects, in-service training and joint teaching can all serve to facilitate this dialogue between ELF researchers and pre- and in-service teachers, which may change mindsets and can support a sustainable implementation of practical changes in the classroom so as to pay tribute to the role of English as a global language and lingua franca.

The following section will finally feed findings from my interactional research on teenage ELF communication and from conceptual considerations as outlined above into more concrete suggestions for classroom implications. It also incorporates ideas which have emerged in conversations with teachers and students and is hoped to encourage further critical examinations and debates from ELF researchers and ELT practitioners alike.

12.2 Classroom implications

Linguacultural awareness-raising "emerges as the bedrock on which an ELF-orientation to pedagogy is founded" (Bowles 2015: 198). Enabling interlocutors to critically reflect and contextually adapt their own communicative behaviour must be considered a pivotal objective for both teacher education and classroom practices in any globally oriented language teaching approach. As language unfolds its communicative potential in a situation-specific way, students need to be offered the chance to practice the decoding and encoding of English messages in a large variety of contexts. If learners are to be taken seriously in their role as present and future users of English in a globalized world, this must include ELF contexts to a substantial degree, as these constitute the vast majority of contact situations in which English is used as a medium of communication.

While building on Byram's (1997) highly influential model and goal of *intercultural communicative competence* (ICC), the present approach operates with a more fluid and hybrid conceptualization of language and culture in Baker's (2011) sense. Baker (2011; 2018) has suggested *intercultural awareness* (ICA) as a central pedagogical goal to strive for, with interculturally aware speakers able to adapt their Englishes to contextual needs. Focussing on communication as a relative and dynamic cultural practice, ICA supersedes Byram's concept of ICC in an ELF-informed approach, which criticizes ICC for its nation-bound, differentialist baseline and its "lack of engagement with the current role of English as a global lingua franca outside of Anglophone settings" (Baker 2018a: 32). Baker (2020: 268) calls for an "expanded range of skills, knowledge, and attitudes related to language, communication, and culture" and an awareness for "the importance of flexibility, process, and contextualisation".

In a specification of Baker's (2018a: 33) concept and educational objective of ICA, I here suggest to particularly emphasize the importance of pragmatics in a situation-specific and co-constructive perspective of communication. At the same time, a transcultural viewpoint allows for a perception of the fluid and hybrid nature of language and culture, and for a perspective on diversity which takes into consideration far more than geographical and national points of reference. *Transcultural pragmatic awareness* (TPA) is hence proposed as a key overall learning target within the framework of an ELF-aware ELT. I conceptualize TPA as an understanding of how cultural influences meet and merge in communicative acts, contributing to a context-dependent and situation-specific use of language. Findings from the TeenELF corpus-based interactional analyses presented in Chapters 6 to 10 are here taken as a starting point for a development of ideas on how to promote TPA in the language classroom. Next to calling for a strengthening of pragmatics, the following sections will explore how the trans-turn can be put into effect and how students can learn to enhance transparency and exploit their multilingual repertoires to communicative success. As Jenkins (2007: 233) points out, reflective competences also allow for a critical consideration of self-concepts, the negotiation of which has been argued to be a central issue for adolescents in particular: "[W]e all – NSs and NNSs [i.e. native speakers and non-native-speakers] of English – need to think about *why* we make our linguistic choices and what attitudes and beliefs (and myths) inform the identities we accept for ourselves and ascribe to others [italics in original]".

12.2.1 Strengthening pragmatics

Students participating in the research project have been shown to employ ELF – consciously or unconsciously – to manifold communicative ends. If ELT succeeds in making learner-users aware of the content-related, interpersonal and identificatory functions of language, which may situationally take on different weights, it can contribute its share to educating "responsible communicators" (Holmes & Dervin 2016: 11), well-equipped for successfully participating in a world of diversity. In response to "the need to increase learners' awareness of the functions and use of [pragmatic] strategies in interaction" (Kaur 2022: 49), pragmatic competence and performance need to receive a stronger focus in ELT.[115]

Contrastive scenarios can help learners explore situation-dependent differences in language use. In a first receptive step, students may be invited to observe how interlocutors adapt their communicative behaviour when situational parameters change. Basic conversation analytic tools such as sequence analysis or knowledge of utterance pair structure (see Section 3.1), and elementary insights into politeness theory, such as Brown and Levinson's (1987) face concept and Leech's (1983) conversational maxims (see Section 3.2), can help advanced language students detect and reflect pragmatic strategies and interactional means. On the basis of receptive awareness-raising, students can then test out impacts of their own communicative behaviour in role-plays with changing settings, which they are invited to reflect upon either orally or in writing. In a peer-learning approach, fellow students may be asked to comment on these role-plays on the basis of pragmatic observation criteria. Learner-users will finally get the chance to apply and further refine their pragmatic competence in authentic interactions (see Figure 32).

If ELT aims at bringing students up to the global reality of English, these opportunities must involve ELF interactions of most various kinds, including situations void of English L1 speakers. In addition to bearing the advantage of immensely widening the possibilities of real-life interactions, this line appears particularly fitting

115 For the German context, this has also been pointed out by the large-scale DESI study (*Deutsch-Englisch Schülerleistungen International*, a study measuring German students' performances in German and English; see Schröder 2007: 295).

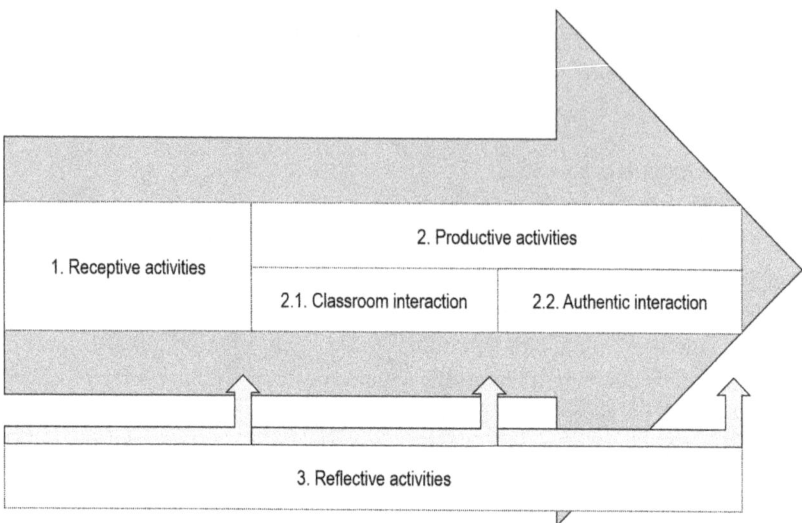

Figure 32: The development of pragmatic competence.

in an experimental and constructive approach to language learning: ELF interlocutors have been found to not take common ground for granted but to expect lingua franca communication to be a constant negotiation space (see e.g. Cogo 2016a: 83), hence acting tolerantly and cooperatively to large degrees. ELF settings may accordingly provide contexts in which learner-users experience the necessary freedom and confidence to put their English to a test in a real-life encounter and engage in processes of negotiation and co-construction. Research on teenage ELF communication suggests that particularly peer interaction in ELF can provide anxiety-free learner-user environments, especially since relational ground proves relatively easy to establish against a backdrop of shared roles, interests and problems. It is hoped that the present study will enrich interactional approaches in language teaching, in which the interdependency of meaning, rapport and identity can be explored.

12.2.2 Putting the trans-turn into effect

While applied linguistics and ELF research have seen a comprehensive trans-turn taking place in recent years (see Section 2.2.3), fluid and hybrid conceptualizations of language, culture and identity have hardly found entry into educational contexts so far. Although teachers often hold fast to stable and monolithic ideas of languages and cultures (see Section 12.1.1), both students and teachers themselves engage in various processes of transculturing and translanguaging, and use transmodal means at the same time. ELF-oriented language teaching should offer learners the possibility to explore and reflect their transcultural identities and consciously exploit their translingual and transmodal repertoires.

Transculturing

While traditional communication models have focused on content-related and interpersonal aspects of language use (see Watzlawick et al. 1967), the present study has exposed an additional identificatory function vividly at play in ELF interactions between teenagers (see Section 5.3). School contexts – especially at secondary level, as questions of identity become particularly salient during adolescence (see Erikson 1959: 88–94) – need to address questions of identity in communication and provide teenagers with ample opportunities to reflect and re-construct their self-concepts. Inter- and transcultural encounters provide most suitable environments as they offer students – and teachers no less – the chance to sharpen their self-concepts in comparing them with various other models at play. In intercultural and transcultural communication, interlocutors engage in a communicative negotiation and co-construction of identities, consciously or subconsciously experiencing the natural fluency and hybridity of (not only) identity, which in turn strongly interacts with language practices and cultural beliefs (see Sections 2.2.2 and 3.3).

Developing transcultural awareness and transcultural competence then become important learning objectives. The construction of transcultural competence can be viewed "as a multidimensional transformative process that challenges [learners'] taken-for-granted frames of references", involving cognitive, affective and social dimensions alike (Jurkova 2021: 108). Clear-cut boundaries between self and other as established in contrastive approaches give way to inclusive understandings of interconnectedness and transculturality (see Jurkova 2021: 102), helping students to comprehend and engage in the increasingly globalized world they live in (see Grimm, Meyer & Volkmann 2015: 163).

ELT can offer various opportunities for an exploration of transcultural identities and for promoting transcultural awareness and competence. While student exchanges of various kinds undoubtedly constitute some of the most effective learning environments in this regard, the realization of face-to-face ELF encounters between learner-users from different linguacultural backgrounds will mostly represent rare highlights restricted in frequency for reasons of time, money, ecology and political or medical reasons. Digital formats such as the globally operating network E-Pals (see Cricket Media n.y.) or the EU based programme E-Twinning (see European Commission n.y.) provide valuable alternatives for a facilitation of intercultural student exchanges to be realized more easily and set up very flexibly.

Learner-users can additionally be encouraged to monitor their private intercultural encounters taking place beyond the classroom, for example when talking to tourists or engaging with people from various parts of the world via social media, where they employ ELF extensively. Transcultural learning, however, can also take place in the absence of real-life interlocutors when students get a chance to engage with cultural artefacts such as music, literature or films. Teachers can offer their students opportunities to reflect their own transcultural identities through providing suitable reading or film material, which may display various contrastive, potentially challenging yet relatable life concepts. It is particularly in these virtual contexts that students can also experiment with alternative identities, for example in producing pieces of writing from various perspectives or slipping into the role of an avatar (see e.g. Oddcast Inc n.y.).

It almost goes without saying that all these activities must be well prepared, adaptively attended and critically reflected if linguacultural learning is to take place. Prior to any intercultural encounter, teachers and students need to engage with their exchange partners' local conditions. Linguistic means for a flexible and situationally adaptable use of ELF, such as a reflective use of repair mechanisms, need to be introduced in class, and discussed, practised and evaluated for their usefulness. Meta-communicative in-between and post-hoc reflections can provide learner-users with ample opportunities to discuss cultural differences and overlaps they experience, as well as transformations they realize taking place within themselves or others. Pair and group discussions, blogs, portfolios and learning diaries can all contribute to enhancing the students' linguacultural awareness and reflective competence.

Translanguaging

Transculturing also transpires in multiple practices of translanguaging (see Section 2.2.4). In line with findings from previous ELF research, the present study has shown adolescent users of ELF to draw on their full linguistic repertoires when negotiating meaning, rapport and identities in intercultural interactions (see Chapter 10).

Answering to a global reality in which multilingualism constitutes the norm rather than the exception and translanguaging takes place in most various forms and settings, pedagogic debates have now started to address multilingualism and translanguaging on a larger scale (see e.g. Schmid & Schmidt 2017; Cenoz 2019). For the European context, this shows for instance in the companion volume to the CEFR (Common European Framework of Reference) where plurilingual and pluricultural competence have been taken up as key concepts (see Council of Europe 2018: 4,

123–128; Burwitz-Melzer 2019), although trans-concepts still remain without explicit mentioning. Multilingualism has been proposed to play a major role in the promotion of language awareness, and vice versa (see Lenz 2009; Schnuch 2015). Raising plurilingually aware speakers who may use their full linguistic resources to further communicative effectiveness now constitutes a central objective.

In spite of its promising potential for second language learning, which large-scale studies have pointed to (e.g. *DESI* study; see Hesse et al. 2008: 214), multilingualism has often been ignored or even actively discouraged in educational contexts (see Schnuch 2015: 130; Jenkins 2015: 79). Accordingly, multilingualism is often perceived as a problem by multilingual students themselves (see Elsner 2015: 73), even though it may constitute a central component of their self-concept at the same time.[116] This deficit approach needs to give way to an encompassing perspective of multilingualism as a pragmatic resource, as suggested by the present study. Multilingualism needs to be acknowledged and harnessed as the point of departure and striven for as a major target in an inclusive language education which aims at appreciating and incorporating all students' resources. This includes an appreciation of translanguaging practices which multilingual speakers naturally employ for communicative purposes.

When it comes to classroom implications, it seems vital to first and foremost help students acknowledge multilingualism as a communicative resource rather than a hindrance (see Busse 2017). For ELT, this requires a replacement of the traditional role model of a monolingual 'native' speaker of English by the model of a competent multilingual ELF speaker (see Galloway & Rose 2015: 208). Students can learn to appreciate their own multilingual identities when experiencing themselves as interactionally successful multilingual users rather than as deficient language learners unable to attain 'native' speaker standards. Exploring the various forms and functions of translanguaging in everyday communication can help sensitize students for the communicative potential of their own multilingual resources. Audio-recordings and transcripts, including examples from the students' own language use, can be integrated to have them systematically investigated by students for different translanguaging phenomena. The taxonomy developed in the present study, which focuses on formal transparency as a structuring criterion (see

---

116 Researchers have pointed to the substantial problem that discriminating, prestige-based differences have frequently been made between those speakers whose multilingualism is accepted, praised and rewarded, and others whose multilingualism either remains invisible or is viewed as a problem (see Weinmann & Arber 2017; Ortega 2018). Migrants' multilingual resources, for instance, may be neglected or viewed as a pedagogical problem if the social discourse on multilingualism is primarily tied to an overall problem-oriented discourse of migration, while multilingualism involving high-prestige school subject languages may actively be promoted at the same time.

Figure 24, Section 10.2.1), can help teachers and students to become aware of the various forms that translanguaging can take.

Teachers can take up spontaneous acts of translanguaging in the classroom, but may also use translanguaging consciously as a pedagogical tool (see Cenoz 2019: 77): they can, for instance, resort to a common L1 to explain challenging contents or help their students exploit cognates from their linguistic repertoire to grasp the meaning of new lexemes in an additional language (see also Council of Europe 2018: 158).

As ELF interlocutors in intercultural encounters draw on different linguacultural repertoires, translanguaging, however, also bears the danger of communicative failure. Transcripts of critical incidents can help students become aware of potential pitfalls. I have suggested transparency as the decisive criterion for the communicative success of translanguaging (see Section 10.2.2), the pedagogic potential of which will be explored in Section 12.2.3.

Transmodalities

The complexity described above for linguistic repertoires of ELF speakers extends beyond verbal semiotic means and includes various modes of expression, which interlocutors again draw on simultaneously. Educational contexts need to make students aware of their multimodal means and help them implement them best for communicative success.

As common ground cannot be taken for granted in intercultural communication (see e.g. Kecskés 2014: 2), interlocutors find themselves in a constant process of negotiation. Research on teenage ELF interactions has revealed the complementing potential offered by a combination of written and oral modes for a successful negotiation of meanings. Some misunderstandings only become apparent when written down and can then be clarified orally, with interlocutors resorting to repetition and rephrasing as needs arise (see e. g. *laugh* vs. *love*, Section 7.4). Writing may also be consciously used to overcome problems in understanding which go down to differences in pronunciation, a phenomenon not uncommon in intercultural interaction (see example of CO_2, Section 7.3). In spiral negotiation processes of meaning making, ambiguities and misunderstandings arising in oral interactions become visible when written down, and can then be re-negotiated, which will result in an overall increase of transparency.

The potential of combining oral and written channels to create more room for the negotiation of understanding can be revealed, practised and internalized in ELT contexts as a tool particularly valid in intercultural contexts. Oral and written tasks may be combined and merged in most various ways and formats in the classroom: students may, for example, summarize spoken dialogues in a written form for posters, school magazines or blogs, engage in silent discussions then to be taken up orally, or watch movies with subtitles to explore the capacity of this interface in its various facets. Intercultural encounters, exchanges and further communicative settings are recommended to be accompanied by meaningful written tasks to be processed in pair or group work – along the lines of the dia|log|books in the present study – so as to enhance the interlocutors' negotiation space and invite students to practice profound interaction. This way it can also be ensured that competences of speaking and hearing, writing and reading are equally addressed.

In a similar way, communicators may resort not only to verbal channels for their en- and decoding of messages, but will also take para- and non-verbal means into account. This becomes particularly relevant in intercultural encounters once again, where verbal means may hit their limits. Research on teenage ELF interactions has, for instance, explored the versatile use of laughter, which has been shown to particularly address the relational side of communication. Students employ laughter amongst others as icebreakers in order to start building rapport, as fill-ins when dealing with interactionally difficult situations, or as an expression of shared joy and happiness (see Section 9.2).

As para- and non-verbal communicative means such as intonation, smiling and laughter, gesture and facial expressions centrally contribute to intercultural interaction in culture-specific ways, language teaching set in a global framework of diversity needs to sensitize learner-users to the multimodality of communication and enable them to read and consciously employ signals on channels other than the verbal. The pragmatic triad of passive reception, active application and meta-communicative reflection (see Figure 32 in Section 12.2.1) offers a helpful scaffold once again for classroom implementations seeking to address this desideratum. Video-recordings can help students realize and reflect their own and others' use of para- and non-verbal instruments. Contrastive approaches playing either on the employment or non-employment of particular means, or on culturally diverse uses of individual channels may help students recognize and assess chances and challenges in the use of para- and non-verbal means in intercultural communication. Exaggerating for the sake of recognition, however, bears the danger of cultural stereotyping once more, which teachers have to reflect and discursively counteract, for instance by providing material which also illustrates individual, intra-ethnic variation, and by explicitly discussing cultural conceptualizations in class.

12.2.3 Enhancing transparency

Working against a backdrop of linguacultural and modal complexity, intercultural communication is often marked by a high degree of explicitness to ensure mutual understanding. Teenage ELF interlocutors in the present study have been shown to employ both pre-empting and repair strategies extensively to make their communicative intentions clear. Repetition, rephrasing, flagging and metalinguistic comments constitute major interactional means, which are successfully exploited to enhance clarity.

In adapting their degree of explicitness, students exhibit reflective awareness and addressee orientation, which are considered highly valued assets in communicative-functional ELT approaches and can further be promoted through intercultural interaction. While pupils in ELT classrooms are often encouraged to practise rephrasing strategies in order to enlarge their expressive potential in the face of lexical constraints, the use of repetition on the other hand tends to be discouraged so as to avoid communicative redundancy. Teenage ELF interactions, however, have laid out the importance of repetition in intercultural interactions on the basis of its clarifying and discourse-structuring potential (see Section 6.2). Especially distant self-repetition, or framing, is extensively used in the TeenELF corpus as a scaffolding strategy to provide a golden thread, emphasizing central aspects and making them as clear or transparent as possible (see Section 6.3). Repetitions hence need to be reflected in ELT in their situational appropriateness and highlighted as a valid tool in intercultural interactions.

In the present study on teenage ELF interactions, transparency has further been exposed as a decisive factor for the communicative success of translanguaging. If interlocutors of diverse linguacultural backgrounds are to exploit their whole linguistic repertoire productively, they need to try and make acts of translanguaging maximum transparent to each other. Transparency in translanguaging has here been suggested to comprise the three interdependent facets of linguistic or formal transparency (F-transparency), speaker transparency (S-transparency) and hearer transparency (H-transparency) (see Section 10.2). The subjective constructs of S- and H-transparency are not only contingent upon the more objective category of F-transparency, which describes the degree of linguistically marked overtness in translanguaging, but also upon each other. The higher the formal transparency, the more likely translanguaging is to be perceived as such by both speaker and hearer. If either speaker or hearer becomes conscious of translanguaging, they can then try to make their interlocutor aware of it, too.

As conversation analysis in teenage ELF interactions has shown communicative success of translanguaging to depend on transparency, pedagogic endeavours should seek to enable students to strive for maximal individual and overall transparency in translanguaging if they want to exploit the communicative potential of translanguaging to the fullest. Interactional transparency builds on reflective awareness, which has been pointed to as a central learning objective above. Communicative acts will appear more transparent for metalinguistically and metaculturally aware interlocutors, who will in turn be able to make their own contributions more transparent for their interlocutors, thus enhancing their overall chance to reach communicative goals.

While metalinguistic awareness may generally help to enhance S- and H-transparency and must hence be emphasized as a central learning objective once more, research on teenage ELF interactions has also shown students to employ a number of linguistically more tangible transparency enhancing devices (TEDs), which ELT can take up in order to provide students with substantial tools to boost their chance for communicative success in intercultural interactions. TEDs include strategies such as flagging with an explicit mentioning of the additional code employed (e.g. "in Swahili, we call it. . ."), metalinguistic comments or questions, repetitions and paraphrasing as well as the provision of conceptual extensions. Inductive and deductive approaches can be used to familiarize students with these strategies.

12.3 Summary of implications

This chapter has explored conceptual as well as practical implications for ELT as they emerge from linguistic research on teenage ELF interactions. It has again emphasized the fluid and hybrid nature of not only language, but also of culture and identity, which are inextricably intertwined though never clearly running along national lines. ELT needs to make students aware of these variable and fluctuating relationships as well as of the situatedness and multifunctionality of language, which serves as a means to negotiate meanings, rapport and transcultural identities.

A strengthening of pragmatics in ELT has been proposed as a major approach, with an enhancing of transcultural pragmatic awareness (TPA) as the central learning objective so as to prepare students for interactions with diverse interlocutors in various settings. At the same time, ELT needs to provide students with methodological and linguistic means to successfully carry out negotiation processes, in which speakers may profit from a conscious exploitation of multimodal means. A negotiation of meanings between interlocutors of linguacultural diverse backgrounds has, for instance, been shown to profit from a combination of written and oral channels. Linking these channels on a regular base can be practised and habitualized within the ELT classroom; it can also provide best possible negotiation spaces in the framework of student exchanges and other extra-curricular learning arrangements. Students also need to be made aware of the importance of para- and non-verbal means as assets particularly valid in circumstances where verbal means may reach their limits. Further communicative potential lies in multilingual speakers' capacity to resort to more than one linguistic code. Strategies of translanguaging must hence not be banned from the language classroom, but need to receive due attention, particularly in ELT, as the global use of English as a Lingua Franca is inextricably linked to multilingualism.

The present research on teenage ELF interactions has demonstrated, however, that translanguaging can only unfold its full interactional potential when interlocutors strive for a maximization of transparency. Transparency enhancing devices (TEDs) such as flagging, repetition and rephrasing need to be explicated and practised as helpful tools for students to make their utterances more explicit in an overall hearer-oriented stance. Some practices often discouraged in the ELT classroom, such as code-switching and repetition, call for a context-specific re-evaluation in the framework of lingua franca oriented ELT concepts.

The analysis of teenage ELF interactions has highlighted the students' communicative potential. Conversations in ELF hence offer speakers a chance to experience themselves as overall successful communicators, able to negotiate meanings, build rapport and co-construct their transcultural identities through their use of English. Allowing ELF settings into ELT classrooms on a large scale will not only reflect the global use of English in a more adequate way and increase the possibilities for authentic interaction, but will also strengthen the learners' language user identity with positive motivational effects. Potentially intimidating experiences of inferiority when language use is primarily measured against monolingual 'native' speaker norms can give way to empowering experiences of communicative success in multilingual ELF interactions, in which the focus shifts from grammatical correctness to mutual intelligibility and communicative appropriateness. At the same time, students will experience the immediate usefulness of a broad base of lexical, grammatical and pragmatic devices for negotiation processes in contexts of diversity.

An encompassing ELF-orientation in ELT will need to affect various levels of teaching and learning. Figure 33 summarizes major aspects with regard to syllabi, teaching materials, methods, and assessment practices, which seem relevant to prepare students for inter- and transcultural communication in diverse contexts. On a systemic level, for instance, ELF, pragmatics and trans-concepts need to be consistently incorporated into curricula at school and university level alike. This should also affect teaching materials, where broad ranges of scenarios and tasks must pay tribute to ELF as a sociocultural reality and educational resource. Students participating in the present study considered different accents the most serious impediment to mutual understanding and evinced the explicit desire to see and particularly hear more of the diversity linked to ELF in the ELT classroom (see Int_GrG; Int_FGf). ELF contexts and authentic material can offer students a motivating chance to discover contexts in which they can apply their linguistic knowledge, and at the same time develop their language awareness in dealing with a *translingua franca*, which offers diverse multilingual references. Methodological approaches need to consider the chances and challenges of transmodality more seriously. On an individual level, it also seems vital that students are granted sufficient space to reflect their experiences, attitudes and self-concepts as multilingual speakers and global citizens, for example in language portfolios and learning diaries, but also in shorter or longer pair and group discussions. Any ELF orientation in ELT classrooms, however, must also take assessment practices into critical account, which bear a central influence on teaching contents and methods. Situational appropriateness rather than grammatical correctness, tested against disputable 'native' speaker standard norms, needs to receive a stronger focus in the setting and marking of assessments (see Section 12.1.3). It is this important area of ELF-oriented assessment practices which has been testified to be in particular need of further exploration and discussion (see Jenkins 2020: 475; for notable exceptions, see e.g. Harding & McNamara 2018; Shohamy 2018).

Classroom practices can only be adapted to the global reality of English by teachers who themselves have developed an awareness of the situated use and formal-functional diversity of English. The changes proposed here hence need to be addressed first and foremost in teacher education (see Cogo 2015: 8) and to be explored and negotiated with prospective and practising teachers so as to render long-term effects in ELT. When (future) teachers are taken on board as active explorers of language practices and encouraged to engage in action research, they can further develop a linguaculturally reflective stance. Participating in and reflecting

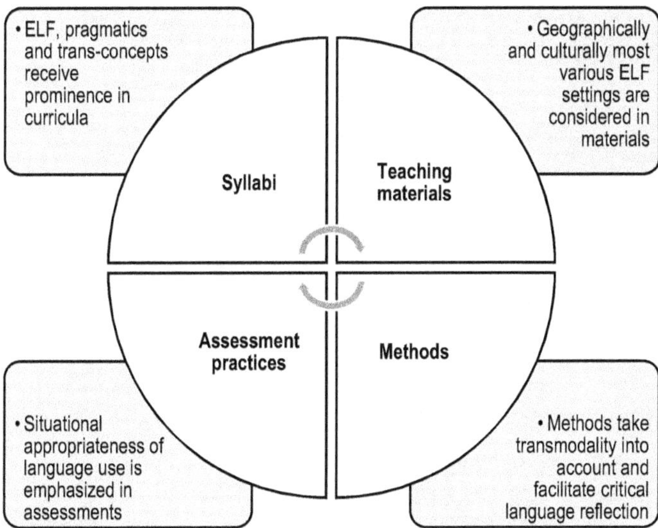

Figure 33: Central components of an ELF-aware and TPA-oriented ELT.

meaningful and authentic interaction of various kinds can open not only students', but also language teachers' eyes to the chances and challenges of English as a globally used medium for a negotiation of variety. It can also instigate further interest in the interactional mechanisms at work and help teachers locate themselves as individuals and social beings in a world of diversity.

13 Outlook

Taking a geographically and socioculturally novel perspective, the present study has generated new insights into communicative practices in English as a Lingua Franca (ELF). Looking at interactions between adolescents from Germany and Tanzania, it has not only provided further evidence for a number of previous results from ELF research, but has also contributed original findings and developed new models. This final chapter will recapitulate major assets, but also some shortcomings of the present study in a nutshell so as to draw conclusions for future research.

The predominantly qualitative interactional linguistic approach has proven methodologically adequate to lay bare and interpret interactional mechanisms and phenomena at work. It has drawn primarily on conversation analysis, but has also profited from triangulation and mixed-methods approaches, gaining valuable insights from complementary ethnographic data and quantitative corpus analyses alike. Future studies are recommended to incorporate retrospective interviews on a larger scale, as they have shown to offer an important interpretative potential by increasing transparency for the researcher while sustaining an emic perspective. In addition, multi-modal analyses based on video-recordings, which for practical reasons could here only be applied as a minor complementary tool (see Section 11.1), would in fact be crucial to enhance our understanding of how facial expressions as well as gestures are employed and how different modes are combined to reach communicative goals in ELF (see e.g. Räisänen 2012; Brunner et al. 2017).

Young ELF speakers in the African-European school context analyzed have emerged from the study as competent communicators and successful users of ELF, applying a wide range of communicative means available to them to reach their interactional goals. Repetition and repair have been used extensively to enhance explicitness in the face of unclear common ground; at the same time, students resort to complimenting a lot, with which they mainly address the relational side of communication. As levels of proficiency may limit articulateness in the target language, the intercultural communicators have been shown to employ their full verbal and non-verbal semiotic repertoire, including laughter and translanguaging.

It has to be emphasized again, however, that all findings presented here have also been situationally determined and must be interpreted within the concrete setting. The present study has opened the field to integrate adolescents and African interlocutors into ELF research, but is restricted with regard to social stratification, for example, as it concentrates on female speakers from an educational elite. More empirical work is needed to shed further light on ELF communication among adolescent speakers from a variety of geographical and social settings so that findings

https://doi.org/10.1515/9783110786576-013

and suggested models in the present exploratory study can be tested and refined against the backdrop of larger and broader databases.

By investigating ELF interactions in an East African setting, the present study has widened the geocultural field of ELF research. Many interactional mechanisms and strategies previously reported for ELF, such as an increase of explicitness or processes of accommodation, have been consolidated here to work more or less independently of cultural influences. At the same time, the exploration of ELF in a new linguacultural surrounding has shed further light on the interplay between language and culture. Cultural influences on ELF have been shown to work on various levels, from covert cultural conceptualizations affecting semantic fields, through influences on the realization of speech acts, to the choice of individual discourse topics. In its interplay with meaning, politeness, rapport, and identity, culture unfolds its capacity as a communicatively relevant category. Beyond providing rich linguistic evidence for this finding, the present data also contain a high discursive potential with students explicitly and implicitly discussing their understandings of culture, interculturality and transculturality. It appears highly rewarding to explore ELF speakers' epistemic beliefs about these concepts in follow-up studies, using qualitative content analyses (see Mayring 2015), for example. An extension of ELF research to cover a wider range of geographical and linguacultural settings as claimed above is expected to also provide further insights into the relationship between language, culture and identity. Intercultural communication research, cultural linguistics and complexity theory can provide frameworks, which in their interplay can both inspire and benefit from ELF research along these lines.

With its focus on adolescent ELF users, most of whom identify as learners of English at the same time, the present study also set out to feed linguistic findings back into ELF-oriented approaches to English language teaching (ELT). The transparency model of translanguaging, which postulates transparency as a decisive factor for communicative success, has been proposed as a promising theoretical concept for teaching approaches which seek to incorporate multilingual resources. Transparency enhancing devices (TEDs) and strategies to increase explicitness have been outlined as clearly identifiable learning objectives, which can also be taken up in the difficult arrangement of ELF-oriented assessments (see e.g. Harding & McNamara 2018: 570). Although debates on pedagogical implications of ELF research are in full swing, ELF-oriented teaching practices remain scarce. The present study has sought to contribute to bridging this theory-practice-gap by providing some concrete classroom suggestions. More empirical research in collaboration with practising teachers and further elaborations on how theoretical considerations can be transformed into classroom practices are desirable. What remains difficult is the overall question of how conceptualizations of languages as fluid and hybrid entities – widely recognized throughout the ELF research community and corroborated in the present study – can gain more acceptance in normative learning contexts. As there is a great deal of authority and power at stake, this question appears worth elaborate future research integrating linguistic and pedagogical approaches.

The present study has contributed a new piece to the larger puzzle. It has revealed interactional principles, cultural influences, contextual factors and idiosyncratic components all at work at the same time – which in fact is the case for any conversation, in ELF contexts and beyond – and has pondered on some pedagogical implications of linguistic findings. English as a Lingua Franca itself has emerged as a versatile transcultural means, which its adolescent speakers successfully appropriate to discuss meanings, manage rapport and negotiate identities in intercultural interactions. Most diverse people will continue to use the language, to transform and be transformed by ELF in various settings, from East Africa to Central Europe, around the globe and back again.

Appendices

Appendix A Transcription key and sample transcript

Appendix A.1 Transcription key

?	Unit-final rising intonation
.	Unit-final falling intonation
↑	Rise in pitch
↓	Fall in pitch
°xyz°	Markedly quiet
XYZ	Markedly loud
(.)	Micropause
(1.5)	Pause in seconds (timed to the nearest half-second)
[xyz]	Overlap
xyz=	Latching
xyz:	Prolongation of sound
xyz-	Cut-off
@	Laughter (approximating syllable number, i.e. hahaha → @@@)
£xyz£	Smiling voice
(xyz)	Uncertain passage
<pvc>	Pronunciation variation/coinage ('standard' English word in curly brackets)
<ipa>	Phonetic representation
<L1xx>	Non-English speech (English translation provided in curly brackets)
<xyz>	Reduced speed of talk
>xyz<	Compressed speed of talk
hhh	Audible outbreath
.hhh	Audible inbreath
{xyz}	Contextual events and non-verbal noises
[CTf/first name]	Anonymization (here: participant's first name)

https://doi.org/10.1515/9783110786576-014

Appendix A.2 Sample transcript

Source: fieldwork Katharina Beuter (N2_326-374)
Transcribed by: Katharina Beuter, September 2017
Checked by: Alice Limmer
Speakers: NTf and NGf
Recording date: 25 October 2016

326 **NGf:** we will visit the <ngorongoro> crat@er
327 **NTf:** hh
328 **NGf:** [in: (.) NEXT week]
329 **NTf:** [it is like heaven there] (.) ↑ah
330 **NGf:** yeah really? ah: [(so great)]
331 **NTf:** [it is ↑so] beautiful. even if you
search the internet you can see (.) the ngorongoro crater
>it's so beautiful< it is like a (.) for example we are
here (.) and it is like a <BI:G ho:le> down there.
332 **NGf:** aha?=
333 **NTf:** =you'll be entering with a car and you'll go [and see]
334 **NGf:** [oh:]
335 **NTf:** also inside there's a sa (.) like an oasis inside there's
water? (.) there's (a) animals moving?
336 **NGf:** mh?
337 **NTf:** but most of the animals are mm: (.) (°what.°) <wide wild>
cows.
338 **NGf:** ↑a[ha].
339 **NTf:** [in] swahili we call them <L1sw> nyati {buffalo} </L1sw>.
340 **NGf:** aha?
341 **NTf:** yes. you'll find them (.) and al- and also find other
types of er animals? (.) it will be such a great
adventu[rous time for you?]
342 **NGf:** [ah::]
343 **NTf:** and (.) i think it will pretty be?
344 **NGf:** i'm looking forw@@ard hh
345 **NTf:** o[°kay°]
346 **NGf:** [real]ly. i've never seen (.) so animals like lions
or elephants or i don't know in the in the NATURE it was
(1.5) every time in zoos (.) behind (.)
347 **NTf:** bars.
348 **NGf:** yeah. behind bars.=

349 **NTf:** =well (.) you'll have to see them (.) on a car.
350 **NGf:** [@]
351 **NTf:** [they'll] (.) be moving in front of your car.
352 **NGf:** ↑oh[::@]
353 **NTf:** [they are going] and moving? (1)
354 **NGf:** so great
355 **NTf:** but if you (.) go: (.) to a wildlife where there are monkeys
356 **NGf:** [@]
357 **NTf:** [just] be £careful£
358 **NGf:** hh okay=
359 **NTf:** =£if you are eating a lollipop it will take it [from you£]
360 **NGf:** [@] really
361 **NTf:** yes.
362 **NGf:** ↑oh
363 **NTf:** monkeys aren't (1) harmful ↓no they are not harmful? hh but when they see something sweet. you know they're just like human beings. for example at the time i went to (.) to a (.) i it is not a wildlife i went to a zoo?
364 **NGf:** @
365 **NTf:** a monkey. (.) a monkey took er my friend's lollipop.
366 **NGf:** ↑a[h@]
367 **NTf:** [he] was ea- she was eating it. (.) and she@
368 **NGf:** oh:[@@ h @]
369 **NTf:** [hh she cr@ied s@o much]
370 **NGf:** .h @@ .hh
371 **NTf:** ↑oh my lollipop [my l@olli↓p@op]
372 **NGf:** [@ .hh]=
373 **NTf:** =and the monkey was eating it (like) [↓mmh]
374 **NGf:** [@ .hh] ↑oh that's f@unny.

Appendix B Fieldwork material

Appendix B.1 Participant information sheet

Intercultural pragmatics: Early ELF interaction in German-Tanzanian student encounters

Informant Information Sheet

Date Informant ID #

Personal information

Age

Gender

○ male ○ female

Nationality

Ethnic Self-Identification

Language(s) used at home while growing up

○ Swahili ○ German

○ other:

Mother's native language

Father's native language

Education Profile

Current school year

Languages learned and used at school

Please use the following abbreviations:
Swahili S, German G, English E, Other O

School year	Language(s) learned as a subject	Language(s) used for teaching and learning in non-language subjects
1		
2		
3		
4		
5		
6		
7		
8		
9		
10		
11		
12		
13		

Mother's highest qualification

Mother's (last) occupation

Father's highest qualification

Father's (last) occupation

Intercultural Experiences

Location Timeline

Please indicate city and state or country.

Age	Location lived at from age 0 – 20
0	
1	
2	
3	
4	
5	
6	
7	
8	
9	
10	
11	
12	
13	
14	
15	
16	
17	
18	
19	
20	

I enjoy intercultural interaction

very much	a little	not a lot	not at all
○	○	○	○

I normally communicate with people speaking languages* other than my home language

daily	weekly	monthly	occasionally	never
○	○	○	○	○

**please specify languages:*

Outside school I communicate in English

daily	weekly	monthly	occasionally	never
○	○	○	○	○

Outside school I communicate in English
(multiple answers possible)

as a tourist	with visitors	with friends	in social networks	in other contexts*
○	○	○	○	○

**please specify:*

Outside school I communicate in English

only with native speakers of English	mainly with native speakers of English	equally with native and non-native speakers of English	mainly with non-native speakers of English	only with non-native speakers of English
○	○	○	○	○

Thank you very much for your participation!

https://doi.org/10.1515/9783110786576-015

Appendix B.2 Task sheet (Day 1) and tasks (Days 2–4)

Day 1: Family and friends

Today you have the chance to find out more about each other's family and friends.

>> **Before you start going, just check whether the red light on the recorder is on. If it is off or flashing, please contact a staff member.** Ignore this message if you do not have a recorder. <<

A) 10 minutes: Talking

Ask your partner questions about things concerning his or her family and friends that you find interesting and answer his or her questions.

In case you run out of ideas, here are some questions that you can choose from:

- What is your full name?
- How old are you?
- Where is your home?
- What does your home look like?
- Who is part of your family?
- How much time do you spend with your family?
- Who are your best friends?
- How much time do you spend with your friends?
- How do you spend the time with your friends?
- Do you have friends of both sexes?

B) 20 minutes: Designing

Use the information you just gathered, the sheet of paper and the stickers in your envelope and a pen to design your first page for our *dia | log | book* together.

Make sure you take the sheet **vertically** ▯ – otherwise it won't fit into the book.

Day 2: Nature and society

- What comes to your mind first when you think of my country?
- Which stereotypes do people in your country have about my country?
- Have you had any intercultural experiences so far?
- What is the climate like in your home country or home region?
- What does the landscape look like in your home country or home region?
- What are your national sports?
- What are major and minor religions in your country? How do they relate?

- How is money distributed in your country?
- What are some of the most serious dangers in your country?

Day 3: School and leisure
- Which subjects are taught at your school?
- When does school start, when does it end?
- How important is school in your life?
- Do you feel motivated to study at school?
- What are your favourite activities outside school?
- What is your favourite sport?
- What kind of music do you like?
- What is the best movie you have ever watched?

Day 4: Present and future
- Are you happy?
- Is there anything lacking in your life?
- Where would you like to live in the future?
- What are your job plans?
- What are you concerned about or afraid of?
- What are your dreams and hopes?

Appendix B.3 Guidelines for interviews

1. General condition and intercultural experiences
   - 1.1. *How are you today?*
   - 1.2. *Do you feel comfortable?*
   - 1.3. *What do you particularly like about your intercultural experience?*
   - 1.4. *What do you experience as difficult?*

2. Communicative and linguistic aspects
   - 2.1. General aspects
     - 2.1.1. *What do you find noticeable here with regard to language use?*
     - 2.1.2. *Do you like speaking English? How do you feel when speaking English (tense/relaxed etc.)?*
     - 2.1.3. *Do you feel you can express yourself as you please in English?*
     - 2.1.4. *What do you find difficult in communicating with your exchange partners?*
     - 2.1.5. *What do you find easier than expected?*

- *2.1.6. Do you feel comfortable when communicating with your exchange partners? Why (not)?*
- *2.1.7. What do you find unusual? What about your exchange partner's communicative behaviour do you find surprising/irritating/unusual?*
- *2.1.8. How do you deal with unexpected communicative behaviour?*

2.2. Problems in understanding
- *2.2.1. Do you often experience difficulties in understanding? If yes, what are the reasons?*
- *2.2.2. What do you do when you notice something you have not understood?*
- *2.2.3. What do you do when you notice that you have not been understood?*

2.3. Managing rapport
- *2.3.1. Do you find it easy to relate to your dialogue partner? Why (not)?*
- *2.3.2. Do you have the impression that you accommodate to your dialogue partner's linguistic or communicative behaviour?*
- *2.3.3. Do you have the impression that your dialogue partner accommodates to your own linguistic or communicative behaviour?*
- *2.3.4. Has the relationship towards your exchange students changed? If yes, in how far?*

2.4. Politeness
- *2.4.1. Is politeness an issue for you? If yes, what makes you think about it?*
- *2.4.2. Do you experience your dialogue partner as friendly/polite?*
- *2.4.3. Do you experience differences in politeness between yourself and your exchange partners? Please specify.*
- *2.4.4. Do you remember a situation in which you perceived your dialogue partner's communicative behaviour as inappropriate for some reason?*
- *2.4.5. Do you consciously try to be friendly/polite? If yes, how?*

3. Metalinguistic awareness
- *3.1. Did you talk about linguistic issues when preparing for this exchange?*
- *3.2. Do you feel your formal education in English has prepared you well for this situation? Please specify.*
- *3.3. Do you discuss linguistic or communicative problems with your fellow students? If yes, in how far?*

4. Miscellaneous
- *4.1. Is there anything else you would like to share?*

Thank you very much for your participation!

Appendix C Cross-corpus comparisons

Table C.1: Information on corpora used in cross-corpus comparisons.

	TeenELF	VOICE	Spoken BNC 1994	Spoken BNC 1994, age 15–24	COLT	Spoken BNC 2014	Spoken BNC 2014, age 15–24	Spoken ICE EA	FOLK
	Corpus of Teenagers' Use of English as a Lingua Franca	Vienna Oxford International Corpus of English	British National Corpus 1994, spoken section	British National Corpus 1994, spoken section, age group 15–24	Bergen Corpus of London Teenage Language	British National Corpus 2014, spoken section	British National Corpus 2014, spoken section, age group 15–24	International Corpus of English, East African component	Forschungs- und Lehrkorpus gesprochenes Deutsch
			Subsection of BNC 1994		Constituent of BNC 1994	Subsection of BNC 2014			
Size (in words)	190,182	1,023,082	10,409,858	594,400	431,528	11,422,617	2,777,761	503,426	2,990,421
Years of data recordings	2016	2001–2007	1991–1994		1993	2012–2016		1990–1996	2003–2020
Age of participants	15 to 19	All ages	All ages	15 to 24	13 to 17	All ages	15 to 24	All ages	1–100
Number of participants	30	753	124		31	668			1251
Provenance of speakers	Germany, Tanzania		Great Britain		London	Great Britain		Kenya, Tanzania	Germany
Major L1s of speakers	German, Swahili	49 different first languages	English		English	English		English, Swahili and others	German

(continued)

https://doi.org/10.1515/9783110786576-016

Table C.1 (continued)

	TeenELF	**VOICE**	**Spoken BNC 1994**	**Spoken BNC 1994, age 15–24**	**COLT**	**Spoken BNC 2014**	**Spoken BNC 2014, age 15–24**	**Spoken ICE EA**	**FOLK**
Number of texts	52	151	910			1251			374
Hours of recording	26 hours	110 hours			50 hours				314 hours
Language	ELF	ELF	British English		British English	British English		East African English	German
Domains	Education	Work, leisure, education	Work, leisure, education etc.		Education	Informal contexts, mainly at home		Education, broadcast etc.	Private, institutional and public contexts
Speech event types	Face-to-face interactions	Naturally occurring face-to-face interactions	Monologues and dialogues		Naturally occurring interactions	Naturally occurring interactions		Unscripted and scripted monologues and dialogues	Interactions
Director(s) or leading researcher(s)	Katharina Beuter	Barbara Seidlhofer	BNC Consortium		Anna-Brita Stenström	Robbie Love		Josef Schmied	Arnulf Deppermann, Martin Hartung, Thomas Schmidt, Silke Reineke
References		VOICE 2013	BNC 2010		COLT 1993; Stenström et al. 2002	BNC2014 2018; Love et al. 2017; Love 2018		Hudson-Ettle & Schmied 1999	IDS 2021; Schmidt 2018

Table C.2: Cross-corpus frequency comparisons of selected items.

	TeenELF	VOICE	Spoken BNC 1994	Spoken BNC 1994, age 15–24	COLT	Spoken BNC 2014	Spoken BNC 2014, age 15–24	Spoken ICE EA	FOLK
words in total	190,182	1,023,082	10,409,858	594,400	431,528	11,422,617	2,777,761	503,426	2,990,421
hits per million									
cool	641.5	51.8	17.6	57.2	192.3	275.4	470.5	11.9	258.2
English	609.9	1310.7	101.5	144.7	319.8	214.8	244.0	224.5	*66.9*[117]
i	29834.6	23764.5	29736.9	42227.5	34936.3	38136.0	43132.9	9628.0	*18763.6*
okay	14428.3	5834.3	1072.7	1054.8	1997.6	1948.9	2337.1	1499.7	2789.6
or so.	68.4	65.5	39.2	21.9	9.3	24.3	13.0	29.8	*746.7*[118]
or what.	42.1	97.7	53.2	70.7	41.7	35.4	30.6	77.5	*270.2*
we	15548.3	16156.1	10415.8	7008.7	4641.6	8008.7	7519.0	12001.8	*7183.9*
wow	552.1	134.9	23.2	89.2	129.8	271.9	295.9	4.0	42.5
you	21616.1	20087.3	25789.3	30842.9	35541.1	27266.1	25088.2	17466.3	*14698.3*[119]

(continued)

117 Numbers in italics in this column indicate that German equivalents of the words in question were counted.

118 As not all corpora presented here include intonational patterns in their transcriptions, numbers for *or so* (resp. 'oder so') and *or what* (resp. 'oder was') have to be treated with special care. In addition to their uses as unit-final discourse markers, both sets can turn up in mid-position of coordinated structures. Examplary in-depth, context-sensitive analyses for *oder so* and *oder was* of randomized samples (n=50) were conducted in FOLK. The results suggest high rates of unit-final discourse marker uses of *oder so* (94% of all cases analyzed) and slightly lower rates for *oder was* respectively (80% of all cases analyzed).

119 This number has been calculated on the basis of all instances of personal pronouns in German in the 2nd person (*du, dich, dir, ihr, euch, Sie, Ihnen*). As FOLK transcripts use lower case letters only, in-depth, context-sensitive analyses of randomized samples (n=50) were conducted for *sie* and *ihnen* to disambiguate between 2nd (*Sie/Ihnen*) and 3rd person pronouns (*sie/ihnen*).

Table C.2 (continued)

	TeenELF	VOICE	Spoken BNC 1994	Spoken BNC 1994, age 15–24	COLT	Spoken BNC 2014	Spoken BNC 2014, age 15–24	Spoken ICE EA	FOLK
absolute hits									
cool	122	53	183	34	83	3146	1307	6	*772*
English	116	1341	1057	86	138	2454	677	113	*200*
i	5674	24313	309557	25100	15076	435613	119813	4847	*56111*
okay	2744	5969	11167	627	862	22261	6492	755	8342
or so.	13	67	408	13	4	278	36	15	*2233*
or what.	8	100	554	42	18	404	85	39	*808*
we	2957	16529	108427	4166	2003	91480	20886	6042	*21483*
wow	105	138	241	53	56	3106	822	2	127
you	4111	20551	268463	18333	15337	311450	69689	8793	*43954*

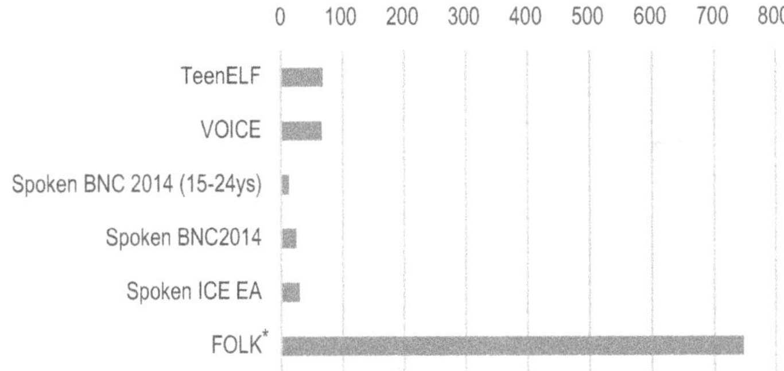

* counts for German *oder so*

Figure C.1: Cross-corpus comparison for *or so* (hits per million).

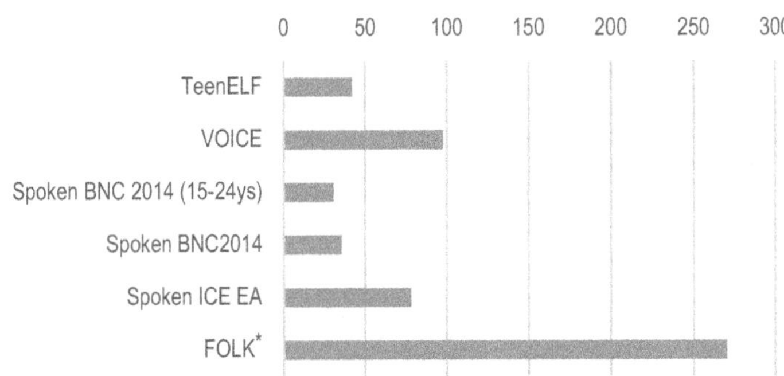

* counts for German *oder was*

Figure C.2: Cross-corpus comparison for *or what* (hits per million).

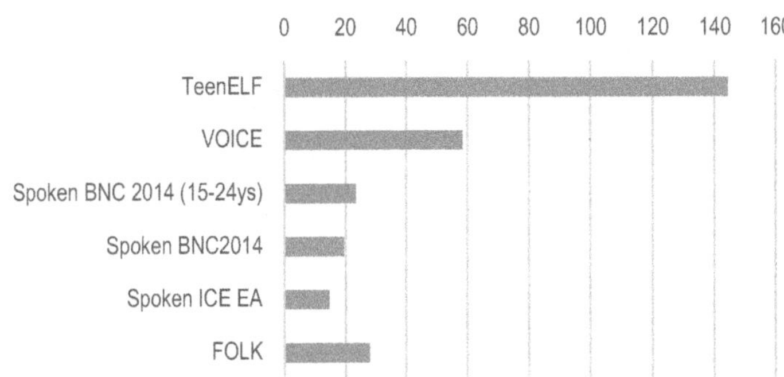

Figure C.3: Cross-corpus comparison for *okay* (hits per ten thousand).

References

Achebe, Chinua. 1975. The African writer and the English language. In Chinua Achebe (ed.), *Morning yet on creation day: Essays*, 55–62. London/Ibadan/Nairobi/Lusaka: Heinemann.

Agar, Michael. 1994. *Language shock: Understanding the culture of conversation*. New York: Morrow.

Alexander, Neville. 2012. The centrality of the language question in post-apartheid South Africa: Revisiting a perennial issue. *South African Journal of Science* 108(9/10). 1–7.

Androutsopoulos, Jannis. 1998. Forschungsperspektiven auf Jugendsprache: Ein integrativer Überblick. In Jannis Androutsopoulos & Arno Scholz (eds.), *Jugendsprache – langue des jeunes – youth language*, 1–34. Frankfurt am Main: Peter Lang.

Androutsopoulos, Jannis. 2018. Digitale Interpunktion: Stilistische Ressourcen und soziolinguistischer Wandel in der informellen digitalen Schriftlichkeit von Jugendlichen. In Arne Ziegler (ed.), *Jugendsprachen/Youth languages: Aktuelle Perspektiven internationaler Forschung/Current perspectives of international research*, 721–748. Berlin/Boston: De Gruyter Mouton.

Androutsopoulos, Jannis & Alexandra Georgakopoulou. 2008. Youth, discourse, and interpersonal management. In Gerd Antos & Eija Ventola (eds.), *Handbook of interpersonal communication*, 457–479. Berlin/Boston: De Gruyter Mouton.

Arundale, Robert B. 2010. Relating. In Miriam A. Locher & Sage L. Graham (eds.), *Interpersonal pragmatics*, 137–165. Berlin/Boston: De Gruyter Mouton.

Arundale, Robert B. 2020. *Communicating & relating: Constituting face in everyday interacting*. New York: Oxford University Press.

Auer, Peter (ed.). 2003. *Code-switching in conversation: Language, interaction and identity*. London: Routledge.

Austin, John L. 1975. *How to do things with words: The William James Lectures delivered at Harvard University in 1955*, 2nd edn. Cambridge, MA: Harvard University Press.

Baird, Robert, Will Baker & Mariko Kitazawa. 2014. The complexity of ELF. *Journal of English as a Lingua Franca* 3(1). 171–196.

Baker, Will. 2011. Intercultural awareness: Modelling an understanding of cultures in intercultural communication through English as a Lingua Franca. *Language and Intercultural Communication* 11(3). 197–214.

Baker, Will. 2015. *Culture and identity through English as a Lingua Franca: Rethinking concepts and goals in intercultural communication*. Berlin/Boston: De Gruyter Mouton.

Baker, Will. 2018a. English as a Lingua Franca and intercultural communication. In Jennifer Jenkins, Will Baker & Martin Dewey (eds.), *The Routledge handbook of English as a Lingua Franca*, 25–36. London: Routledge.

Baker, Will. 2018b. Transcultural communication and ELF: New perspectives on language, culture and intercultural communication. Keynote speech presented at the ELF conference *ELF, migration and multilingualism* (ELF 11), London, 5–7 July, 2018.

Baker, Will. 2020. English as a Lingua Franca and transcultural communication: Rethinking competences and pedagogy for ELT. In Christopher J. Hall & Rachel Wicaksono (eds.), *Ontologies of English: Conceptualising the language for learning, teaching, and assessment*, 253–272. Cambridge: Cambridge University Press.

Baker, Will. 2021. From intercultural to transcultural communication. *Language and Intercultural Communication* 1(1). 1–14.

Baker, Will & Chittima Sangiamchit. 2019. Transcultural communication: language, communication and culture through English as a Lingua Franca in a social network community. *Language and Intercultural Communication* 19(6). 471–487.

https://doi.org/10.1515/9783110786576-017

Baker, Will & Tomokazu Ishikawa. 2021. *Transcultural communication trough global Englishes: An advanced textbook for students*. London/New York: Routledge.

Bamberg, Michael G. W., Anna de Fina & Deborah Schiffrin (eds.). 2007. *Selves and identities in narrative and discourse*. Amsterdam: Benjamins.

Bamford, Anne. 2009. *The wow factor: Global research compendium on the impact of the arts in education*, 2nd edn. Münster/München/Berlin: Waxmann.

Barth-Weingarten, Dagmar. 2008. Interactional linguistics. In Gerd Antos & Eija Ventola (eds.), *Handbook of interpersonal communication*, 77–106. Berlin/Boston: De Gruyter Mouton.

Bauman, Zygmunt. 2004. *Identity*. London: Polity.

Baumert, Jürgen & Mareike Kunter. 2011. Das Kompetenzmodell von COACTIV. In: Mareike Kunter, Jürgen Baumert, Werner Blum & Michael Neubrand (eds.), *Professionelle Kompetenz von Lehrkräften: Ergebnisse des Forschungsprogramms COACTIV*, 29–54. Münster: Waxmann.

Bayyurt, Yasemin & Sumru Akcan (eds.). 2015. *Current perspectives on pedagogy for English as a Lingua Franca*. Berlin/Boston: De Gruyter Mouton.

Bayyurt, Yasemin & Martin Dewey. 2020. Locating ELF in ELT. *English Language Teaching Journal* 74(4). 369–376.

Beneke, Jürgen. 1991. Englisch als *lingua franca* oder als Medium interkultureller Kommunikation? In Renate Grebing (ed.), *Grenzenloses Sprachenlernen: Festschrift für Reinhold Freudenstein*, 54–66. Berlin: Cornelsen & Oxford University Press.

Beuter, Katharina. 2019a. Beziehungsmanagement durch Lachen und Humor in interkulturellen Schülerbegegnungen: Gesprächsanalytische Betrachtungen in einem deutsch-tansanischen Kontext. In Ute Franz (ed.), *Kolloquium Forschende Frauen 2018: Beiträge Bamberger Nachwuchswissenschaftlerinnen*, 9–29. Bamberg: Bamberg University Press.

Beuter, Katharina. 2019b. Repair in English as a Lingua Franca interactions between Tanzanian and German school students: A qualitative approach. In Juhani Härmä, Hartmut E. H. Lenk, Begoña Sanromán Vilas & Elina Suomela-Härmä (eds.), *Studies in comparative pragmatics*. Cambridge: Cambridge Scholars Publishing.

Beuter, Katharina. 2019c. Sprachen vermitteln, Welten sichten: Konzeptualisierungen und Zusammenhänge von Sprache und Kultur in Bildungskontexten. In Katharina Beuter, Benjamin Bauer, Adrianna Hlukhovych, Konstantin Lindner & Sabine Vogt (eds.), *Sprache und kulturelle Bildung: Perspektiven für eine reflexive Lehrerinnen- und Lehrerbildung und einen heterogenitätssensiblen Unterricht*, 13–29. Bamberg: Bamberg University Press.

Beuter, Katharina. fthc. Positioning the self and other in English lingua franca interactions: Reference systems and the dynamics of identification in a German-Tanzanian school exchange. In Minna Nevala & Minna Palander-Collin (eds.), *Self- and other-reference in social contexts: From global to local discourses*. Cambridge: Cambridge University Press.

Bhabha, Homi K. 1994. *The location of culture*. Abingdon: Routledge.

Bhatt, Rakesh M. 2008. In other words: Language mixing, identity representations, and third space. *Journal of Sociolinguistics* 12(2). 177–200.

Biebighäuser, Katrin. 2014. *Fremdsprachenlernen in virtuellen Welten: Empirische Untersuchung eines Begegnungsprojekts zum interkulturellen Lernen*. Tübingen: Narr.

Blair, Andrew. 2017. Standard language models, variable lingua franca goals: How can ELF-aware teacher education square the circle? *Journal of English as a Lingua Franca* 6(2). 345–366.

Block, David. 2015. Researching language and identity. In Brian Paltridge & Aek Phakiti (eds.), *Research methods in applied linguistics: A practical resource*, 527–540. London: Bloomsbury.

Blum-Kulka, Shoshana, Juliane House & Gabriele Kasper (eds.). 1989. *Cross-cultural pragmatics: Requests and apologies*. Norwood, NJ: Ablex.

Bondi, Marina. 2017. Corpus linguistics. In Edda Weigand (ed.), *The Routledge handbook of language and dialogue*, 46–61. New York/London: Routledge.

Bowles, Hugo. 2015. ELF-oriented pedagogy: Conclusions. In Hugo Bowles & Alessia Cogo (eds.), *International perspectives on English as a Lingua Franca: Pedagogical insights*, 194–208. Basingstoke: Palgrave Macmillan.

Bowles, Hugo & Alessia Cogo (eds.). 2015. *International perspectives on English as a Lingua Franca: Pedagogical insights*. Basingstoke: Palgrave Macmillan.

Brown, Penelope & Stephen C. Levinson. 1987. *Politeness: Some universals in language use*. Cambridge: Cambridge University Press.

Brunner, Marie-Louise & Stefan Diemer. 2018. "You are struggling forwards, and you don't know, and then you . . . you do code-switching . . .": Code-switching in ELF Skype conversations. *Journal of English as a Lingua Franca* 7(1). 59–88.

Brunner, Marie-Louise, Stefan Diemer & Selina Schmidt. 2017. ". . . okay so good luck with that ((laughing))?": Managing rich data in a corpus of Skype conversations. *Studies in Variation, Contacts and Change in English 19: Big and Rich Data in English Corpus Linguistics: Methods and Explorations* 19. https://varieng.helsinki.fi/series/volumes/19/brunner_diemer_schmidt/ (20 June, 2022.)

Bucholtz, Mary & Kira Hall. 2005. Identity and interaction: A sociocultural linguistic approach. *Discourse Studies* 7(4/5). 585–614.

Burwitz-Melzer, Eva. 2019. Konzepte und Skalen zur Plurikulturalität und Plurilingualität im Companion Volume (2018). *Zeitschrift für Fremdsprachenforschung* 30(2). 181–198.

Busch, Dominic. 2015. Culture is leaving conversation analysis, but is it really gone?: The analysis of culturalist performances in conversation. *Journal of Intercultural Communication* 39. 1–17.

Busch, Florian. 2018. Digitale Schreibregister von Jugendlichen analysieren: Ein linguistisch-ethnographischer Zugang zu Praktiken des Alltagsschreibens. In Arne Ziegler (ed.), *Jugendsprachen/Youth languages: Aktuelle Perspektiven internationaler Forschung/Current perspectives of international research*, 829–857. Berlin/Boston: De Gruyter Mouton.

Busse, Vera. 2017. Zur Förderung positiver Einstellungen gegenüber sprachlicher Diversität als europäisches Bildungsziel: Status quo und Desiderate. *Zeitschrift für Fremdsprachenforschung* 28(1). 53–75.

Bwenge, Charles. 2012. English in Tanzania: A linguistic cultural perspective. *International Journal of Language, Translation and Intercultural Communication* 1(1). 167–182.

Byram, Michael. 1997. *Teaching and assessing intercultural communicative competence.* Clevedon: Multilingual Matters.

Canagarajah, Suresh. 2007. Lingua franca English, multilingual communities, and language acquisition. *The Modern Language Journal* 91(5). 923–939.

Canagarajah, Suresh. 2011. Codemeshing in academic writing: Identifying teachable strategies of translanguaging. *The Modern Language Journal* 95(3). 401–417.

Cenoz, Jasone. 2019. Translanguaging pedagogies and English as a Lingua Franca. *Language Teaching* 52(1). 71–85.

Choi, Koun & Yongcan Liu. 2020. Challenges and strategies for ELF-aware teacher development. *English Language Teaching Journal* 74(4). 442–452.

Chomsky, Noam. 1957. *Syntactic structures.* Berlin/Boston: De Gruyter Mouton.

Chovan, Miloš. 2006. Kommunikative Stile sozialen Abgrenzens: Zu den stilistischen Spezifika sozial-distinktiver Handlungen in der Interaktion Jugendlicher. In Christa Dürscheid & Jürgen Spitzmüller (eds.), *Perspektiven der Jugendsprachforschung – Trends and developments in youth language research*, 135–150. Frankfurt am Main: Peter Lang.

Clift, Rebecca. 2016. *Conversation analysis.* Cambridge: Cambridge University Press.
Cogo, Alessia. 2009. Accommodating difference in ELF conversations: A study of pragmatic strategies. In Anna Mauranen & Elina Ranta (eds.), *English as a Lingua Franca: Studies and findings*, 254–273. Newcastle upon Tyne: Cambridge Scholars Publishing.
Cogo, Alessia. 2012. ELF and super-diversity: A case study of ELF multilingual practices from a business context. *Journal of English as a Lingua Franca* 1(2). 287–313.
Cogo, Alessia. 2015. English as a Lingua Franca: Descriptions, domains and applications. In Hugo Bowles & Alessia Cogo (eds.), *International perspectives on English as a Lingua Franca: Pedagogical insights*, 1–12. Basingstoke: Palgrave Macmillan.
Cogo, Alessia. 2016a. English as a Lingua Franca in Europe. In Andrew R. Linn (ed.), *Investigating English in Europe: Contexts and agendas*, 79–89. Berlin/Boston: De Gruyter Mouton.
Cogo, Alessia. 2016b. Conceptualizing ELF as a translanguaging phenomenon: Covert and overt resources in a transnational workplace. *Waseda Working Papers in ELF* 5, 61–77.
Cogo, Alessia. 2018a. ELF and multilingualism. In Jennifer Jenkins, Will Baker & Martin Dewey (eds.), *The Routledge handbook of English as a Lingua Franca*, 357–368. London: Routledge.
Cogo, Alessia. 2018b. "What is English as a Lingua Franca?: An introduction to the field." *Goldsmiths.* https://www.gold.ac.uk/glits-e/back-issues/english-as-a-lingua-franca/ (20 June, 2022.)
Cogo, Alessia. 2020. The role of translanguaging in ELF advice sessions for asylum seekers. In Anna Mauranen & Svetlana Vetchinnikova (eds.), *Language change: The impact of English as a Lingua Franca*, 336–355. Cambridge: Cambridge University Press.
Cogo, Alessia. 2021. ELF and translanguaging: Covert and overt resources in a transnational workplace. In Kumiko Murata (ed.), *ELF research methods and approaches to data and analyses: Theoretical and methodological underpinnings*, 38–54. London: Routledge.
Cogo, Alessia & Martin Dewey. 2012. *Analysing English as a Lingua Franca: A corpus-driven investigation.* London: Continuum.
Cogo, Alessia & Juliane House. 2018. The pragmatics of ELF. In Jennifer Jenkins, Will Baker & Martin Dewey (eds.), *The Routledge handbook of English as a Lingua Franca* (Routledge Handbooks in Applied Linguistics), 210–223. London: Routledge.
Council of Europe. 2018. *Common European Framework of Reference for languages, learning, teaching, assessment: Companion volume with new descriptors*. https://rm.coe.int/cefr-companion-volume-with-new-descriptors-2018/1680787989 (20 June, 2022.)
Couper-Kuhlen, Elizabeth & Margret Selting. 1996. Towards an interactional perspective on prosody and a prosodic perspective on interaction. In Elizabeth Couper-Kuhlen & Margret Selting (eds.), *Prosody in conversation: Interactional studies*, 11–56. Cambridge: Cambridge University Press.
Couper-Kuhlen, Elizabeth & Margret Selting. 2001. Introducing interactional linguistics. In Margret Selting & Elizabeth Couper-Kuhlen (eds.), *Studies in interactional linguistics*, 1–22. Amsterdam: Benjamins.
Couper-Kuhlen, Elizabeth & Margret Selting. 2018. *Interactional linguistics: An introduction to language in social interaction.* Cambridge: Cambridge University Press.
Creese, Angela & Adrian Blackledge. 2015. Translanguaging and identity in educational settings. *Annual Review of Applied Linguistics* 35. 20–35.
Cricket Media. n.y. *ePals*. https://www.epals.com/#/connections (18 June, 2022.)
Crystal, David. 2010. *The Cambridge encyclopedia of language*, 3rd edn. Cambridge/New York: Cambridge University Press.
Crystal, David. 2012a. *English as a global language*, 2nd edn. Cambridge/New York: Cambridge University Press.

Crystal, David. 2012b. August 23. The story of English spelling. *The Guardian*, https://www.theguardian.com/books/2012/aug/23/david-crystal-story-english-spelling (20 June, 2022.)

Culpeper, Jonathan & Michael Haugh. 2014. *Pragmatics and the English language*. Basingstoke: Palgrave Macmillan.

D'Andrea, Maria L. 2012. *English as a Lingua Franca: Examples from students' production and teachers' perception: A case study in the Italian school context.* Verona: University of Verona, Unpublished PhD dissertation.

Danesi, Marcel & Andrea Rocci. 2009. *Global linguistics: An introduction.* Berlin/Boston: De Gruyter Mouton.

Day, Dennis & Johannes Wagner. 2008. Ethnomethodology and conversation analysis. In Gerd Antos & Eija Ventola (eds.), *Handbook of interpersonal communication*, 33–51. Berlin/Boston: De Gruyter Mouton.

Deppermann, Arnulf. 2007. Using the other for oneself: Conversational practices of representing out-group members among adolescents. In Michael G. W. Bamberg, Anna de Fina & Deborah Schiffrin (eds.), *Selves and identities in narrative and discourse*, 273–301. Amsterdam: Benjamins.

Dervin, Fred & Anthony J. Liddicoat. 2013a. Introduction: Linguistics for intercultural education. In Fred Dervin & Anthony J. Liddicoat (eds.), *Linguistics for intercultural education*, 1–25. Amsterdam: Benjamins.

Dervin, Fred & Anthony J. Liddicoat (eds.). 2013b. *Linguistics for intercultural education.* Amsterdam: Benjamins.

Deutsch, Charles & Dirk Rohr. 2018. *Lehr- und Praxisbuch für Peer Learning: Peer-Projekte initiieren, begleiten und beraten.* Weinheim: Beltz.

Deutscher, Guy. 2011. *Through the language glass: Why the world looks different in other languages.* London: Arrow Books.

Dewey, Martin. 2009. English as a Lingua Franca: Heightened variability and theoretical implications. In Anna Mauranen & Elina Ranta (eds.), *English as a Lingua Franca: Studies and findings*, 60–83. Newcastle upon Tyne: Cambridge Scholars Publishing.

Dewey, Martin. 2012. Towards a post-normative approach: Learning the pedagogy of ELF. *Journal of English as a Lingua Franca* 1(1), 141–170.

Dewey, Martin. 2013. The distinctiveness of English as a Lingua Franca. *English Language Teaching Journal* 67(3). 346–349.

Dewey, Martin. 2021. English language teachers in context: Who teaches what, where and why?. In Andy Kirkpatrick (ed.), *The Routledge handbook of World Englishes*, 2nd edn., 609–623. Abingdon/New York: Routledge.

Dingemanse, Mark & Simeon Floyd. 2014. Conversation across cultures. In Nicholas J. Enfield, Paul Kockelman & Jack Sidnell (eds.), *The Cambridge handbook of linguistic anthropology*, 447–480. Cambridge: Cambridge University Press.

Djenar, Dwi Noverini, Michael C. Ewing & Howard Manns. 2018. *Style and intersubjectivity in youth interaction.* Berlin/Boston: De Gruyter Mouton.

Dorleijn, Margreet, Marten Kossmann & Jacomine Nortier. 2020. Urban youth speech styles in multilingual settings. In Evangelia Adamou and Yaron Matras (eds.), *The Routledge handbook of language contact*, 366–382. London/New York: Routledge.

Dröschel, Yvonne. 2011. *Lingua Franca English: The role of simplification and transfer*. Bern: Lang.

Duan, Yuanbing. 2011. A pragmatic research report on compliment speech act. *Theory and Practice in Language Studies* 1(4). 356–360.

DYLAN. 2011. *Set of postcards.* http://www.dylan-project.org/Dylan_en/dissemination/final/postcards/postcards.php (4 August, 2019.)

Eberhard, David M., Gary F. Simons & Charles D. Fennig (eds.). 2019. *Ethnologue: Languages of the world*, 22nd edn. Dallas, TX: SIL International. Online version: http://www.ethnologue.com. (4 September, 2019.)

Eberhard, David M., Gary F. Simons & Charles D. Fennig (eds.). 2022. *Ethnologue: Languages of the world*, 25th edn. Dallas, TX: SIL International. Online version: http://www.ethnologue.com. ejournals.um.edu.mt (23 June, 2022.)

Eckert, Hartwig & William Barry. 2005. *The phonetics and phonology of English pronunciation: A coursebook with CD-ROM*. Trier: Wissenschaftlicher Verlag.

Ehrhart, Sabine. 2015. Continua of language contact. In Gerald Stell & Kofi Yakpo (eds.), *Code-switching between structural and sociolinguistic perspectives*, 305–316. Berlin/Boston: De Gruyter Mouton.

Elsner, Daniela. 2015. Inklusion von Herkunftssprachen: Mehrsprachigkeit als Herausforderung und Chance. In Christiane M. Bongartz & Andreas Rohde (eds.), *Inklusion im Englischunterricht*, 71–94. Frankfurt am Main: Peter Lang.

Erikson, Erik H. 1959. *Identity and the life cycle: Selected papers*. New York: International Universities Press.

European Commission. n.y. *eTwinning*. https://www.etwinning.net/de/pub/about.htm (18 June, 2022.)

Ferguson, Charles A. 1982. Foreword. In Braj B. Kachru (ed.), *The other tongue: English across cultures*, vii–xii. Urbana: University of Illinois Press.

Fina, Anna de. 2010. The negotiation of identities. In Miriam A. Locher & Sage L. Graham (eds.), *Interpersonal pragmatics*, 205–224. Berlin/Boston: De Gruyter Mouton.

Firth, Alan. 1996. The discursive accomplishment of normality: On 'lingua franca' English and conversation analysis. *Journal of Pragmatics* 26(2). 237–259.

Firth, Alan. 2009. The lingua franca factor. *Intercultural Pragmatics* 6(2). 147–170.

Frank, Roslyn M. 2015. A future agenda for research on language and culture. In Farzad Sharifian (ed.), *The Routledge handbook of language and culture*, 493–512. London: Routledge.

Friedrich, Paul. 1989. Language, ideology, and political economy. *American Anthropologist* 91(2). 295–312.

Gagliardi, Cesare & Alan Maley. 2010. *EIL, ELF, global English: Teaching and learning issues*. Bern: Lang.

Galloway, Nicola & Heath Rose. 2015. *Introducing global Englishes*. London: Routledge.

García, Ofelia. 2009. Education, multilingualism, and translanguaging in the 21st century. In Tove Skutnabb-Kangas, Robert Phillipson, Ajit K. Mohanty & Minati Panda (eds.), *Social justice through multilingual education*, 140–158. Bristol/Buffalo: Multilingual Matters.

García, Ofelia & Li Wei 2014. *Translanguaging: Language, bilingualism and education*. Basingstoke/Hampshire/New York: Palgrave Macmillan.

Gardner, Rod. 2006. Conversation analysis. In Alan Davies (ed.), *The handbook of applied linguistics*, 262–284. Malden, MA: Blackwell.

Garfinkel, Harold. 1967. *Studies in ethnomethodology*. Englewood Cliffs, NJ: Prentice Hall.

Geertz, Clifford. 1973. *The interpretation of cultures: Selected essays*. New York: Basic Books.

Geluykens, Ronald. 2007. On methodology in cross-cultural pragmatics. In Bettina Kraft & Ronald Geluykens (eds.), *Cross-cultural pragmatics and interlanguage English*, 21–72. München: LINCOM.

Glaznieks, Aivars & Jennifer-Carmen Frey. 2018. Dialekt als Norm? Zum Sprachgebrauch Südtiroler Jugendlicher auf Facebook. In Arne Ziegler (ed.), *Jugendsprachen/Youth languages: Aktuelle Perspektiven internationaler Forschung/Current perspectives of international research*, 859–889. Berlin/Boston: De Gruyter Mouton.

Glenn, Phillip J. 2003. *Laughter in interaction*. Cambridge: Cambridge University Press.

Glenn, Phillip J. & Elizabeth Holt. 2013. Introduction. In Phillip J. Glenn & Elizabeth Holt, *Studies of laughter in interaction*, 1–22. London: Bloomsbury.

Gnutzmann, Claus (ed.). 1999. *Teaching and learning English as a global language.* Tübingen: Stauffenburg.

Goffman, Erving. 1967. *Interaction ritual: Essays on face-to-face behaviour.* New York: Pantheon Books.

Golato, Andrea. 2005. *Compliments and compliment responses: Grammatical structure and sequential organization*. Philadelphia/Amsterdam: Benjamins.

Goldberg, Adele E. 2013. Constructionist approaches. In Thomas Hoffmann & Graeme Trousdale (eds.), *The Oxford handbook of construction grammar*, 15–31. Oxford: Oxford University Press.

Görke, Adrian. 2018. Jugendsprachliche Merkmale als Ausdruck glokaler jugendsprachlicher Tendenzen. In Arne Ziegler (ed.), *Jugendsprachen/Youth languages: Aktuelle Perspektiven internationaler Forschung/Current perspectives of international research*, 97–121. Berlin/Boston: De Gruyter Mouton.

Graddol, David. 2006. *English next: Why global English may mean the end of 'English as a Foreign Language'.* London: British Council.

Grice, Herbert P. 1975. Logic and conversation. In Peter Cole & Jerry L. Morgan (eds.), *Speech acts*, 5th edn., 41–58. New York: Academic Press.

Grimm, Nancy, Michael Meyer & Laurenz Volkmann. 2015. *Teaching English*. Tübingen: Narr Francke Attempto.

Gumperz, John J. 1999. On interactional sociolinguistic method. In Srikant Sarangi (ed.), *Talk, work and institutional order: Discourse in medical, mediation and management settings*, 453–471. Berlin/Boston: De Gruyter Mouton.

Gumperz, John J. & Jenny Cook-Gumperz. 1981. Ethnic differences in communicative style. In Charles A. Ferguson and Shirley B. Heath (eds.), *Language in the USA*, 430–445. Cambridge: Cambridge University Press.

Halliday, Michael A. K. 1976. *Explorations in the functions of language*. London: Arnold.

Halliday, Michael A. K. 1979. *Language as social semiotic: The social interpretation of language and meaning.* London: Arnold.

Harding, Luke & Tim McNamara. 2018. Language assessment: The challenge of ELF. In Jennifer Jenkins, Will Baker & Martin Dewey (eds.), *The Routledge handbook of English as a Lingua Franca*, 570–582. London: Routledge.

Haß, Frank (ed.). 2011. *Fachdidaktik Englisch: Tradition, Innovation, Praxis.* Stuttgart: Klett.

Hawkins, Margaret R. 2018. Transmodalities and transnational encounters: Fostering critical cosmopolitan relations. *Applied Linguistics* 39(1). 55–77.

Hawkins, Margaret R. & Junko Mori. 2018. Considering 'trans-' perspectives in language theories and practices. *Applied Linguistics* 39(1). 1–8.

Herbert, Robert K. 1990. Sex-based differences in compliment behavior. *Language in Society* 19(2). 201–224.

Herder, Johann Gottfried von. 1774. *Auch eine Philosophie der Geschichte zur Bildung der Menschheit.* Riga: Hartknoch.

Hesse, Hermann-Günter, Kerstin Göbel & Johannes Hartig. 2008. Sprachliche Kompetenzen von mehrsprachigen Jugendlichen und Jugendlichen nicht-deutscher Erstsprache. In DESI-Konsortium (ed.), *Unterricht und Kompetenzerwerb in Deutsch und Englisch: Zentrale Befunde der Studie Deutsch-Englisch-Schülerleistungen-International (DESI)*, 208–230. Frankfurt am Main: Deutsches Institut für Internationale Pädagogische Forschung.

Hollington, Andrea & Nico Nassenstein. 2015. Youth language practices in Africa as creative manifestations of fluid repertoires and markers of speakers' social identity. In Nico Nassenstein & Andrea Hollington (eds.), *Youth language practices in Africa and beyond*, 1–22. Berlin/Boston: De Gruyter Mouton.

Hollington, Andrea & Nico Nassenstein. 2018. African youth language practices and social media. In Arne Ziegler (ed.), *Jugendsprachen/Youth languages: Aktuelle Perspektiven internationaler Forschung/ Current perspectives of international research*, 807–828. Berlin/Boston: De Gruyter Mouton.

Holmes, Janet. 1986. Compliments and compliment responses in New Zealand English. *Anthropological Linguistics* 28(4). 485–508.

Holmes, Janet. 1988. Paying compliments: A sex-preferential politeness strategy. *Journal of Pragmatics* 12(4). 445–465.

Holmes, Prue & Fred Dervin. 2016. Introduction – English as a Lingua Franca and interculturality: Beyond orthodoxies. In Prue Holmes & Fred Dervin (eds.), *The cultural and intercultural dimensions of English as a Lingua Franca*, 1–30. Bristol/Buffalo/Toronto: Multilingual Matters.

Horner, Kristine & Jean J. Weber. 2018. *Introducing multilingualism: A social approach*. London/New York: Routledge.

House, Juliane. 1999. Misunderstanding in intercultural communication: Interactions in English as Lingua Franca and the myth of mutual intelligibility. In Claus Gnutzmann (ed.), *Teaching and learning English as a global language*, 73–89. Tübingen: Stauffenburg.

House, Juliane. 2003. English as a Lingua Franca: A threat to multilingualism?. *Journal of Sociolinguistics* 7(4). 556–578.

House, Juliane. 2010. The pragmatics of English as a Lingua Franca. In Anna Trosborg (ed.), *Pragmatics across languages and cultures*, 363–387. Berlin/Boston: De Gruyter Mouton.

House, Juliane. 2014. English as global lingua franca: A Threat to multilingual communication and translation? *Language Teaching* 47(3). 363–376.

Huang, Yan. 2014. *Pragmatics*, 2nd edn. Oxford: Oxford University Press.

Hudson-Ettle, Diana M. & Josef Schmied. 1999. *Manual to accompany the East African component of the International Corpus of English: Background information, coding conventions and lists of source texts*. Chemnitz University of Technology.

Huensch, Amanda. 2017. How the initiation and resolution of repair sequences act as a device for the co-construction of membership and identity. *Pragmatics and Society* 8(3). 355–376.

Humboldt, Wilhelm Freiherr von. 1836. *Über die Verschiedenheit des menschlichen Sprachbaues und ihren Einfluss auf die geistige Entwicklung des Menschengeschlechts*. Berlin: Dümmler.

Hüllen, Werner. 1982. Teaching a foreign language as 'lingua franca'. *Grazer Linguistische Studien* 16. 83–88.

Hülmbauer, Cornelia. 2007. 'You moved, aren't?' – The relationship between lexicogrammatical correctness and communicative effectiveness in English as a Lingua Franca. *Vienna English Working Papers* 16(2). 3–35.

Hülmbauer, Cornelia. 2009. "We don't take the right way. We just take the way that we think you will understand" – The shifting relationship between correctness and effectiveness in ELF. In Anna Mauranen and Elina Ranta (eds.), *English as a Lingua Franca: Studies and findings*, 323–347. Newcastle upon Tyne: Cambridge Scholars Publishing.

Hülmbauer, Cornelia. 2011. Old friends?: Cognates in ELF communication. In Alasdair N. Archibald, Alessia Cogo & Jennifer Jenkins (eds.), *Latest trends in ELF research*, 139–162. Newcastle upon Tyne: Cambridge Scholars Publishing.

Hülmbauer, Cornelia. 2016. Multi, pluri, trans . . . and ELF: Lingualisms, languaging and the current lingua franca concept. In Marie-Luise Pitzl & Ruth Osimk-Teasdale (eds.), *English as a Lingua Franca: perspectives and prospects: Contributions in honour of Barbara Seidlhofer*, 193–203. Berlin/ Boston: De Gruyter Mouton.

Hundt, Marianne. 2015. World Englishes. In Douglas Biber & Randi Reppen (eds.), *The Cambridge handbook of English corpus linguistics*, 381–400. Cambridge: Cambridge University Press.

Hymes, Dell. 1964. Introduction. In Dell Hymes (ed.), *Language and culture in society*, 3–14. New York: Harper & Row.
Hymes, Dell. 1972. On communicative competence. In John B. Pride and Janet Holmes (ed.), *Sociolinguistics: Selected readings*, 269–293. Harmondsworth: Penguin.
Hymes, Dell. 1983. Notes towards a history of linguistics anthropology. In Dell Hymes (ed.), *Essays in the history of linguistic anthropology*, 1–57. Amsterdam/Philadelphia: Benjamins.
Hymes, Dell. 1996. *Ethnography, linguistics, narrative Inequality: Toward an understanding of voice.* London/Bristol: Taylor & Francis.
Illés, Éva. 2016. Issues in ELF-aware teacher education. *Journal of English as a Lingua Franca* 5(1). 135–145.
Imo, Wolfgang. 2013. *Sprache in Interaktion: Analysemethoden und Untersuchungsfelder*. Berlin/Boston: De Gruyter Mouton.
Ishamina, Athirah G. & David Deterding. 2018. Pronunciation and miscommunication in ELF interactions: An analysis of initial clusters. In Jennifer Jenkins, Will Baker & Martin Dewey (eds.), *The Routledge handbook of English as a Lingua Franca*, 224–232. London: Routledge.
Ishikawa, Tomokazu. 2022. English as a multilingual franca and 'trans-' theories. *Englishes in Practice* 5(1). 1–24.
Ishikawa, Tomokazu & Will Baker. 2021. Multi-, inter-, and trans-? 'Confusing' terms for ELF researchers. *ELF The Centre for English as a Lingua Franca forum* 1(1). 21–30.
Ivankova, Nataliya V. & Jennifer L. Greer. 2015. Mixed methods research and analysis. In Brian Paltridge & Aek Phakiti (eds.), *Research methods in applied linguistics: A practical resource*, 63–81. London: Bloomsbury.
Jefferson, Gail. 2004. Glossary of transcript symbols with an introduction. In Gene H. Lerner (ed.), *Conversation analysis: Studies from the first generation*, 13–23. Philadelphia, PA: Benjamins.
Jenkins, Jennifer. 2000. *The phonology of English as an international language: New models, new norms, new goals*. Oxford: Oxford University Press.
Jenkins, Jennifer. 2006. Current perspectives on teaching World Englishes and English as a Lingua Franca. *Teaching English to Speakers of Other Languages Quarterly* 40(1). 157–181.
Jenkins, Jennifer. 2007. *English as a Lingua Franca: Attitude and identity*. Oxford: Oxford University Press.
Jenkins, Jennifer. 2015. Repositioning English and multilingualism in English as a Lingua Franca. *Englishes in Practice* 2(3). 49–85.
Jenkins, Jennifer. 2017. English as a Lingua Franca in the expanding circle. In Markku Filppula, Juhani Klemola and Devyani Sharma (eds.), *The Oxford handbook of World Englishes*, 549–566. New York: Oxford University Press.
Jenkins, Jennifer. 2018. The future of English as a Lingua Franca? In Jennifer Jenkins, Will Baker & Martin Dewey (eds.), *The Routledge handbook of English as a Lingua Franca*, 594–605. London: Routledge.
Jenkins, Jennifer. 2020. Where are we with ELF and language testing?: An opinion piece. *English Language Teaching Journal* 74(4). 473–479.
Jenkins, Jennifer, Will Baker & Martin Dewey (eds.). 2018. *The Routledge handbook of English as a Lingua Franca*. London: Routledge.
Jenkins, Jennifer, Alessia Cogo & Martin Dewey. 2011. Review of developments in research into English as a Lingua Franca. *Language Teaching* 44(3). 281–315.
Jiang, Fei, Stephen Michael Croucher & Deqiang Ji. 2021. Editorial: Historicizing the concept of transcultural communication. *Journal of Transcultural Communication* 1(1). 1–4.
Joseph, John E. 2004. *Language and identity: National, ethnic, religious*. Basingstoke: Palgrave Macmillan.

Jørgensen, Normann J. 2008. Polylingual languaging around and among children and adolescents. *International Journal of Multilingualism* 5(3). 161–176.

Jurkova, Sinela. 2021. Transcultural competence model: An inclusive path for communication and interaction. *Journal of Transcultural Communication* 1(1). 102–119.

Kachru, Braj B. 1985. Standard, codification and sociolinguistic realism: The English language in the outer circle. In Randolph Quirk & Henry G. Widdowson (eds.), *English in the world: Teaching and learning the language and literatures*, 11–30. New York: Cambridge University Press.

Kachru, Braj B. 1992. Teaching World Englishes. In Braj B. Kachru (ed.), *The other tongue: English across cultures*, 2nd edn., 355–365. Urbana: University of Illinois Press.

Kachru, Braj B. 1996. English as a Lingua Franca. In Hans Goebl, Peter H. Nelde, Zdenek Stary & Wolfgang Wölck (eds.), *Kontaktlinguistik: Ein internationales Handbuch zeitgenössischer Forschung = Contact linguistics: An international handbook of contemporary research*, 906–913. Berlin/Boston: De Gruyter Mouton.

Kachru, Braj B. 2017. *World Englishes and culture wars*. Cambridge: Cambridge University Press.

Kalocsai, Karolina. 2014. *Communities of practice and English as a Lingua Franca: A study of Erasmus students in a central European context*. Berlin/Boston: De Gruyter Mouton.

Kasper, Gabriele & Johannes Wagner. 2014. Conversation analysis in applied linguistics. *Annual Review of Applied Linguistics* 34. 171–212.

Kaur, Jagdish. 2009. Pre-empting problems of understanding in English as a Lingua Franca. In Anna Mauranen & Elina Ranta (eds.), *English as a Lingua Franca: Studies and findings*, 107–123. Newcastle upon Tyne: Cambridge Scholars Publishing.

Kaur, Jagdish. 2011. Raising explicitness through self-repair in English as a Lingua Franca. *Journal of Pragmatics* 43(11). 2704–2715.

Kaur, Jagdish. 2016a. Conversation analysis and ELF. In Marie-Luise Pitzl & Ruth Osimk-Teasdale (eds.), *English as a Lingua Franca: perspectives and prospects: Contributions in honour of Barbara Seidlhofer*, 161–168. Berlin/Boston: De Gruyter Mouton.

Kaur, Jagdish. 2016b. Intercultural misunderstanding revisited: Cultural difference as a (non) source of misunderstanding in ELF communication. In Prue Holmes & Fred Dervin (eds.), *The cultural and intercultural dimensions of English as a Lingua Franca*, 134–156. Bristol/Buffalo/Toronto: Multilingual Matters.

Kaur, Jagdish. 2022. Pragmatic strategies in ELF communication: Key findings and a way forward. In Ian Walkinshaw (ed.), *Pragmatics in English as a Lingua Franca: Findings and developments*, 35–54. Berlin/Boston: De Gruyter Mouton.

Kecskés, István. 2011. Intercultural pragmatics. In Dawn Archer & Peter Grundy (eds.), *The pragmatics reader*, 371–386. London: Routledge.

Kecskés, István. 2014. *Intercultural pragmatics*. Oxford: Oxford University Press.

Kecskés, István. 2016. A dialogic approach to pragmatics. *Russian Journal of Linguistics* 20(4). 26–42.

Kecskés, István & Jesús Romero-Trillo. 2013. Introduction. In István Kecskés & Jesús Romero-Trillo (eds.), *Research trends in intercultural pragmatics*, 1–3. Berlin/Boston: De Gruyter Mouton.

Kirkpatrick, Andy. 2007. *World Englishes: Implications for international communication and English language teaching*. Cambridge: Cambridge University Press.

Kitzinger, Celia. 2013. Repair. In Jack Sidnell & Tanya Stivers (eds.), *The handbook of conversation analysis*, 229–256. Chichester, UK: Wiley-Blackwell.

Klimpfinger, Theresa. 2009. "She's mixing the two languages together": Forms and functions of code-switching in English as a Lingua Franca. In Anna Mauranen & Elina Ranta (eds.), *English as a Lingua Franca: Studies and findings*, 348–371. Newcastle upon Tyne: Cambridge Scholars Publishing.

Knapp, Karlfried. 1985. Englisch als internationale lingua franca und Richtlinien. In Karl-Richard Bausch, Herbert Christ, Werner Hüllen & Hans-Jürgen Krumm (eds.), *Forschungsgegenstand Richtlinien: Arbeitspapiere der 5. Frühjahrskonferenz zur Erforschung des Fremdsprachenunterrichts*, 84–90. Tübingen: Narr.

Kohn, Kurt. 2018. MY English: A social constructivist perspective on ELF. *Journal of English as a Lingua Franca* 7(1), 1–24.

Kordia, Stefania. 2020. ELF awareness in the task-based classroom: A way forward. *English Language Teaching Journal* 74(4). 398–407.

Könning, Benjamin. 2018. Peer-Kommunikation in der Schule: Empirische und methodische Zugänge. In Arne Ziegler (ed.), *Jugendsprachen/Youth languages: Aktuelle Perspektiven internationaler Forschung/Current perspectives of international research*, 247–267. Berlin/Boston: De Gruyter Mouton.

Kraft, Bettina & Ronald Geluykens. 2007. Defining cross-cultural and interlanguage pragmatics. In Bettina Kraft & Ronald Geluykens (eds.), *Cross-cultural pragmatics and interlanguage English*, 3–20. München: LINCOM.

Kramsch, Claire J. 2016. Multilingual identity and ELF. In Marie-Luise Pitzl & Ruth Osimk-Teasdale (eds.), *English as a Lingua Franca: perspectives and prospects: Contributions in honour of Barbara Seidlhofer*, 179–186. Berlin/Boston: De Gruyter Mouton.

Krogull, Susanne & Sigrun Landes-Brenner. 2009. Qualitätsstandards für Begegnungsreisen im Nord-Süd-Kontext. *Zeitschrift für internationale Bildungsforschung und Entwicklungspädagogik* 32(2). 14–19.

Krug, Manfred G. & Julia Schlüter. 2013. Preface. In Manfred G. Krug & Julia Schlüter (eds.), *Research methods in language variation and change*, xxi–xxv. Cambridge: Cambridge University Press.

Krug, Manfred G. & Katrin Sell. 2013. Designing and conducting interviews and questionnaires. In Manfred G. Krug & Julia Schlüter (eds.), *Research methods in language variation and change*, 69–98. Cambridge: Cambridge University Press.

Kuße, Holger. 2011. Kulturwissenschaftliche Linguistik. In Csaba Földes (ed.), *Interkulturelle Linguistik im Aufbruch: Das Verhältnis von Theorie, Empirie und Methode*, 117–136. Tübingen: Narr.

Labov, William. 1972. *Sociolinguistic patterns.* Philadelphia: University of Pennsylvania Press.

Languages of Tanzania Project. 2009. *Atlasi ya Lugha za Tanzania.* Das es Salaam: Mradi wa Lugha za Tanzania, Chuo Kikuu cha Dar es Salaam.

Larsen-Freeman, Diane. 2018. Complexity and ELF. In Jennifer Jenkins, Will Baker & Martin Dewey (eds.), *The Routledge handbook of English as a Lingua Franca*, 51–60. London: Routledge.

Leech, Geoffrey N. 1983. *Principles of pragmatics*. London: Taylor & Francis.

Leech, Geoffrey N. 2014. *The pragmatics of politeness*. Oxford: Oxford University Press.

Lenz, Annina. 2009. Fremdsprachenübergreifende Vokabelarbeit im Englischunterricht als Methode zur Förderung von Sprachbewusstheit. *Forum Sprache* 1(2). 42–60.

Levinson, Stephen C. 1983. *Pragmatics.* Cambridge: Cambridge University Press.

Li, Wei. 2011. Moment analysis and translanguaging space: Discursive construction of identities by multilingual Chinese youth in Britain. *Journal of Pragmatics* 43(5). 1222–1235.

Li, Wei. 2018. Translanguaging as a practical theory of language. *Applied Linguistics* 39(2). 9–30.

Lichtkoppler, Julia. 2007. 'Male. Male.' – 'Male?' – 'The sex is male.' – The role of repetition in English as a Lingua Franca conversations. *Vienna English Working Papers* 16(1). 39–65.

Liddicoat, Anthony J. 2011. *An introduction to conversation analysis*, 2nd edn. London: Continuum.

Locher, Miriam A. & L. G. Sage. 2010. Introduction to interpersonal pragmatics. In Miriam A. Locher & Sage L. Graham (eds.), *Interpersonal pragmatics*, 1–13. Berlin/Boston: De Gruyter Mouton.

Love, Robbie. 2018. The British National Corpus 2014: User manual and reference guide. http://corpora.lancs.ac.uk/bnc2014/documentation.php (4 September, 2019.)

Love, Robbie, Claire Dembry, Andrew Hardie, Vaclav Brezina & Tony McEnery. 2017. The Spoken BNC2014: Designing and building a spoken corpus of everyday conversations. *International Journal of Corpus Linguistics* 22(3). 319–344.

Mair, Christian. 2013. Using 'small' corpora to document ongoing grammatical change. In Manfred G. Krug & Julia Schlüter (eds.), *Research methods in language variation and change*, 181–194. Cambridge: Cambridge University Press.

Manes, Joan. 1983. Compliments: A mirror of cultural values. In Nessa Wolfson & Elliot Judd (eds.), *Sociolinguistics and language acquisition*, 96–102. Cambridge, MA: Newbury House.

Manes, Joan & Nessa Wolfson. 1981. The compliment formula. In Florian Coulmas (ed.), *Conversational routine: Explorations in standardized communication situations and prepatterned speech*, 115–132. Berlin/Boston: De Gruyter Mouton.

Mauranen, Anna. 2006. Signaling and preventing misunderstanding in English as a Lingua Franca communication. *International Journal of the Sociology of Language* 177. 123–150.

Mauranen, Anna. 2009. Introduction. In Anna Mauranen & Elina Ranta (eds.), *English as a Lingua Franca: Studies and findings*, 1–9. Newcastle upon Tyne: Cambridge Scholars Publishing.

Mauranen, Anna. 2012. *Exploring ELF: Academic English shaped by non-native speakers*. Cambridge: Cambridge University Press.

Mauranen, Anna. 2013. Lingua franca discourse in academic contexts: Shaped by complexity. In John Flowerdew (ed.), *Discourse in context*, 225–245. London: Bloomsbury.

Mauranen, Anna. 2018a. Conceptualizing ELF. In Jennifer Jenkins, Will Baker & Martin Dewey (eds.), *The Routledge handbook of English as a Lingua Franca*, 7–24. London: Routledge.

Mauranen, Anna. 2018b. Second Language Acquisition, World Englishes, and English as a Lingua Franca (ELF). *World Englishes* 37(1). 106–119.

Mayer, Horst O. 2008. *Interview und schriftliche Befragung: Entwicklung, Durchführung und Auswertung*, 4th edn. München: Oldenbourg.

Mayring, Philipp. 2015. *Qualitative Inhaltsanalyse: Grundlagen und Techniken*, 12th edn. Weinheim: Beltz.

Meierkord, Christiane. 2002. 'Language stripped bare' or 'linguistic masala'?: Culture in lingua franca conversation. In Karlfried Knapp & Christiane Meierkord (eds.), *Lingua franca communication*, 109–133. Frankfurt am Main: Peter Lang.

Meierkord, Christiane. 2012. *Interactions across Englishes: Linguistic choices in local and international contact situations*. Cambridge: Cambridge University Press.

Mesthrie, Rajend (ed.). 2010. *Varieties of English 4: Africa, South and Southeast Asia*. Berlin/Boston: De Gruyter Mouton.

Mohr, Susanne & Dunlop Ochieng. 2017. Language usage in everyday life and in education: current attitudes towards English in Tanzania. *English Today* 33(4). 12–18.

Mortensen, Janus. 2017. Transient multilingual communities as a field of investigation: Challenges and opportunities. *Journal of Linguistic Anthropology* 27(3), 271–288.

Mortensen, Janus & Spencer Hazel. 2017. Lending bureaucracy voice: Negotiating English in institutional encounters. In Markku Filppula, Juhani Klemola, Anna Mauranen and Svetlana Vetchinnikova (eds.), *Changing English*, 255–275. Berlin/Boston: De Gruyter Mouton.

Müller-Hartmann, Andreas & Maike Grau. 2004. Nur Tourist sein oder den Dialog wagen?: Interkulturelles Lernen in der Begegnung. *Der Fremdsprachliche Unterricht Englisch* 7(70). 2–9.

Murray, Neil. 2012. English as a Lingua Franca and the development of pragmatic competence. *ELT Journal* 66(6). 318–326.

Mustajoki, Arto. 2017. Miscommunication in everyday life and in lingua franca conversation. In István Kecskés & Stavros Assimakopoulos (eds.), *Current issues in intercultural pragmatics*, 55–74. Amsterdam/Philadelphia: Benjamins.

Myers-Scotton, Carol. 1993. *Duelling languages: Grammatical structure in code-switching*. Oxford: Oxford University Press.

Nelson, Gaylel, Mahmoud Al-Batal & Erin Echols. 1996. Arabic and English compliment responses: Potential for pragmatic failure. *Applied Linguistics* 17(4). 411–432.

Nortier, Jacomine. 2008. Youth Languages. In Arne Ziegler (ed.), *Jugendsprachen/Youth languages: Aktuelle Perspektiven internationaler Forschung/Current perspectives of international research*, 3–23. Berlin/Boston: De Gruyter Mouton.

Oddcast Inc. n.y. *Voki*. https://l-www.voki.com/ (18 June, 2022.)

Omoniyi, Tope & Goodith White. 2006. *The sociolinguistics of identity*. London: Bloomsbury.

O'Neal, George. 2019. Systematicity in linguistic feature selection: Repair sequences and subsequent accommodation. *Journal of English as a Lingua Franca* 8(2). 211–233.

Ortega, Lourdes. 2018. Multilingualism and ELF: A (mostly SLA-informed) outsider perspective. London. Keynote speech presented at the ELF conference *ELF, migration and multilingualism* (ELF 11), London, 5–7 July, 2018.

Pakir, Anne. 2009. English as a Lingua Franca: Analyzing research frameworks in International English, World Englishes, and ELF. *World Englishes* 28(2). 224–235.

Palacios Martínez, Ignacio M. 2018. Lexical innovation in the language of teenagers. In Arne Ziegler (ed.), *Jugendsprachen/Youth languages: Aktuelle Perspektiven internationaler Forschung/Current perspectives of international research*, 363–390. Berlin/Boston: De Gruyter Mouton

Palmer, Gary B. 1996. *Toward a theory of cultural linguistics*. Austin: University of Texas Press.

Pennycook, Alastair. 2007. *Global Englishes and transcultural flows*. London: Routledge.

Petzell, Malin. 2012. The linguistic situation in Tanzania. *Moderna Språk* 106(1). 136–144.

Pietikäinen, Kaisa S. 2014. ELF couples and automatic code-switching. *Journal of English as a Lingua Franca* 3(1). 1–26.

Piller, Ingrid. 2007. Linguistics and intercultural communication. *Language and Linguistic Compass* 1(3). 208–226.

Pitzl, Maire-Luise. 2016. World Englishes and creative idioms in English as a Lingua Franca. *World Englishes* 35(2). 293–309.

Pitzl, Marie-Luise. 2018a. *Creativity in English as a Lingua Franca: Idiom and metaphor*. Berlin/Boston: De Gruyter Mouton.

Pitzl, Marie-Luise. 2018b. Transient international groups (TIGs): exploring the group and development dimension of ELF. *Journal of English as a Lingua Franca* 7(1). 25–58.

Pitzl, Marie-Luise. 2022. From cross to inter to trans – *cultural pragmatics on the move: The need for expanding methodologies in lingua franca research. In Ian Walkinshaw (ed.), *Pragmatics in English as a Lingua Franca: Findings and developments*, 55–80. Berlin/Boston: De Gruyter Mouton.

Pölzl, Ulrike & Barbara Seidlhofer. 2006. In and on their own terms: The "habitat factor" in English as a Lingua Franca interactions. *International Journal of the Sociology of Language* 177. 151–176.

Pomerantz, Anita. 1978. Compliment responses: Notes on the co-operation of multiple constraints. In Jim Schenkein (ed.), *Studies in the organization of conversational interaction*, 79–112. New York: Academic Press.

Pratt, Mary L. 1991. Arts of the contact zone. *Profession* 91. 33–40.

Pullin, Patricia. 2018. Humour in ELF interaction: A powerful, multifunctional resource in relational practice. In Jennifer Jenkins, Will Baker & Martin Dewey (eds.), *The Routledge handbook of English as a Lingua Franca*, 333–344. London: Routledge.

Quirk, Randolph. 2012. *A comprehensive grammar of the English language*, 24th edn. Harlow/Essex: Longman.

Ra, Jaewon Jane. 2021. The perceptions of translanguaging trough English as a Lingua Franca among international students in Korean higher education. *Journal of English as a Lingua Franca* 10(1). 59–87.

Räisänen, Tiina. 2012. Processes and practices of enregisterment of business English, participation and power in a multilingual workplace. *Sociolinguistic Studies* 6(2). 309–331.

Rampton, Ben. 1995. *Crossing: Language and ethnicity among adolescents*. London: Longman.

Risager, Karen. 2006. *Language and culture: Global flows and local complexity*. Clevedon: Channel View Publications.

Risager, Karen. 2012. Linguaculture and transnationality: The cultural dimensions of language. In Jane Jackson (ed.), *The Routledge handbook of language and intercultural communication*, 101–115. London: Routledge.

Roever, Carsten. 2013. Researching pragmatics. In Brian Paltridge & Aek Phakiti (eds.), *Continuum companion to research methods in applied linguistics*, 240–255. London: Bloomsbury.

Rotne, Lene. 2018. "I don't have time for tits": An investigation of Italian and Danish adolescents' writing on Facebook and in school essays. In Arne Ziegler (ed.), *Jugendsprachen/Youth languages: Aktuelle Perspektiven internationaler Forschung/Current perspectives of international research*, 891–914. Berlin/Boston: De Gruyter Mouton.

Rose, Heath & Nicola Galloway. 2019. *Global Englishes for language teaching*. Cambridge/New York: Cambridge University Press.

Rosen, Anna. 2014. *Grammatical variation and change in Jersey English*. Amsterdam/Philadelphia: Benjamins.

Rudwick, Stephanie. 2021. *The ambiguity of English as a Lingua Franca: Politics of language and race in South Africa*. London: Routledge.

Russell, Joan. 2010. *Complete Swahili beginner to intermediate: Learn to read, write, speak and understand a new language with Teach Yourself*. London: Hodder Education. (Kindle edition, no pages)

Sacks, Harvey, Emanuel A. Schegloff & Gail Jefferson. 1974. A simplest systematics for the organization of turn-taking for conversation. *Journal of the Linguistic Society of America* 50(4). 696–735.

Sapir, Edward. 1929. The status of linguistics as a science. *Language* 5(4). 207–214.

Saussure, Ferdinand de. 1916. *Cours de linguistique générale: Avec la collaboration de Albert Riedlinger.* Lausanne/Paris: Payot.

Schegloff, Emanuel A. 1996a. Confirming allusions: Toward an empirical account of action. *American Journal of Sociology* 102(1). 161–216.

Schegloff, Emanuel A. 1996b. Turn organization: One intersection of grammar and interaction. In Elinor Ochs, Emanuel A. Schegloff & Sandra A. Thompson (eds.), *Interaction and grammar*, 52–133. Cambridge: Cambridge University Press.

Schegloff, Emanuel A. 2000. When 'others' initiate repair. *Applied Linguistics* 21(2). 205–243.

Schegloff, Emanuel A. 2007. *Sequence organization in interaction*. Cambridge: Cambridge University Press.

Schegloff, Emanuel A., Gail Jefferson & Harvey Sacks. 1977. The preference for self-correction in the organization of repair in conversation. *Language* 53(2). 361–382.

Schlüter, Julia. 2019. Variante oder Fehler?: Der Beitrag der englischen Korpuslinguistik zur Lehrerinnen- und Lehrerbildung. In Katharina Beuter, Benjamin Bauer, Adrianna Hlukhovych, Konstantin Lindner & Sabine Vogt (eds.), *Sprache und kulturelle Bildung: Perspektiven für eine reflexive Lehrerinnen- und Lehrerbildung und einen heterogenitätssensiblen Unterricht*, 185–224. Bamberg: Bamberg University Press.

Schmid, Euline C. & Torben Schmidt. 2017. Migration-based multilingualism in the English as a Foreign Language classroom: Learners' and teachers' perspectives. *Zeitschrift für Fremdsprachenforschung* 28(1). 29–52.

Schmidt, Thomas. 2018. *FOLK: Informationen zum Forschungs- und Lehrkorpus Gesprochenes Deutsch.* Mannheim. http://agd.ids-mannheim.de/folk.shtml (accessed 04 September 2019)

Schmied, Josef. 2010. East African English (Kenya, Uganda, Tanzania): Phonology. In Rajend Mesthrie (ed.), *Varieties of English 4: Africa, South and Southeast Asia*, 150–163. Berlin/Boston: De Gruyter Mouton.

Schmitt, Holger. 2016. *Teaching English pronunciation: A textbook for the German-speaking countries.* Heidelberg: Winter.

Schneider, Edgar W. 2016. World Englishes and English as a Lingua Franca: Relationships and interfaces. In Marie-Luise Pitzl & Ruth Osimk-Teasdale (eds.), *English as a Lingua Franca: Perspectives and prospects: Contributions in honour of Barbara Seidlhofer*, 105–113. Berlin/Boston: De Gruyter Mouton.

Schneider, Klaus P. & Anne Barron. 2008. *Variational pragmatics: A focus on regional varieties in pluricentric languages*. Amsterdam: Benjamins.

Schnuch, Johanna. 2015. Inklusion und Mehrsprachigkeit: Die Rolle von Sprachbewusstheit im multilingualen Spracherwerb. In Christiane M. Bongartz & Andreas Rohde (eds.), *Inklusion im Englischunterricht*, 117–143. Frankfurt am Main: Peter Lang.

Schnurr, Stephanie. 2010. Humour. In Miriam A. Locher & Sage L. Graham (eds.), *Interpersonal pragmatics*, 307–326. Berlin/Boston: De Gruyter Mouton.

Schröder, Ulrike. 2014. Interkulturelle Kommunikation zwischen Deutschen und Brasilianern im Lichte von Strategien der (Un-)höflichkeit, divergierenden Konfliktstilen und Formen des Beziehungs-managements. In Csaba Földes (ed.), *Interkulturalität unter dem Blickwinkel von Semantik und Pragmatik*, 207–224. Tübingen: Narr.

Scollon, Ronald, Suzanne B. K. Scollon & Rodney H. Jones. 2012. *Intercultural communication: A discourse approach*. Chichester: Wiley-Blackwell.

Searle, John R. 1969. *Speech acts: An essay in the philosophy of language.* Cambridge: Cambridge University Press.

Searle, John R. 1979. *Expression and meaning: Studies in the theory of speech acts*. Cambridge: Cambridge University Press.

Seedhouse, Paul. 1998. CA and the analysis of foreign language interaction: A reply to Wagner. *Journal of Pragmatics* 30(1). 85–102.

Seedhouse, Paul. 2005. Conversation analysis as research methodology. In Keith Richards & Paul Seedhouse (eds.), *Applying conversation analysis*, 251–266. Basingstoke: Palgrave Macmillan.

Seidlhofer, Barbara. 2001. Closing a conceptual gap: The case for a description of English as a Lingua Franca. *International Journal of Applied Linguistics* 11(2). 133–158.

Seidlhofer, Barbara. 2002. The shape of things to come?: Some basic questions about English as a Lingua Franca. In Karlfried Knapp & Christiane Meierkord (eds.), *Lingua franca communication*, 269–302. Frankfurt am Main: Peter Lang.

Seidlhofer, Barbara. 2004. Research perspectives on teaching English as a Lingua Franca. *Annual Review of Applied Linguistics* 24. 209–239.

Seidlhofer, Barbara. 2007. English as a Lingua Franca and communities of practice. In Sabine Volk-Birke & Julia Lippert (eds.), *Proceedings/Anglistentag 2006, Halle*, 307–319. Trier: Wissen-schaftlicher Verlag Trier.

Seidlhofer, Barbara. 2009. Orientations in ELF research: Form and function. In Anna Mauranen & Elina Ranta (eds.), *English as a Lingua Franca: Studies and findings*, 37–59. Newcastle upon Tyne: Cambridge Scholars Publishing.

Seidlhofer, Barbara. 2010. DYLAN – Language dynamics and management of diversity: Forschungsprogramm und Fragestellungen eines Verbundprojekts. In Cornelia Hülmbauer, Eva Vetter & Heike Böhringer (eds.), *Mehrsprachigkeit aus der Perspektive zweier EU-Projekte: DYLAN meets LINEE*, 59–72. Frankfurt am Main: Peter Lang.

Seidlhofer, Barbara. 2011. *Understanding English as a Lingua Franca*. Oxford: Oxford University Press.

Seidlhofer, Barbara. 2017. English as a Lingua Franca and multilingualism. In Jasone Cenoz, Durk Gorter & Stephen May (eds.), *Language awareness and multilingualism*, 391–404. Cham: Springer.

Seidlhofer, Barbara. 2018. Standard English and ELF variation. In Jennifer Jenkins, Will Baker & Martin Dewey (eds.), *The Routledge handbook of English as a Lingua Franca*, 85–100. London: Routledge.

Seidlhofer, Barbara & Henry Widdowson. 2020. What do we really mean by ELF-informed pedagogy?: An enquiry into converging themes. In Mayu Konakahara & Keiko Tsuchiya (eds.), *English as a Lingua Franca in Japan: Towards multilingual practices*, 323–331. Cham: Palgrave Macmillan.

Sharifian, Farzad. 2015. Cultural linguistics. In Farzad Sharifian (ed.), *The Routledge handbook of language and culture*, 473–492. London: Routledge.

Sharifian, Farzad. 2017. *Cultural linguistics: Cultural conceptualisations and language*. Amsterdam/ Philadelphia: Benjamins.

Shohamy, Elana. 2018. ELF and critical language testing. In Jennifer Jenkins, Will Baker & Martin Dewey (eds.), *The Routledge handbook of English as a Lingua Franca*, 583–593. London: Routledge.

Sidnell, Jack. 2009. Conversational analytic approaches to culture. In Jacob Mey (ed.), *Concise encyclopedia of pragmatics*, 2nd edn., 169–172. Amsterdam: Elsevier.

Siebenhaar, Beat. 2018. Funktionen von Emojis und Altersabhängigkeit ihres Gebrauchs in der WhatsApp-Kommunikation. In Arne Ziegler (ed.), *Jugendsprachen/Youth languages: Aktuelle Perspektiven internationaler Forschung/Current perspectives of international research*, 749–772. Berlin/Boston: De Gruyter Mouton.

Sifakis, Nicos C. & Natasha Tsantila (eds.). 2019. *English as a Lingua Franca for EFL contexts*. Bristol/Blue Ridge Summit: Multilingual Matters.

Sifakis, Nicos C., Natasha Tsantila, Aristea Masina & Katerina Vourdanou. 2020. Designing ELF-aware lessons in high-stakes exam contexts. *English Language Teaching Journal* 74(4). 463–472.

Simon, Bernd. 2004. *Identity in modern society: A social psychological perspective.* Malden, MA: Blackwell.

Simons, Gary F. & Charles D. Fennig (eds.). 2018. *Ethnologue: Languages of Africa and Europe,* 21st edn. Dallas, TX: SIL International. Online version: http://www.ethnologue.com. (4 September, 2019.)

Sönning, Lukas. 2020. *Phonological variation in German learner English.* Bamberg: Otto-Friedrich-Universität.

Spencer-Oatey, Helen. 2005. Rapport management theory and culture. *Intercultural Pragmatics* 2(3). 335–346.

Spencer-Oatey, Helen. 2007. Theories of identity and the analysis of face. *Journal of Pragmatics* 39. 639–656.

Spencer-Oatey, Helen. 2008. Face, (im)politeness and rapport. In Helen Spencer-Oatey (ed.), *Culturally speaking: Culture, communication and politeness theory*, 2nd edn., 11–47. London: Continuum.

Spencer-Oatey, Helen & Peter Franklin. 2009. *Intercultural interaction: A multidisciplinary approach to intercultural communication.* Basingstoke: Palgrave Macmillan.

Spreckels, Janet & Helga Kotthoff. 2010. Communicating identity in intercultural communication. In David R. Matsumoto (ed.), *APA handbook of intercultural communication*, 123–143. Washington, DC: American Psychological Association.

Starfield, Sue. 2013. Ethnographies. In Brian Paltridge & Aek Phakiti (eds.), *Continuum companion to research methods in applied linguistics*, 50–65. London: Bloomsbury.

Stenström, Anna-Brita, Gisle Andersen & Ingrid K. Hasund. 2002. *Trends in teenage talk: Corpus compilation, analysis, and findings*. Amsterdam/Philadelphia: Benjamins.

Svendsen, Bente A. 2015. Language, youth and identity in the 21st century: Content and continuations. In Jacomine Nortier & Bente A. Svendsen (eds.), *Language, youth and identity in the 21st century: Linguistic practices across urban spaces*, 3–23. Cambridge: Cambridge University Press.

Tagliamonte, Sali A. 2016. So sick or so cool?: The language of the youth on the internet. *Language in Society* 45(1). 1–32.

Taguchi, Naoko & Noriko Ishihara. 2018. The pragmatics of English as a Lingua Franca: Research and pedagogy in the era of globalization. *Annual Review of Applied Linguistics* 38. 80–101.

Tannen, Deborah. 2007. *Talking voices: Repetition, dialogue, and imagery in conversational discourse*, 2nd edn. Cambridge: Cambridge University Press.

Tatsioka, Zoi, Barbara Seidlhofer, Nicos C. Sifakis & Gibson Ferguson (eds.). 2018. *Using English as a Lingua Franca in education in Europe: English in Europe, Volume 4*. Berlin/Boston: De Gruyter Mouton.

Thode Hougaard, Tina & Marianne Rathje. 2018. Emojis in the digital writings of young Danes. In Arne Ziegler (ed.), *Jugendsprachen/Youth languages: Aktuelle Perspektiven internationaler Forschung/ Current perspectives of international research*, 773–806. Berlin/Boston: De Gruyter Mouton.

Thompson, Alan. 2022. Interjections in spoken ELF interactions. In Ian Walkinshaw (ed.), *Pragmatics in English as a Lingua Franca: Findings and developments*, 147–163. Berlin/Boston: De Gruyter Mouton.

Thiong'o, Ngũgĩ wa. 1986. *Decolonising the mind: The politics of language in African literature*. London/ Nairobi/Portsmouth, NH: James Currey; East African Educational Publishers; Heinemann.

Topping, Keith J., Céline Buchs, David Duran & Hilde van Keer. 2017. *Effective peer learning: From principles to practical implementation.* London/New York: Routledge.

Trosborg, Anna. 2010a. Introduction. In Anna Trosborg (ed.), *Pragmatics across languages and cultures*, 1–39. Berlin/Boston: De Gruyter Mouton.

Trosborg, Anna (ed.). 2010b. *Pragmatics across languages and cultures*. Berlin/Boston: De Gruyter Mouton.

Tsuchiya, Keiko. 2020. Mediation and translanguaging in a BELF casual meeting. In Mayu Konakahara and Keiko Tsuchiya (eds.), *English as a Lingua Franca in Japan: Towards multilingual practices*, 255–278. Cham: Palgrave Macmillan.

UNDESA. n.y. Definition of Youth. http://undesadspd.org/Youth.aspx (21 March, 2022.)

Verschueren, Jef. 1999. *Understanding pragmatics*. London: Arnold.

Vetter, Fabian. 2022. Comparing approaches to (micro-)register variation: The press editorials sections in the British, Canadian and Jamaican components of ICE. In Julia Schlüter & Ole Schützler (eds.), *Data and methods in corpus linguistics: Comparative approaches*, 75–100. Cambridge: Cambridge University Press.

Vettorel, Paola. 2013. ELF in international school exchanges: Stepping into the role of ELF users. *Journal of English as a Lingua Franca* 2(1). 147–173.

VOICE Project. 2007. *VOICE Transcription Conventions* [2.1]. http://www.univie.ac.at/voice/voice.php?page=transcription_general_information. (24 April, 2019.)

Walkinshaw, Ian. 2022. Findings and developments in ELF pragmatic research: An introduction. In Ian Walkinshaw (ed.), *Pragmatics in English as a Lingua Franca: Findings and developments*, 1–14. Berlin/Boston: De Gruyter Mouton.

Walkinshaw, Ian & Andy Kirkpatrick. 2014. Mutual face preservation among Asian speakers of English as a Lingua Franca. *Journal of English as a Lingua Franca* 3(2). 269–291.
Walkinshaw, Ian & Andy Kirkpatrick. 2022. Where to now?: Future directions in ELF pragmatics research. In Ian Walkinshaw (ed.), *Pragmatics in English as a Lingua Franca: Findings and developments*, 221–236. Berlin/Boston: De Gruyter Mouton.
Van der Walt, Christa & Rinelle Evans. 2018. Is English the lingua franca of South Africa? In Jennifer Jenkins, Will Baker & Martin Dewey (eds.), *The Routledge handbook of English as a Lingua Franca*, 186–198. London: Routledge.
Watzlawick, Paul, Janet H. Beavin & Don D. Jackson. 1967. *Pragmatics of human communication: A study of interactional patterns, pathologies, and paradoxes.* New York: Norton.
Weinmann, Michiko & Ruth Arber. 2017. Orientating multilingualism: Navigating languages teacher identities. *Curriculum Perspectives* 37(2). 173–179.
Weisser, Martin. 2015. Speech act annotation. In Karin Aijmer & Christoph Rühlemann (eds.), *Corpus pragmatics: A handbook*, 84–114. Cambridge: Cambridge University Press.
Welsch, Wolfgang. 2010. Was ist eigentlich Transkulturalität? In Lucyna Darowska, Thomas Lüttenberg & Claudia Machold (eds.), *Hochschule als transkultureller Raum?: Kultur, Bildung und Differenz in der Universität*, 39–66. Bielefeld: Transkript Verlag.
Wenger, Etienne. 1998. *Communities of practice: Learning, meaning, and identity*. Cambridge: Cambridge University Press.
WHO. n.y. "Adolescent health: Adolescent health in the South-East Asia Region." *Health topics*. https://www.who.int/southeastasia/health-topics/adolescent-health (21 March, 2022.)
Widdowson, Henry G. 1994. The ownership of English. *Teaching English to Speakers of Other Languages Quarterly* 28(2). 377–389.
Widdowson, Henry G. 2012. ELF and the inconvenience of established concepts. *Journal of English as a Lingua Franca* 1(1). 5–26.
Widdowson, Henry G. 2015. ELF and the pragmatics of language variation. *Journal of English as a Lingua Franca* 4(2). 359–372.
Widdowson, Henry G. 2018. Historical perspectives on ELF. In Jennifer Jenkins, Will Baker & Martin Dewey (eds.), *The Routledge handbook of English as a Lingua Franca*, 101–112. London: Routledge.
Widdowson, Henry G. 2021. Research perspectives on ELF: Linguistic usage and communicative use. In Kumiko Murata (ed.), *ELF research methods and approaches to data and analyses: Theoretical and methodological underpinnings*, 21–28. London: Routledge.
Williams, Cen. 2002. *A Language gained: A study of language immersion at 11–16 years of age*. Bangor: School of Education. http://www.bangor.ac.uk/addysg/publications/Language_Gained%20.pdf. (26 August, 2019.)
Wittgenstein, Ludwig. 1921. Tractatus logico-philosophicus: Logisch-philosophische Abhandlung. *Annalen der Naturphilosophie* 14. 185–266.
Wolff, Ekkehard. 2016. *Language and development in Africa: Perceptions, ideologies and challenges.* Cambridge: Cambridge University Press.
Wolfson, Nessa. 1983. An empirically based analysis of complimenting in American English. In Nessa Wolfson & Elliot Judd (eds.), *Sociolinguistics and language acquisition*, 82–95. Cambridge, MA: Newbury House.
Wolfson, Nessa. 1986. The bulge: A theory of speech behaviour and social distance. *Working Papers in Educational Linguistics* 2(1). 55–83.
Wray, Alison & Aileen Bloomer. 2006. *Projects in linguistics: A practical guide to researching language*, 2nd edn. London: Hodder Education.

Yuan, Yi. 2002. Compliments and compliment responses in Kunming Chinese. *Pragmatics* 12(2). 183–226.
Yule, George. 2002. *Pragmatics,* 6th edn. Oxford: Oxford University Press.
Yule, George. 2017. *The Study of Language*. 6th edn. Cambridge: Cambridge University Press.

Corpora, dictionaries and software

ACE. 2014. *The Asian Corpus of English*. https://corpus.eduhk.hk/ace/ (20 June, 2022.)
Audiotranskription. n.y. *f4.* Marburg: Dr. Dresing & Pehl GmbH. www. audiotranskription.de (23 June, 2022.)
BNC. 2010. *The British National Corpus* (Version 4.3). Bodleian Libraries, University of Oxford. http://www.natcorp.ox.ac.uk/ (29 August, 2019.)
BNC2014. 2018. *British National Corpus 2014.* http://corpora.lancs.ac.uk/bnc2014/ (31 August, 2019.)
COLT. 1993. *The Bergen Corpus of London Teenage English.* http://clu.uni.no/icame/colt/ (1 August, 2019.)
Dudenredaktion. n.y. *Duden online.* https://www.duden.de/ (1 August, 2019.)
ELFA. 2008. *The Corpus of English as a Lingua Franca in Academic Settings.* http://www.helsinki.fi/elfa/elfacorpus (24 September, 2018.)
IDS. 2021. *Datenbank für Gesprochenes Deutsch (DGD): FOLK.* http://dgd.ids-mannheim.de (28 June, 2022.)
Langenscheidt (ed.). n.y. *Langenscheidt Online-Wörterbuch.* Stuttgart: Klett. https://de.langenscheidt.com/ (4 September, 2019.)
OED. n.y. *OED online*. Oxford: Oxford University Press. http://www.oed.com/ (1 August, 2019.)
PONS (ed.). n.y. *PONS Online-Wörterbuch.* Stuttgart: Klett. https://de.pons.com/ (24 June, 2022.)
VERBI Software. 2022. *MaxQDA* (Version 2018). Berlin: VERBI Software. www.maxqda.de (23 June, 2022.)
VOICE. 2013. *The Vienna-Oxford International Corpus of English* (Version 2.0 online). http://voice.univie.ac.at (1 August, 2019.)
WrELFA. 2015. *The Corpus of Written English as a Lingua Franca in Academic Settings,* http://www.helsinki.fi/elfa/wrelfa.html (24 September, 2018.)

Introductory quote by David Crystal taken from:

Dico, Joy Lo. 2010. March 14. Watch what you're saying!: Linguist David Crystal on Twitter, texting and our native tongue. *The Independent*, http://independent.co.uk/arts-entertainment/books/features/watch-what-you-re-saying-linguist-david-crystal-on-twitter-texting-and-our-native-tongue-1919271.html (30 April, 2023)

Index

https://doi.org/10.1515/9783110786576-018

www.ingramcontent.com/pod-product-compliance
Lightning Source LLC
Chambersburg PA
CBHW050517170426
43201CB00013B/1990

* 9 7 8 3 1 1 2 2 1 4 1 5 2 *